# THE MUSIC OF MICHAEL NYMAN

for Tania, ac i'm rhieni

# The Music of Michael Nyman

## Texts, Contexts and Intertexts

PWYLL AP SIÔN
*University of Wales, Bangor, UK*

**ASHGATE**

Published by
Ashgate Publishing Limited
Gower House
Croft Road
Aldershot
Hants GU11 3HR
England

Ashgate Publishing Company
Suite 420
101 Cherry Street
Burlington, VT 05401-4405
USA

Ashgate website: http://www.ashgate.com

**British Library Cataloguing in Publication Data**

Pwyll ap Siôn
  The music of Michael Nyman
  1. Nyman, Michael – Criticism and interpretation
  I. Title
  780.9′2

**Library of Congress Cataloging-in-Publication Data**

Pwyll ap Siôn
  The music of Michael Nyman : texts, contexts, and intertexts / by Pwyll ap Siôn.
    p. cm.
  Includes bibliographical references (p. 215) and index.
  ISBN-13: 978-1-85928-210-6 (alk. paper)
  1. Nyman, Michael–Criticism and interpretation. 2. Music–20th century–History
  and criticism. I. Title.
  ML410.N935P99 2007
  780.92—dc22

                                                                    2006032541

ISBN 978-1-85928-210-6

Printed and bound in Great Britain by TJ International Ltd, Padstow, Cornwall.

# Contents

# List of Tables, Figures and Music Examples

**Tables**

**Figures**

**Music examples**

# Foreword

During the 1970s the Ladbroke Grove area of West London was a hotbed of experimental music activity. The Experimental Music Catalogue operated from a flat at 208 Ladbroke Grove and Michael Nyman lived and worked a few doors away. When I first visited him 'at home' I stumbled into a landscape of clutter. Incongruous objects and extraordinary artefacts filled every corner. Papers, scores and books were scattered everywhere along with children's toys and games. And he sat at a large round table working as a music copyist late into the night. By day he clattered away at an IBM typewriter producing amazing reviews, articles and features about music that most people were yet to hear. The walls were covered with paintings, drawings and photographs. Many of the photographs featured large gatherings of nineteenth century gentlemen with full beard and the stiffest of bib and tucker; they clustered around long dining tables at huge banquets. These were photographs of the 'Banquet Years'; not the well documented Banquet Years famously celebrated in Paris but banquets that had occurred in England. The sheer numbers of gentlemen celebrated a notion of the bizarre. At the edges of one photograph the wide-angle lens enlarged and extended the gentlemen's ears producing an image of fantastic and off-beat eccentricity. I realized many years later that these photographs, especially the image of the eccentric ears, were in fact a metaphor for the world that Nyman inhabited. It is a world he has never left.

Nyman is a collector, an assembler of clutter, a guardian of the forgotten. Through layers of discarded gems he burrows connecting wormholes. His references are gathered from sources well outside the dominant culture; fuelled by an insatiable curiosity he deliberately seeks out the arcane, the overlooked and the abandoned. In the late 1970s, when he began to compose again, he worked on a beaten up old piano that stood on the landing outside his kitchen. At one time his family and visitors were obliged to clamber around an enormous microfilm reader he had borrowed and installed next to the piano. He peered into its dimly lit screen and, with his right hand, whirled yards of microfilmed scores through the machine. His left hand was poised over the piano keys ready to play anything that caught his eye. He was looking for repeating rhythmic patterns, clumps of quavers and semiquavers or curious syncopations. He also had an eye, and an ear, open for harmonies that defied functionality, arresting time by suspending the music in a fragile stillness.

Tonality and an identifiable pulse were anathema to the music establishment in the 1970s. Post-serialism ruled. The European avant-garde were still working their way through the legacy of Schoenberg's dissonance. So the idea of clumps of quavers or chord sequences that went nowhere seemed like pure folly. And the idea of beginning work on a new piece by kidnapping existing music seemed like cheating. Composers had always appropriated folk tunes or politely quoted fragments from other composers, but to shamelessly lift whole chunks of other people's music seemed positively vulgar. Nonetheless Nyman was always very honest about his methods; an early concert by the Campiello Band was entitled 'No Way To Treat The Originals'. He wasn't hiding anything, and he wasn't simply stealing music because the originals were always a springboard to his own work. The results of his appropriations always sounded like Nyman; they were new, they were fresh, and they were unlike anything that had been heard before.

This book tells the story of Nyman's work, it reveals the sources and explains the processes of his compositional methodology. It uncovers and displays some of the items in his musical curiosity cabinet and, like the distorted banquet photographs, it presents us with the extended and eccentric ears that hear those enigmatic harmonies.

© Robert Worby 2006

# Acknowledgements

A substantial number of people have given of their time generously and freely during the preparation and writing of this book. Four names deserve particular mention. Clearly without Michael Nyman's musical presence there would not have been a book to write, but his personal involvement and support has also been invaluable, confirming my belief that in studying the work of a living composer one is often afforded access to untold privileges and advantages. Not only was I given permission to view manuscripts, sketches, scores and recordings in Nyman's London home, but he also found time during an enormously demanding schedule of concert tours and recordings to email answers to queries, read through draft versions of the book, and provide detailed annotations and observations. Robert Adlington, Andrew F. Wilson and Tristian Evans also read through earlier drafts of the text, submitting constructive comments and suggestions with the kind of generosity of spirit that makes such an undertaking seem all the more worthwhile. Robert's impartial assessment of the book's structure and content in particular encouraged me to revisit and reconsider specific areas, while Andrew's steadfast support over the years in supplying vast amounts of films and recordings, articles, videos, newspaper reports and reviews generated much needed momentum and purpose. Tristian provided invaluable assistance with layout and indexing.

Robert Worby supplied a fascinating foreword and kindly shared with me his formidable knowledge of Nyman's music while Domenico De Gaetano proffered similar advice on the films of Peter Greenaway at various stages during the book's gestation. I am thankful to have been able to call on Robert Pascall's redoubtable musical knowledge when various analytical problems presented themselves; indeed, many past and present staff and student members at the University of Wales, Bangor, who listened patiently to my embryonic impressions on the subject during the School of Music's weekly research seminar series will no doubt recognize their timely contributions in the spaces between these words. Sally Harper in particular provided much encouragement, in addition to advice on formatting and presentation. Many academics readily responded to a variety of questions and requests for assistance, including David Clarke, Dai Griffiths, Paul Griffiths, Rebecca Leydon, Steen K. Nielsen and Fred Ritzel.

Marsha and Phineas de Thornley Head were at hand during the early stages of my research to send relevant scores and supply useful information, as did harpist and improviser Rhodri Davies. Indeed, looking at Phineas' tracing of musical interconnections in Nyman's music led me to concentrate specifically on this aspect in my book. Another vital presence was Peter Harrison, whose extensive archive of early Nyman recordings and videos plugged some gaping holes in my knowledge at the time. Sadly, he is no longer present to read the fruits of our many discussions; the book is dedicated to his memory. Geraint Lewis and Iwan Llewelyn-Jones also provided fresh perspectives when most needed.

In sourcing scores and material for Nyman's early works I was assisted in no small measure by Richard Chester, Lucy Telfer (née Berthoud) and Clarissa Machin (née Melville). I also received some fascinating recollections of Nyman's apprenticeship at the Royal Academy of Music from fellow composers Richard Stoker and David Lyon. Christopher Hobbs sent along some valuable scores and recordings from the heyday of the English experimental music movement, while James Clements put me on the right track regarding Heinrich Biber.

A whole team of friends and colleagues facilitated the translation of important texts into English. Peter Hemming Larsen's lucid translation from Danish of parts of Steen K. Nielsen's MA dissertation on Nyman was enthusiastically received, as were Martin Rigby's fastidious corrections to my inaccurate translations of German interviews and articles. Eirwyn Vaughan laboured tirelessly over a substantial Nyman interview in the Greenaway *Dis Voir* publication, while Laura Rorato supplied cogent translations from Italian. Any inaccuracies are of course entirely my own fault. The following all reacted positively to requests for articles, videos, books, and recordings: Beate Haungs at SWR Media-Gmbh, video artist Andreas Siefert, Paul Rolfe, Ian Oliver, Claudia Caruso and Jasmine Hornabrook.

All those dealing with Nyman's catalogue at Chester Music over the years have without exception responded swiftly to requests for scores; John Fosbrook in particular has been enormously helpful, but also before him Karen Price, Catherine Long, Jane Carter, Katie Rook and Jakob Faurholt at Edition Wilhelm Hansen all provided assistance at various times. At Ashgate Publishing, my commissioning editor Heidi May and her predecessor Rachel Lynch demonstrated loyalty and patience beyond all reasonable expectation in dealing with my poor time keeping and phobia for deadlines. I thank them for their fortitude and perseverance. Any errors, anomalies, or inconsistencies contained herein are entirely my own. Finally, I wish to thank my wife Tania and our families both in Cornwall and on Ynys Môn for selflessly and readily providing support and care for our two boys Tomos and Osian when required.

All examples from Nyman's music are © Copyright (1974–2000) Chester Music Limited, apart from the *Canzona* and *Divertimento* (© Michael Nyman) and the theme from Gattaca © Copyright Colpix Music (1997). Reproduced by permission of Chester Music & Novello & Co.

# Introduction

I first came into contact with Nyman's music when he accepted an invitation to give a talk at a seminar organized by the Oxford Contemporary Music Group during Trinity Term, 1989. Having serendipitously recognized him on Oxford Station platform without previous means of identification, I later had to confess to him in the Faculty of Music's common room that I had in fact heard very little of his music.

Although he had been composing solidly for some ten years up to this point, Nyman was (and maybe even still is) regarded as something of an outsider in music establishment terms.[1] Recognized primarily in those days as an exponent of what in some musical circles has been traditionally viewed as a more 'lowly' art form – that of film composition – the only recording I had discovered in St Aldate's music library prior to Nyman's lecture talk was not of a soundtrack, but his chamber opera *The Man who Mistook his Wife for a Hat*. In some respects the work represented an atypical introduction to Nyman's style, despite containing features that were common to his compositions as a whole. In particular it lacked the kind of distinctive sound world developed by Nyman in his many soundtracks for Peter Greenaway's films. Indeed, with the notable exception of his film scores, Nyman's music was relatively infrequently recorded during the 1980s, a situation that changed dramatically during the following decade with the success of *The Piano*.

Nyman's Oxford lecture consisted of a detailed and, at times, technical account of the processes and procedures applied to the second movement of Mozart's *Sinfonia Concertante* K. 364 for his soundtrack to Greenaway's film *Drowning by Numbers*. I remember being struck for the first time with the idea that music could be directly related to a previous composition, either by being modelled upon it, or by directly referring through quotation, commentary or any other means. The notion that every piece of music exists in a vacuum was unceremoniously renounced by Nyman, and given further credence by the fact that his music often operated within the multimedia sphere of film, as one component amongst many. To form a view on Nyman's music inevitably led one to form views about a whole host of other disciplines, from art history to genetic engineering.

Indeed the full impact of Nyman's music could only be truly appreciated within the context of image and movement, as I was to witness a few weeks later when I saw for the first time in the cramped surroundings of Oxford's *Moulin Rouge* cinema *The Cook, the Thief, his Wife and her Lover*. Here was a film unlike anything I had seen

---

1 Evidence of this is partly suggested by his omission from Paul Griffiths' collection of interviews conducted during the first half of the 1980s called *New Sounds, New Personalities*. He was not the only one to be disregarded: both Michael Finnissy and Howard Skempton were also conspicuous by their absence (Griffiths 1985).

before or have witnessed since: a film that evoked revulsion and wonderment in equal measure. Of course, the pulsating drama of death and debauchery was underpinned by Nyman's visceral soundtrack, this time using passages not from Mozart but from Purcell's *King Arthur*.

It soon became clear to me that here was a composer who possessed a unique and distinctive creative voice, yet the irony remained that his music was often composed out of the voices of others. In the pop sphere this situation would have hardly appeared extraordinary, where borrowing and appropriating is considered standard practice. Indeed Nyman's music was (and again, still is) more readily accepted and appreciated by pop audiences. Judged according to the elevated aesthetic standard of the music establishment again, Nyman's music seemed to fare less well.

As outlined in Chapter 1, Nyman's recourse to quoted materials in many of his compositions has been the cause of critical consternation and disapproval. My argument here is that these judgments are often informed by a stubborn reliance on post-Kantian notions of creative individuality, where 'the work' forms the focus for any aesthetic judgement or response. Clearly, without wishing to discredit entirely the Kantian ideal, I suggest here that alternative methods should be adopted in framing quotation in Nyman's music, based not so much on their internal forms and features but rather on the contexts surrounding them.

That quotation is, indeed, an important aspect of Nyman's music is demonstrated in Maarten Beirens' observation that he has 'turned quotation into one of the cornerstones of his musical language', developing a number of complex compositional stratagems linked with borrowing and of recycling musical material (Beirens 2005, p. 414). In drawing upon three centuries of classical music as material for his own work, quotation 'has become a substantial part of [Nyman's] style, to the extent that his oeuvre reads as a "who's who in western music history"' (ibid., p. 404). In many respects, then, Nyman's use of quotation is an obvious starting point for any discussion of his music. It draws one's attention to the kind of symbiotic relationship his music has developed with the past, while remaining firmly rooted in the present. Difficulties lie not so much in one's understanding of the nature and function of quotation in Nyman's music, but rather in one's perception of it. What are we supposed to make of it, and what is Nyman really trying to say? If a more balanced critical assessment of his borrowings and appropriations is to take place, then Nyman's techniques and methods require further contextualization.

Context can, of course, suggest a variety of different meanings. If a general theme does run through this book, however, then it relates to placing Nyman 'in context' and applying a variety of contexts – both analytical and theoretical – to his music. Chapters 2 and 3 aim to outline the broadest possible contextual overview to Nyman's music by looking at his background and upbringing, student compositions, his work as critic and the general aesthetic and stylistic foundations upon which his music was formed during the 1970s. Focusing further on context brought into play Nyman's important writings on music, which formed a kind of pretext to his own musical 'texts'. One is maybe stating the obvious in saying that his own music relates to the kind of values and opinions represented in his writings. Nevertheless, the range and diversity of his writings perhaps more accurately indicate why Nyman has felt the need to allow the past to feed into his music. Talking of musical texts and their inter-relationships necessitated providing a definition of the term 'intertext' since theories developed from intertextuality would naturally serve to orientate my own approach, illuminate Nyman's working methods, and provide a key to unlocking some of its meanings. Defined initially through terms belonging to literary theory, art criticism and music theory and practice, Chapter 4 supplies a framework upon which a general typography of Nyman's intertextual methods could be mapped.

If Chapter 4 forms the basis for further intertextual explorations of Nyman's music, the following chapters focus on particular areas, genres and specific compositions in order to illuminate his working methods in more detail. Chapter 5 provides a general intertextual overview of Nyman's film collaborations with Peter Greenaway. Composing film music is by its very nature a piecemeal process, and may partly explain why Nyman decided to turn to the larger architectural design of opera in order to integrate more completely intertextual aspects in his work. He first attempted this in *The Man who Mistook his Wife for a Hat*, which forms the basis of Chapter 6. Here the intertextual component serves to open up other areas, such as narrativity in music, while also shedding further light on the dramatic function and meaning of the work. While there are no direct quotes from other composers in Nyman's follow-up opera *Facing Goya*, the work nevertheless advances the notion of 'borrowing' from pre-existing sources to even greater and more ambitious levels; this time by using material derived from a multiplicity of sources from his own work, as seen in the closing chapter.[2] In between these two large-scale compositions, I explore the plurality of intertextual approaches in a single genre – the string quartet – in Chapter 7, and seek to place the impact of quotation within the diegetic and non-diegetic function of musical cues presented in Nyman's most successful score, *The Piano*, in Chapter 8.

Clearly not all of Nyman's music is based on borrowing or quotation, nor does it always explicitly rework ideas from earlier compositions, but this intertextual element nevertheless forms a crucial and at times controversial part of his musical language. In concentrating mainly on this aspect of his work, my book inevitably emphasizes certain issues and marginalizes others. A follow-up study would wish to address inherently 'textual' characteristics of Nyman's musical language – the distinguishing features of each work – rather than examining elements that connect them, as I have done here. Indeed recent compositions, such as the opera *Man and Boy: Dada* (2003), the *Violin Concerto* (2003) and the electronically generated soundtrack to Shobana Jeyasingh's multimedia dance production *Flicker* (2005), suggest that Nyman is placing increasingly less emphasis on intertextual and inter-referential aspects in his music.

---

2  I discount the fact that, of the three intervening stage works, the first (*Vital Statistics*) was withdrawn, and the other two (*Letters, Riddles and Writs* and *Noises, Sounds and Sweet Airs*) are respectively a TV-opera and (in its original format) an opera-ballet.

Other significant areas have not been covered in any systematic fashion here, such as Nyman's lifelong obsession with Laurence Sterne's rambling encyclopaedic account of *The Life and Opinions of Tristram Shandy, Gentleman*, his enduring passion for football and its connections with his music,[3] his enthusiasm for collaborative projects which have brought him into contact with other media (such as dance and film) or his interest in extending stylistic boundaries through interacting with non-Western classical traditions and cultures. Some of these issues are addressed in passing, but usually – as in the case of Nyman's music for film – from an intertextual perspective. No attempt has therefore been made here to provide a detailed critique of the relationship between sound and image in his work, which in itself would be an ambitious but potentially rewarding undertaking.

Likewise, in analysing intertextuality in Nyman's music, the significance of certain genres has been magnified at the expense of others. Two of his operas and one of his quartets have been afforded generous space, for example, while songs and choral works are hardly touched upon. I hope that my reasons for doing this will become evident from the conclusions I draw from the study of these pieces. While any discussion of Nyman's music inevitably deals with aspects of sound, colour and timbre, I have again not set out to provide a systematic analysis of these features, or traced changes in the Nyman 'sound' from one decade to the next. The Nyman 'sound' is discussed only in so far as it links in with the intertextual focus of my study. My primary concern has therefore been with Nyman's treatment of musical material: its presentation, re-presentation and shaping of method and technique in the composer's work, although this approach has led me to look at related areas.

This book should not be understood as 'the last word' on the music of Michael Nyman; a notion that – self-evidently in intertextual terms – would be considered absurd in any case. Neither should it be viewed merely as an apologia of his methods. My aim has been to contextualize Nyman's music by applying what I hope will be seen as relevant and useful intertextual theories and methodologies. Given that this is, as far as I am aware, the first book-length study in English on Nyman, I have also attempted to summarize and conflate present thoughts and opinions about his music from writers engaged in a variety of disciplines. Nyman's appeal is wide-ranging, as witnessed in writings from film theory and criticism, popular music magazines, cultural studies and musicology (much of which resides in German, Italian and French publications). I hope that the present study will serve to elicit further reaction, response and research in these areas, forming another textual link along an intertextual chain of future critical discourses on the music of Michael Nyman.

---

3  Some work has already been undertaken in this area (see Schoonderwoerd 2005).

# Chapter 1

# Nyman 'On Trial'

At one point during Nyman's TV-opera homage to Mozart, *Letters, Riddles and Writs* (1991),[1] an eighteenth-century style mock courtroom scene is held where the composer is brought to trial for committing 'blatant intellectual theft'. In short, he has been accused of musical plagiarism. The prosecutor is none other than Joseph Haydn, who substantiates the charge by inviting a court composer, acted out in the scene by Nyman himself, to play the 'offending' extract; a passage some seven bars into the development section of the first movement of Mozart's String Quartet in $E^\flat$ major, K. 428. Witnessing his music being reused in this way, an androgynous-looking Mozart (played by singer Ute Lemper) exclaims, 'he has taken my chords, he has slowed them down.' At this point the nineteenth-century Swiss musicologist Georg Nägeli is called upon to provide a case for the defence. He does so by quoting a passage from Carl Czerny's manual *School of Practical Composition*, which in turn has been lifted from Haydn's own advice: '[one] must compose according to chosen models, taking the same key, time, phrase structure, number of bars and even modulation, following them strictly.' The scene ends with a talking bust of Beethoven solemnly declaring, 'what Mr Nyman has done is merely project these models two hundred years into the future', while Mozart appears to become more absorbed in the methods used to recompose his music.[2]

On the surface, this fictitious scenario represents nothing more than a musical joke, a *buffa*-style comic interlude, where puns are played on regal and legal court establishments. Furthermore, the allegations of 'brazen plagiarism' are made to appear weak and absurd, but the scene also masks a deeper and more serious grievance. Nyman's rise to international prominence during the past three decades has made him one of the world's most successful living composers. His soundtrack to Jane Campion's film *The Piano* (1993) alone sold three million copies. His band has toured the globe for over twenty years, performing in venues from Melbourne to Mexico City. Festivals regularly pay homage to his music, especially in Italy and Spain, where his music engenders passion bordering on fanaticism. He has developed a large fan base in the Far East, is often courted as a rock musician, and is admired by many rock stars, including Blur's Damon Albarn and Neil Hannon of The Divine Comedy. Demand for his music has been met with an increased rate in productivity, making him one of the most prolific composers of his generation.

---

1 The 'plot' for *Letters, Riddles and Writs*, written and directed by Jeremy Newson and Pat Gavin, was devised entirely by Nyman (see *Not Mozart* [CAV 026]).

2 Carlo Cenciarelli has also taken this scene as a starting point for analysing connections between Nyman and Mozart's music (Cenciarelli 2006).

Nyman's popularity, however, has only been matched by the degree of critical opprobrium levelled against him. Admired and condemned in equal measure, Nyman has become a victim of his own success. While the substance of such criticisms occasionally touches upon a perceived limitation in technique or method, Nyman's detractors often use his 'parasitic' borrowing of other composers' music or of his own persistent self-borrowing as grist to their mill (see Schwarz 1996, p. 200). Any inherent value belonging to these methods has been questioned by some in order to challenge the very notion that Nyman is a composer at all. Keith Potter once expressed a view commonly held by some critics (though not necessarily shared by him), who believed that 'Nyman's adherence to a repetitive manner, crossed with borrowings from classical music and presented with more than a nod in the direction of rock, leads him inevitably to become not merely a bad composer but ... not a composer at all' (Potter 1990, p. 212). Meirion Bowen provided a similar argument when he stated that if Nyman 'has any status as a composer – and that I doubt – he has acquired it by steadily annihilating all past composers, from Purcell and Mozart onwards' (Bowen 1995).[3] Nyman's music thus elicits extreme responses of approval or dissent, and is understood as either 'blasphemy of the coarsest kind, or a compelling postmodern reinterpretation of the musical past' (Schwarz 1996, p. 200).

Such stern disapproval has called into question the very integrity and credibility of Nyman's music. It is hardly surprising that he has felt as if placed on trial. The courtroom drama played out in *Letters, Riddles and Writs* is a parody of those who have taken Nyman to task for his alleged misguided actions, but it also provides a historical and cultural context from which borrowing or self-borrowing might be understood. In an interview with Jonathan Webster, Nyman has responded to the accusation of 'unoriginal borrowing' by stating:

> [This] is nothing new. My detractors state that my technique is to take little segments from previous composers' works and repeat them with only the most superficial variation. While I would not deny the accusation of borrowing, only about 20 per cent of my music is based upon reworked material from other composers. I would also strongly contend that I always transform what I take into something totally fresh and musically challenging, in just the same way that Stravinsky might have done. Besides, whenever I borrow ... I always credit my sources. (Webster 1995, p. 14)

Nyman has pointed out that borrowing or appropriating features from another composition is not in itself revolutionary. Indeed, his approach is symptomatic of wider conflicts between modernism and postmodernism. Questions of authenticity and originality or simulacra and mimesis have underpinned aesthetic discussions on the value and purpose of both old and new cultural forms. 'To quote or unquote?' has fuelled further debate in this area. Held up by modernists as a betrayal of truth, authenticity and self-presence, advocated by postmodernists as a paradigm of plurality and multiplicity, quotation is misunderstood yet widely employed. Cultural

---

3  It is interesting to note that in another review Potter has argued the opposite view, that Nyman's success is because of 'the [pre-existing musical] models' (Potter 1990, p. 213).

plundering is enacted on a daily basis in the multi-referential sphere of film, media and popular culture in general. Modernism has resisted and repelled these forms, or attempted to absorb them into its own set of belief-systems.

To his critics, then, Nyman's borrowings demonstrate a lack of originality indicative of much postmodern cultural production. However, part of the problem in understanding Nyman's music lies in one's definition and understanding of 'originality' and how it is contextualized. In order to move towards a more balanced understanding of the nature and function of originality in relation to quotation, the issue of borrowing will be examined in this chapter from three perspectives: first, within the more general context of music historiography, secondly, in terms of its transformation in twentieth-century culture (through art in particular), and finally, by analysing a specific example from Nyman's work.

## Historical concepts of originality

In Webster's phrase 'unoriginal borrowing' the use of pre-existing words, images or sounds suggests a lack of creativity. Quotation transgresses originality and is therefore seen as a sign of creative weakness or inadequacy. This view has not been shared by all generations. In deciding to locate a courtroom scene on musical plagiarism during Mozart's age, *Letters, Riddles and Writs* draws the viewer's attention to the fact that the idea of originality would have been understood somewhat differently at this time. It had not acquired the venerable sheen of authority and legitimacy later bestowed by Romantic aesthetics.

The pretext and motivation for 'being original' was, on the contrary, questioned and discouraged by enlightenment thought. Originality inhabited a grey area where only either a bold or foolish composer would dare tread. While inventiveness was regarded as evidence of a sure technical grasp, only composers skilful enough to blend the rules of their art with innate creativity were deemed to truly possess its more capricious and unpredictable companion. Haydn's famous comment to Griesinger that when as Kapellmeister to Prince Esterházy from 1761–90 he was forced 'to become original' was spoken at a time when the cultural shift from Classicism/ Romanticism was already well underway (see Sisman 1997, p. 3). Haydn's acute sense of historical awareness may have motivated him to instil the notion of originality with a significance that gained value in subsequent eras.

Haydn's musical originality in fact lay as much in his willingness to depart from '"textbook rules" for aesthetic reasons [and] on the basis of his "free spirit", even "genius", than on the wilful pursuance and flaunting of individuality *per se*' (ibid., p. 8). Indeed, when Haydn deviated from the norm he was often admonished for doing so. *Sturm und Drang*'s appearance during the 1770s coincided with a popular resurgence in Shakespearean tragedy, providing Haydn with both an opportunity to utilize greater dramatic contrasts and employ extreme disruptions in his music. Many considered such bold gestures extravagant because they unbalanced the neat patterns and restrained sensibility of the prevailing *stile galant*. Yet at the same time these innovative techniques provided further weight to the importance of individual expression and originality.

When, towards the end of his life, Haydn spoke his famous words to Griesinger, he had been since Mozart's death arguably the leading figure of his generation. He may therefore have wished to present himself as the creative force behind the emerging Romantic Movement.[4] Haydn's championing of originality was also passed directly on to Beethoven – as famously predicted by Count Waldstein in 1792.[5] In historiographical terms, Beethoven's bold reinterpretation of the term in his musical aesthetic was subsequently idealized and mythologized by nineteenth-century writers and inherited by subsequent generations during the twentieth century.

Lawrence Kramer has supported this idea, observing, '[the] ideal of originality ... dates from the mid-eighteenth century, when the work expected of the artist began to change from imitation and emulation to original creation. The artist as original genius siphons off collective memory into his own charisma' (Kramer 2002, p. 265). Beethoven's music thus became one of the most powerful representations of a quintessentially Romantic spirit, where unbridled individuality, bold innovation and expressive freedom were all justified in the name of originality and made possible only through the genius's creative vision. Such views also formed an aesthetic backdrop against which twentieth-century art was duly judged and appreciated. Linda Hutcheon, for example, sees the dismissal in more recent art criticism of twentieth-century trends such as parody as evidence of 'the continuing strength ... of a Romantic aesthetic that [places value upon] genius, originality, and individuality ...' (Hutcheon 1985, p. 4).

Certainly the twin concepts of creative autonomy and artistic genius were already being reshaped and reconfigured during the age of Haydn and Mozart. Jean-Jacques Rousseau, for example, claimed in 1768 that an artist 'would never be thought a genius if he lacked originality' (Rousseau, in le Huray and Day 1988, p. 86). Kant later echoed this idea in his *Critique of Judgment* (1790) when he stated, 'the foremost property of genius must be originality' (Kant 1987, p. 175). Christine Battersby supports this view by maintaining that Kant believed the artist to be a kind of god 'who literally [thinks] himself into existence ... art grows out of individuality' (Battersby, in McCartney 2000). Such comments anticipated the shift towards stylistic and technical innovation that took place during the late-Classical and early-Romantic periods. Originality was not ignored or marginalized before the nineteenth century however: it was merely viewed according to different cultural and aesthetic values.

Lydia Goehr has claimed that the emergence of the concept of the musical work at the turn of the nineteenth century changed the character and function of musical production and reception, allowing a composer of Beethoven's genius to consciously display openly striking and original features in his music (Goehr 1992,

---

4  Haydn was considered by nineteenth-century music critic E.T.A. Hoffmann to be a 'romantic' composer (see Rosen 1976, p. 19).

5  Quoted in Rosen (ibid., p. 19).

p. 206).[6] In the Baroque and early Classical eras, however, the musical work was viewed as a more fluid concept, easily adaptable and broken down to the specific contexts in which it was required to serve. The adaptability and variability of musical works during this time was reflected in the fact that many compositions shared common materials and origins. Compositions were not generally viewed as independent, autonomous constructions, nor were they necessarily expected to develop some aspect of technical innovation or aesthetic progress. Such examples would have been greeted with suspicion from the arbiters of enlightenment taste and sensibility. Goehr states that compositions at this time

> involved significant overlap and repetition of musical material. And such overlap would not just have existed within a single composer's output, but among compositions by any number of composers. The general sense of borrowing was comparable ... to the general use of a language for which there is no uniqueness or ownership of any given expression. Musicians could almost say the same thing as often as they wanted. (Ibid., p. 183)

## Classical music and signification

Goehr's description of the classical approach to composition as a 'shared employment of musical language' (ibid., p. 185) where composers could draw from a common pool of materials, characters, gestures, figures and structures has been used in other discussions about this period. Leonard Ratner's study of the late-eighteenth-century style tacitly assumes that the music was not composed *ex nihilo*, but rather emerged out of a complex cultural network of shared signs and associations, exchanged by composers and perceived by its audience (Ratner 1980). A sign-based, semiotic nature of musical production also informs Kofi Agawu's analysis of classical music where units of meaning are seen to possess a dual function, operating within specific contexts while at the same time referring outside themselves (Agawu 1991, pp. 26–79). Agawu coins the terms 'introversive' and 'extroversive' semiosis to describe these binary associations.

In fact modern linguistic theory since Ferdinand de Saussure has attempted to articulate similar functions of intrinsic and extrinsic signification in language, or in more general terms between absolute and referential meaning. Linguistic structures suggested to Saussure a form of intrinsic signification, in Jameson's words 'a perpetual present, with all the possibilities of meaning implicit in every moment' (Jameson 1972, p. 6). Subsequent writers, including Julia Kristeva, preferred to see textual meaning as extrinsically constructed, in her words 'as a mosaic of quotations; any text is the absorption and transformation of another' (Kristeva 1980, p. 66). Indeed it was Kristeva who coined the term 'intertextuality' to describe what she considered to be 'the radical plurality of the sign' (Allen 2000, p. 6). Roland Barthes redefined the function of the linguistic sign in such a way that the author became 'a compiler

---

6 For an opposing view not discussed here, see Erauw 1998.

or arranger of pre-existent possibilities within the language system' (ibid., p. 14). A more detailed definition of intertextuality will be undertaken later, but for now it is clear that the idea of referring to or borrowing from existing musical texts was not an alien concept to eighteenth-century composers. A composer's role was essentially to draw upon the surrounding established and accepted range of cultural signs.

While in principle the concept of a shared language involved the reapplication of generic figures and formal archetypes to new musical contexts, in practice composers were nevertheless unafraid to borrow or quote from their immediate predecessors or fellow practitioners. Johann Mattheson once claimed that Handel had extracted a complete and unaltered melody from one of Mattheson's operas and used it in one of his own works. Surprisingly enough, at least from the twenty-first-century viewpoint of copyright acts, Mattheson did not begrudge Handel this deed. That Handel was indeed guilty of indulging in acts of 'brazen plagiarism' became a more common complaint during the nineteenth century when writers such as Samuel Wesley observed how he 'pilfered from all Manner of Authors ... although it is certain that what he has taken he has generally improved on' (Wesley, in Goehr 1992, p. 185). Such comments point to the fact that during the Romantic era 'the demand for originality translated into a demand that each composer should create his works from scratch' (ibid., p. 220). Prior to this, the musical work was viewed not as an indestructible object but rather as a malleable structure, where the sum of its parts were considered to be greater than the whole due to the almost endless adaptability and versatility of musical gestures, phrases, turns and figures belonging to the Baroque and Classical styles.

## Postmodern precursor: Dada

Nyman's use of musical quotation may therefore be more easily understood and accurately explained from the perspective of seventeenth- and eighteenth-century compositional practice. Indeed it may be significant that his sources often belong to this period, ranging from Bull and Purcell to Biber and Mozart. But to view Nyman as a kind of guardian of musical antiquities would be misleading. As Beethoven wryly observes in *Letters, Riddles and Writs*, Nyman's use of Mozart's musical ideas is still 'projected into the future'. Therein lies its paradox. Nyman's attitude may resemble that of an eighteenth-century composer but its sounds and gestures could only belong to that of the late twentieth century.

This fusion of old and new partly explains why Nyman has often been described as a postmodernist. In his assessment of Nyman's collaborative work with film director Peter Greenaway, Domenico De Gaetano views postmodernism as a self-conscious reclamation of the past through its use of baroque artifice, evolving 'from the figurative and musical structuralism of the early seventies to the present neo-baroque age, the latest offshoot of postmodern aesthetics' (De Gaetano 1994, p. 17). De Gaetano uses 'baroque' in the sense applied by Jorge Luis Borges here, as a 'style which deliberately exhausts (or tries to exhaust) all its possibilities and which borders on its own parody' (Borges 1973, p. 12). Focillon's four stages of art also culminate in baroque sublimation, 'whereby the embellishments become the substance or content of the work' (Focillon, in Denham 1993, p. 52). Laura Denham has also described Nyman's music as 'a type of minimalist-baroque, where elements of modernism (minimalism) and postmodernism (intertextuality and baroque) ... come together. The point at which at which modernism ends and postmodernism begins is nebulous' (ibid., pp. 15–16).

Nyman's baroque artifice is only one aspect of his poly-modal approach to the past. Kramer sees postmodernity as both decentred and culturally omnivorous, '[having] no place of origin to which we can refer or aspire, of being part of a universal diaspora from nowhere, and the experience, on the other hand, of living in a whirligig of repetitions, citations free to become endless recitations, pasts that are constantly re-presenting themselves' (Lawrence Kramer 2002, p. 286). Postmodernists therefore adopt signs from the cultural past to suit their own ends, and Kramer evokes the figure of the *revenant* to articulate this sense of 'past present'. Defined by him as a 'ghost, a phantom, one who haunts, who returns, who walks again', Kramer sees revenants imbuing postmodern compositions with literally a spirit of the past, but one which at the same time resists any form of historical consciousness (ibid., p. 263). The revenant's presence throws into doubt any modernist notions of originality or authenticity:

> Revenants do not have to worry about originality. What they bring is not difference, but that of estrangement within sameness by which sameness becomes compelling. Not difference, but what Derrida named *différence*, the continuous distinction and deferral of the same from itself. Musical revenants throw into question the romantic and modernist ideal of originality. They suggest that there is no need to seek difference from the past because difference is already present, in the present. The sameness of the revenant is the form in which that difference is overcome, the form in which the past lives on – but not as it was, not exactly. The same returns in order to live on – differently. (Ibid., pp. 263–4)

Originality in postmodern consciousness has no memory of history and does not struggle to define itself according to canonic practice. While Kramer is referring here to more recent examples, such attitudes are also found in earlier examples, including the avant-garde art movement from the early twentieth century called Dadaism. Emerging from the debris of the First World War (1914–18), Dada drew attention to the futility, paradox and schizophrenia of war as it raged across Europe. Dada's heterogeneous nature, springing almost simultaneously from a number of different places, ultimately led to the movement's lack of cohesion and momentum, but its impact remained strong on subsequent generations of artists, writers and composers. Though born according to most accounts in the *Cabaret Voltaire* performances taking place in Zurich in 1916, similar activities soon flourished in other cultural centres, including New York, Berlin, Hanover and (somewhat later) Paris. In its diverse appropriation of cabaret, concert, art exhibition, poetry reading and a host of other forms of theatre and performance, Dada often thrived on its ability to surprise, confuse, shock and sometimes offend.

While revelling in a rich profusion of contradictions Dada displayed some common characteristics, including what Hanne Bergius has identified as 'a predilection for *indifference* and *irony*' (Bergius 1980, p. 29). The effects of irony and in particular parody have been far-reaching in twentieth-century culture. Dada's use of ironic forms was intended to cast doubts over the fetishization of the art object, generating new creative intensities by reinstating life at the centre of artistic experience. Francis Picabia emphasized this when he stated, 'wherever art appears, life disappears' (Picabia, in Stangos 1981, p. 113). Ironic play was often achieved in Dadaist art by replacing the work with common, everyday objects, and artists such as Marcel Duchamp and Picabia would often make use of *objets trouvés* (or ready-mades) in their work. The principles underlying Dada art were therefore inherently intertextual, although the intention was to create a sense of alienation through the unconventional presentation of familiar images.

Another artist working according to these principles was Kurt Schwitters, whose life and work became the subject of Nyman's third opera, *Man and Boy: Dada* (2002). Schwitters did not align himself with any Dada 'school' or centre, maintaining in his work a level of independence, clarity and coherence lacking in the avant-garde excesses of his fellow artists. A relatively isolated existence away from the many other centres of activity resulted in his development of a highly individual form of Dada art called *Merz*, where everyday items of junk and refuse were assembled and mounted onto drawings, pictures, collages or became incorporated into parts of larger installations. Although his use of discarded objects and materials suggests an affinity with Duchamp's ready-mades, or the Berlin school, Schwitters was not a nihilist and wished to preserve the autonomy of the art object:

> Schwitters was absolutely, unreservedly, 24-hours-a-day PRO-art … [there] was no talk of the 'death of art', or 'non-art', or 'anti-art' with him. On the contrary, every tram-ticket, every envelope, cheese wrapper or cigar-brand, together with old shoe-soles or shoe-laces, wire, feathers, dishcloths – everything that had been thrown away – all this he loved, and restored to an honoured place by means of his art. (Richter 1965, p. 138)

Unlike Duchamp, who emigrated from Paris to New York and set about to negate the very principles upon which art was constructed and understood, Schwitters remained in Europe and was committed to the notion of 'the artist'. There are parallels here with Nyman, who although influenced by American experimentalism and minimalism has nevertheless remained close to his European roots. Nyman once stated, '[my] tradition is European, and I get all my musical kicks and ideas from the European symphonic tradition' (in Schwarz 1996, p. 197). This fits in with Beirens' observation that European minimalism's willingness to refer to past models and forms can be explained in terms of its closer proximity to that tradition than was the case with American minimalism (Beirens 2005, p. 405). In entering into 'an ongoing dialogue with music history', Nyman thus affirms his European musical roots and identity (ibid., p. 410).

## *In Re* Michael Nyman

Although he has commented on many occasions about his admiration for the two composers most closely associated with Dadaism, Satie and Cage, it would be misleading to view Nyman as a Dada composer.[7] Nevertheless, Roger Cardinal's observation on the meaning of Dada art provides a context from which a clearer understanding of Nyman's music may be gained. In an article on the 'cultures of collecting' he sees the inclusion of 'worthless' everyday objects in Schwitters's paintings as, '[obliging] the viewer to engage in different ways of looking ... ways regulated less by aesthetic models and refined cultural connotation, than by [a] commonsensical, associative semiotics on which we rely in our everyday lives' (Cardinal 1994, p. 90). Cardinal's 'associative semiotics' is closely related to the notion of intertextual practice. Both suggest a site where meaning is contextualised, negotiated and deferred. As with Dada's use of ready-made objects, a whole network of intertextual associations are built around Nyman's compositions. These occur on both implicit and explicit levels, as discussed in greater detail in Chapter 4. For now it is worth noting that a general quality of openness in his music suggests an implicit (that is non-specific) intertextuality, while compositions such as *In Re Don Giovanni* (1977), being structurally autonomous, also refer explicitly to pre-existing music.

*In Re Don Giovanni* (hereafter *In Re*) is an obvious starting point for any discussion of Nyman's music. As with *Letters, Riddles and Writs*, *In Re*'s title also has legal connotations, where 'in re' is used as a formula in documentation to literally mean 'in the matter of'. Often regarded as Nyman's first truly 'original' composition to some, to others, *In Re*'s 'originality' can only at best be understood paradoxically or ambiguously. After all, every single note is generated from the opening sixteen bars of Mozart's 'Il Catalogo' (or 'Catalogue') aria from *Don Giovanni*, hence the title (in fact the pattern amounts to fifteen bars, end-to-end, as seen in Example 1.1).

Beirens has noted that Nyman's only input here is to subject the given material 'to a strict process of elimination and reconstruction' (Beirens 2005, p. 424). In certain respects, criticisms directed towards the music's 'pseudo-individuality' are symptomatic of Cardinal's comments relating to pre-conceived opinions of 'aesthetic models and refined cultural connotation'. Could there be another way to view this music, based instead on Cardinal's alternative suggestion? Could the music be understood according to some kind of 'associative semiotics', through a network of references?

The content of *In Re* self-evidently belongs to Mozart, although somewhat ironically Mozart quotes and parodies other eighteenth-century composers and styles in his opera. The aria provides all the melodic, rhythmic and harmonic substance, immediately establishing a 'classical' chain of musical references and associations.

---

7  Neither composer belonged to the movement, however. Satie has rightly been recognized as a forerunner of Dada and Cage one of its descendants (see Nancy Perloff 1993, p. 66, and Marjorie Perloff 1994, p. 100).

**Example 1.1**   *Mozart's 'Il Catalogo' aria (piano reduction)*

But Nyman makes some important choices regarding Mozart's material. First, he consciously sets out to restrict the choice of material to only one short section from the aria and a mere fragment from the opera as a whole. In his re-arrangement of this section, Nyman turns the 15-bar sequence into a kind of perpetual canon or round. Four equal blocks are each repeated twice, resulting in eight repetitions of the complete cycle, rounded off with a short coda (see Table 1.1 for a brief summary of the work's structure). His approach is almost like that of a Schenkerian analyst, building up musical layers from harmonic background through contrapuntal middleground to melodic foreground, or even applying in reverse the principles underpinning Hans Keller's theory of 'functional analysis'. Nyman thus self-consciously separates out,

**Table 1.1    Nyman's *In Re Don Giovanni***

| Section | Bar number | Material | Bar number and instrumentation in Mozart |
|---|---|---|---|
| 1 | 1–15 | Harmonic accompaniment | 1–15 (violin II, viola) |
| 2 | 16–30 | Harmonic accompaniment and bass-line | 1–15 (violin II, viola, cello and double bass) |
| 3 | 31–45 | Harmonic accompaniment, bass-line and treble-part imitation of bass-line | 1–15 (violin I, violin II, viola, cello and double bass) |
| 4 | 46–60 | Harmonic accompaniment, bass-line, treble-part imitation of bass-line and vocal melody | 1–15 (bass-baritone voice, violin I, violin II, viola, cello and double bass) |
| 5 | 61–2 | D major chord | 1–2 |

or 'deconstructs', the original material into its component parts (harmonic, melodic and counter-melodic elements) before reordering them back together again.[8]

What effects do these changes have on one's perception of the music? Nyman's cutting and re-pasting of the original serves at once to magnify many incidental features contained in the original. One's attention is drawn initially to the propulsive rhythmic energy of the repeated quaver patterns first heard on strings and piano. Largely omitted thereafter from Mozart's original aria, where it merely provides a galant-style accompaniment, Nyman's relentless emphasis on the repeated quaver results in some 960 repetitions during the course of the piece (more if the quavers heard at the very end are also included). Some 5.5 quavers are heard on average per second of music (though it is worth noting that, from the perspective of a performance practice of Nyman's music, the original tempo of *In Re* has increased significantly since its first recording in 1981). Ratner's observation about Mozart's mechanistic accompaniment signifying a kind of 'counting machine' is therefore taken literally by Nyman to almost extreme measures (Ratner 1980, p. 403). As is often the case in pop music – with which *In Re* shares its condensed three-minute format – musematic (or note-to-note) repetition controls and directs the overall form. But whereas the rhythmic frame of pop is almost always made visible through the presence of strong and weak beats articulated on drums and percussion, Nyman reduces this aspect to what Dave Laing in his analysis of punk rock has described as the 'rhythmic monad': a series of regular, undifferentiated beats based on 1-1-1-1 rather than 1-2-1-2.[9] The comparison with punk may be less than coincidental since *In Re* was composed when

---

8   Beirens makes a similar observation when he states that *In Re* 'sounds like an analysis of [Mozart], its components slowly being put together again almost as if to demonstrate how the music works' (Beirens 2005, p. 424).

9   A discussion of the 'rhythmic monad' may be found in Moore 1993, p. 113.

the movement was at its height and Nyman is known to have collaborated with some of its proponents, including David Cunningham and The Flying Lizards.

Other pop references lie hidden within the relentless rhythmic forward motion of *In Re*. The rapid reiteration of a single chord is often avoided in modern music.[10] On the other hand repetition is a common feature of the visceral playing of rock 'n' roll pianists such as Little Richard and Jerry Lee Lewis. Lewis's recordings during the late 1950s practically reinvented a new kind of performance practice, where high octane repetition became symbolic of 'sound made physical', brought alive through and by means of the body's reanimation of it. Nyman accidentally discovered this aspect of rock performance when, having 'played [the Mozart sequence] like Jerry Lee Lewis ... I [simultaneously] discovered an approach to texture, an approach to piano playing, and a piano style which dictated the dynamic, articulation and texture of everything I've subsequently done. It was born in one complete package' (Ford 1993, p. 194).

*In Re* resembles pop music in its replication of the three-minute pop song layout, rhythmic movement and direct tonal language. Yet it maintains a strong connection with the past. The music's eighteenth-century syntax is retained in the accompaniment's phrase structure, with its arched ascent from A to D then back down again creating an almost symmetrical shape. Likewise, the imitative dialogue between treble and bass suggests a 'conversational' style typical of classical music while at the same time evoking pop's 'call and response' form. Nyman's gradual reintroduction of these elements successively rather than simultaneously allows many subsidiary lines to be brought unequivocally to the surface. He also emphasizes the interlocking and imitative nature of the contrapuntal dialogue, echoing the repeating patterns of minimalist composer Steve Reich. Further canonic effects are created when the vocal line is added as the final layer in Nyman's Mozart 'mix', most notably in bar 10, where it appears to anticipate the arpeggiated descent of the bass line. In constructing from the aria taxonomies of elements such as melody, accompaniment, secondary theme and its imitation, Nyman deliberately plays on the subject matter of the original. A 'catalogue' is by definition an ordered collection of objects, 'a systematic or methodical arrangement' according to the Oxford English Dictionary. Nyman's composition is by definition a catalogue of musical characteristics.

Replete with lists, inventories, classifications and types taken from both 'high' and 'low' spheres, musical and literary allusions, historical and art-historical references, Nyman's music combines elements of structural and modernist logic with post-structural freedom. Osborne has compared the music's poly-stylistic effect with that of '*A Summer Place* in a devilish arrangement by Tartini, [pulsating] over harmonic sequences from *Sgt. Pepper* or *The House of the Rising Sun* in a sheet music transcription by Northern Songs' (Osborne 1983, p. 40). Nyman adopts certain chord sequences precisely because they belong to an almost universal range of harmonic

---

10 Exceptions are usually of an ironic or conceptual nature, such as Stockhausen's *Klavierstücke IX* (1961), with its 'famous repeated chord' (Maconie 1976, p. 147).

archetypes, from Baroque chaconne to 12-bar rhythm and blues. *In Re*'s opening harmonic pattern, with its open-ended I-VI-II-VII sequence, is a variant of the classic I-VI-IV-V sequence commonly found in 1950s American doo-wop and one which forms the basis of many re-workings by Nyman.

Nyman therefore composes with his ear towards the past as if it were a rich quarry to mine. He works like a musical archaeologist, uncovering artefacts and chiselling fresh and vibrant sonic edifices out of them. While the musical substance of *In Re* may belong to the late eighteenth century, its material *character* and re-presentation is still rooted in that of the late twentieth century. Rich in historical connotation, history is paradoxically given a synchronic, simultaneous dimension. Nyman's music tells us that harmonic and melodic components only form part of music's overall 'composition' or physiognomy. He does to Mozart what surrealist or pop artists such as René Magritte, Roy Lichtenstein or Andy Warhol did to a Van Gogh or Cézanne. The original's sense of form or appearance has been preserved, but the surface image is changed in order to foreground representation, reproduction and the simulacrum, and to question modernist notions of originality and authenticity. This approach is also found in many films directed by Greenaway to which Nyman supplied soundtracks (see Woods 1996, p. 35).[11]

Such observations may ultimately do little to convince Nyman's detractors of any redeeming features belonging to his musical borrowings. He has gone to great lengths to justify his actions, however, arguing that precisely *because* of his fascination with, respect for and an admiration of the original material, his relationship with it often becomes all-consuming. He has found some classical materials 'fascinating in themselves [because] they suggest to me – ways of working' (Nyman, in Ford 1993, p. 194), and in another interview points out,

> What I do looks deeply into Mozart's musical language and makes discoveries about it … [all right] the music is remodelled, I impose a post-modern aesthetic on it, so it doesn't come away unscathed; but I *do* treat it with respect. There's a vein of educationalism in me. I'm saying: here's a few notes you mightn't notice in an opera house or concert hall – this is what they can do. (White 1991, p. 17)

How should these references be understood? Are they intended to be playful or serious, ironic or straight-faced? In truth the answer lies somewhere in between. If *In Re Don Giovanni* is indeed ironic, then it is of a detached nature, commenting on its subject from a distance. What emerges is a juxtaposition of form (minimalism, rock 'n' roll) and content (Baroque, classical). At the music's centre remains Nyman's own complex and thoroughgoing engagement with it as a 'text', and with the texts of music. As I hope to demonstrate in the following chapters, Nyman's approach goes much further than haphazardly quoting bits of 'old' music. His methods draw parallels with those of structural linguistics and post-structural theory and provide it

---

11 Dadaists such as Duchamp had previously explored similar areas in paintings such as LHOOQ (in which a postcard representation of the Mona Lisa is literally 'defaced' by him).

with a self-conscious semiotic design. To use *In Re* again, Nyman adopts a method not dissimilar to Saussure's two basic linguistic operations of generating grammatical structures: the syntagmatic (the process of joining words together) and paradigmatic (selecting and choosing from a list of common terms). Nyman's selection of elements from Mozart's musical 'language' (rhythm, harmony, melody and so on) is therefore paradigmatic, while the manner with which they are recombined is syntagmatic.

If Nyman's musical-textual critiques resemble that of structuralism, he nevertheless turns the text's autonomy on its head by using a found object – a musical intertext – as his material, suggesting that an important post-structural element also forms part of his musical aesthetic. The concept of intertextuality – the relationship between texts – and its application is essential to any understanding of Nyman's work. While it is unlikely that he will ever be completely exonerated from future allegations of 'intellectual misconduct', it is hoped that an intertextual study of his music will at least provide a valid context from which a more balanced assessment of his music may be gained. Before examining specific examples, however, a brief biographical account of his formative years will be undertaken in the following chapter, casting light on the background to these methods. Even Nyman's student compositions demonstrate a stylistic openness while also indicating disaffection with avant-garde techniques, and his subsequent reaction to modernism is detailed in Chapter 3 through a study of his writings on music. This chapter also examines Nyman's early work against the backdrop of the experimental scene in the 1970s in order to show how his experiences in a variety of music-related areas formed the basis for the pluralist, postmodern and inherently intertextual approach adopted by him from the mid-1970s onwards.

# Chapter 2

# Man and Boy: The Early Years

Michael Laurence Nyman was born in Stratford, part of the London Borough of Newham, on 23 March 1944 but was brought up in Chingford, North East London. His parents were not particularly musical and worked in the fur-trade industry. Although Nyman was not brought up an orthodox Jew, his parents encouraged him to respect certain orthodoxies that even secular Jews were expected to observe. He eventually reacted against this during early adolescence when, instead of attending Barmitzvah classes, he would play truant by taking 'bus journeys to St Albans or Woolwich' (Nyman 2004, p. 16). In doing so he cultivated an interest in collecting London bus tickets, which later developed into a fascination with ordering and grouping objects and creating lists in general. Nyman was not alone in wishing to 'make something significant out of the ... urban chaos' of post-war London (ibid., p. 16). Michael Hastings, librettist for Nyman's opera *Man and Boy* recalls that he and many others of his generation (including art critic Roger Cardinal and music critic Michael Church) all 'shared a feeling that by collecting ephemera we were perhaps unconsciously trying, as kids, to restore order to the ruined city and the wasted fields around us' (Hastings 2004, p. 8). As mentioned in Chapter 1, the culture of collecting mirrored the interests of Dada artist Kurt Schwitters, who incorporated found and discarded objects in his paintings. Although there is little on the surface tying together the 'paste-up process' of Schwitters's paintings and Nyman's own musical methods, they both share a common interest in identifying, gathering, arranging and ordering visual or musical objects into categories, classes and collections (Nyman 2004, p. 17).

## Childhood and upbringing

Nyman's musical upbringing was nothing if not unconventional. His parents' employment in the fur-trade industry involved, '[cutting] skins and [sewing] them together to make larger skins which ... were then sent off to fur-coat makers' (Nyman 2000). Nyman's approach to compositional 'material', in which found or created musical ideas are constantly reused, reworked, recombined and recomposed, bears some resemblance to his parents' artisan methods of utilizing every single scrap of material. As a child, any music Nyman may have heard did not come from domestic music-making but rather through radio and television (Russell and Young 2000, p. 95). Therefore latent musical interests remained largely undeveloped during childhood and early education. Indeed Nyman once joked that as a young pupil at Yardley Lane Primary School he was refused admission into the school choir on account of being a 'tuneless "growler"' (Hill 1991, p. 26).

Circumstances significantly altered when, at the age of around eight, Nyman moved to the Sir George Monoux Grammar School in Walthamstow and was brought to the attention of the school's music teacher, Leslie Winters. He was the first person to identify Nyman's potential and set about to nurture, develop and realize it. Winters exerted a powerful influence over Nyman's early musical development, providing him for ten years with a 'broad and intensive musical education' (Russell and Young 2000, p. 95). For the first time he attended live concerts and operas, including Sadler's Wells' production of *Don Giovanni*, and Mahler's epic song-cycle *Das Lied von der Erde*. Both works proved influential. *Don Giovanni* furnished Nyman with the necessary materials for his own intertextual analysis and re-composition of it, while Mahler's output in general, with its use of quotation, allusion and conscious juxtaposition of high and low musical signifiers, provided Nyman with a compelling historical precedent.

Due to the absence of any musical instruments at home, Nyman was effectively integrated into his music teacher's household and allowed to practice on their piano. Adopted by a middle class North Chingford household from the traditionally working-class South, Nyman soon lost his pronounced East End accent and was taught to write using his teacher's elegant italic handwriting. His musical ability soon flourished. At the age of thirteen he started composing, but most efforts remained unfinished. Nyman later recalled that there were 'notebooks lying around at home with lots of beginnings, a few middles and absolutely no ends' (Ford 1993, p. 192). At the age of fourteen he was being employed as a part-time music copyist (Sutcliffe 1984, p. 9). Suffice to say that Winters effectively groomed Nyman for study at the Royal Academy of Music, and he was duly accepted there in September 1961 as a seventeen-year-old student: a quite remarkable achievement for someone who had not benefited from any privileged musical upbringing.[1]

## The Academy years

Although he had started to compose before arriving at the Royal Academy, composition did not assume a central place for Nyman during his time there, and he later admitted that 'composition was not [my] principal focus' (Ford 1993, p. 192). Nyman studied with equal enthusiasm music history, piano, and also harpsichord with Geraint Jones.[2] Fellow composer at the Academy, David Lyon, recalls that at the time Nyman's primary interest was in seventeenth-century music:

Composition was not regarded by [Nyman] or anyone else as his main activity [during this time]. He was essentially a pianist and musicologist, whose main interest was

1  Winters' brother Geoffrey, a composer, had previously studied with Alan Bush at the Royal Academy and therefore recommended Nyman to him.

2  One of Jones's other pupils at the time, harpsichordist Virginia Black, later commissioned, performed and recorded Nyman's music.

Purcell and German Baroque. When, in 1964, my wife and I invited him for a meal at our flat in [London] ... together with the [music] critic Bernard Jacobson, he and Bernard became engrossed in an intense discussion on the finer points of Bach scholarship ... . (Lyon 2004)

Nyman's preference for musicology may have resulted in him being assigned to Alan Bush for composition lessons rather than the more established Lennox Berkeley. Bush's somewhat dogmatic methods were not to everyone's liking, but Nyman revered him, later stating that he exerted 'a powerful influence on my life' (Nyman 1998). In stark contrast to Berkeley's highly respectable position, Bush had by the early 1960s been driven out by the predominantly conservative middle-class forces within the classical music establishment after declaring support for Marxism and Communism. Working in relative isolation and anonymity, Bush nevertheless formulated during the years preceding the Second World War a compositional technique based on what he described as 'the principle of thematic composition' (Bush 1946). This 'thematic' approach attempted to resolve what many recognized as the perennial compositional problem of the mid-twentieth century by providing a synthesis of the two 'mutually contradictory theories [of] Schoenberg's 12-tone system ... and Hindemith's theoretical re-establishment of tonality as a basic and therefore unavoidable ingredient in the fabric of musical art' (Bush 1980, p. 47). Although Bush maintained that he excluded 'in principle from the general [composition] course [at the Academy] this technique of thematic composing as [practised] personally', his political outlook and compositional methods probably influenced Nyman's own efforts during this time. Bush's attempt to resolve the serial *versus* neo-classical dichotomy alerted Nyman to the need later to provide his own musical solution to the modern or postmodern problem that faced him in the mid-1970s.

Bush's admiration for Shostakovich (in particular his *Preludes and Fugues*) and his belief in Hindemith's use of 'diatonicised chromaticism' as a viable alternative to the serial *impasse* represented by the Second Vienna School impressed Nyman, who later declared, '[when] I was a student ... I wrote in a kind of Hindemith–Shostakovich style' (Schwarz 1996, p. 195). While openly renouncing what he perceived as severe methodological constraints imposed by the dodecaphonic system, Bush was at the same time keen to embrace a chromatic free-play that had been gained as a consequence, but within a clearly prescribed tonal context. Mason and Cole have identified in Bush's music, '[some] sort of serial melodic structure ... and there are 12-note themes in the first and slow movements of the C major symphony and of the Violin concerto ... [these] series, however, are used in a tonal context, with an accompaniment of, or as an accompaniment to, freely moving ... other parts' (Mason and Cole 1980, p. 502). Berkeley adopted similar melodic devices in his music. His Sonatina for Oboe and Piano, op. 61 (1962) opens with a twelve-note statement then reverts to more conventional tonal syntax. In addition to Hindemith, Shostakovich, Bush and Berkeley, Nyman's stylistic indebtedness to Bartók and Stravinsky suggests at this time that he was veering away from Austro-German atonality towards Eastern European neoclassicism. In particular the kind of thematic chromaticism generated by Bartók's superimposition of two or more modal regions regularly appears in Nyman's early works (see Antokoletz 1984, pp. 52–4).

Another important element to have emerged from his studies with Bush was Nyman's use of predominantly seventeenth- and eighteenth-century formal devices. His teacher employed similar formal structures in compositions dating from the 1950s and early 1960s, such as the Pavane for the Castleton Queen, Dorian Passacaglia and Fugue, op. 52, or the Suite for Harpsichord or Piano, op. 54. Nyman adopted similar models for his formative compositions, clearly reflecting an early interest in Baroque formal design and the rhythmic character of dance music. Although a radical shift in style and approach took place during the intervening eighteen years (the completion of his soundtrack to *The Draughtsman's Contract* in 1982 is generally considered to be Nyman's first major work), he continued to pursue an interest in the formal structures and processes of Baroque music.

Bush's socialist beliefs may have influenced Nyman more than in purely music-stylistic terms. His teacher's polemical writings on the failings and shortcomings of capitalist society drew Nyman at the end of the 1960s towards another powerful advocate of communism, Cornelius Cardew. If Bush and Cardew allowed their political beliefs to determine their musical characters to strikingly different ends, Nyman's mature compositional style represents a kind of double-edged critique of the work-as-object. That is to say, in a typical performance of a Nyman composition the Michael Nyman Band may symbolize on one level a kind of proletarian-style 'collective accountability' and unity of purpose, echoing Cardew and Frederic Rzewski's musical and political approach. At the same time his music's commercial appeal and economic value would appear to contradict this notion. One could draw from these observations that Nyman is subverting the cultural fabric and dynamic of late capitalism from within. Unlike his predecessors' negative critique of Western capitalism, Nyman is therefore seen to adopt a post-capitalist, postmodern stance in relation to the musical 'object'.

### Stylistic features of the early works

Nyman's student compositions were mainly written for performances at the Academy between late 1962 and early 1964. Some four works were premiered during this time but only two are believed to have survived. This period of continuous (though hardly intense) compositional activity did not go unnoticed by the college authorities, who awarded Nyman the 'Howard Carr Memorial Prize' for composition in July 1964, the first formal recognition of his creative efforts. An indication of the dilemma facing him after leaving the Academy is provided by the fact that Nyman's musical criticism had also been acknowledged during the previous year when he received a prize for 'Best Résumé of Review Week Lectures'.

Of the four compositions in question, the Introduction and Allegro Concertato for Wind Quartet, and the Divertimento for Flute, Oboe and Clarinet were both performed at Royal Academy concerts on 31 January and 13 June 1963 respectively. The Divertimento was also performed at a Macnaghten concert held on 13 December 1963, the well-known and highly regarded series founded by Anne Macnaghten, Iris Lemare and Elisabeth Lutyens in 1931 with the primary purpose of promoting new music. The Introduction and Allegro Concertato – since lost – received its first public performance by the Nash Ensemble in January 1965. Finally a *Canzona* for solo Flute, probably composed during early 1964, was also performed at a Macnaghten concert in November the same year. This last work and the Divertimento provide some indication of the kinds of creative concerns occupying Nyman around this time. Although it would be incorrect to read too much into these works, they do reveal Nyman's interest in past models, variation techniques and neo-classical thought processes.

Nyman's programme note on the *Canzona* describes it as providing 'in form, though not in spirit ... a free approximation to the Italian variation canzona of the [seventeenth] century' (Nyman, 1964a). The piece consists of a series of alternating slow and fast sections, with an introductory theme forming the basis for a set of five freely derived variations followed by a cadenza, and concluding with an abridged recapitulation of the opening theme. The theme is somewhat unusual in that it employs all twelve chromatic notes, suggesting that Nyman may have had in mind one of Bush's twelve-note themes (see Ex. 2.1). As with his teacher's chromatic melodies, Nyman does not develop or expand on the serial potential of the theme. In fact, a shorter three-note figure heard at the end of the first measure provides a basis for further thematic development. This cell-like pattern appears some ten times in all during the opening sixteen-bar statement, preceded either by a tied note, a rest or a short pause (indicated by the brackets in Example 2.1).

**Example 2.1** *Opening theme of Nyman's* Canzona

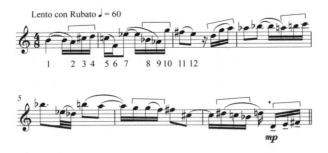

A feature of these tri-chords is that they almost always turn in on themselves by way of oblique chromatic motion, calling to mind Bartók's angular melodic shapes. An opening A-C$^\sharp$-D pattern is 'filled in' by C$^\natural$, B$^\flat$-A$^\flat$-G by F$^\sharp$, D-G-A by A$^\flat$, A-B-C by B$^\flat$, and so on. Similar eleven- or twelve-note 'rows' generated from three-note segments also appear elsewhere in Nyman's early style, notably in the second movement of the Divertimento.

The *Canzona*'s theme creates contrast by encompassing an entire chromatic gamut from D above middle C to C two octaves above, but it also relies heavily on rhythmic repetition and restatement in order to preserve its cell-like identity. Rhythmic repetition is in fact one of its most striking features. The first variation, for example, repeats a quaver pattern in compound time, the second a triplet figure, and the third a semiquaver idea similar to the opening theme. Even when a cadenza-like section is introduced towards the end, any sense of rhythmic and metric freedom is negated by the appearance of repeated rhythms. It would be misleading to suggest that this piece anticipates the repetitive patterns of Nyman's later style, but it is nevertheless useful to note that in a composition which deviates in so many other respects from Nyman's later works, rhythm serves as the primary means of controlling and regulating melodic motion.

Such features also permeate the opening measures of the second movement Siciliano from a slightly earlier work, the Divertimento. According to composer Richard Stoker, who was present at the Macnaghten concert premiere in December 1963, its 'continuously evolving' textures, and 'extensive use of ostinato' anticipate Nyman's later style more than any other of his compositions. The opening four-note statement with its crab-like motion, suggesting Bartók again, is heard some eight times before any kind of thematic variation is introduced (see Ex. 2.2).

**Example 2.2**   *Theme from Nyman's* Divertimento *(Second Movement)*

Such examples of fixed repetition, though common in popular music, would have been comparatively rare in a modern composition. It is tempting with hindsight to view the passage not only as an early indication of musical minimalism but also as encapsulating in microcosm Nyman's later compositional style. However, the context of the Siciliano is both conceptually and aesthetically distinct from minimalist music. As a movement, minimalism had yet to be established when Nyman was writing this piece. To many it occurred in America a year later with Terry Riley's landmark composition *In C*. In fact, rather than suggest minimalism, the inversional characteristics of the theme and its development lean more towards dodecaphonic techniques, but one which again foregrounds rhythmic repetition. The opening four-note pattern consists of a whole-tone dyad and its inversion a minor third higher (D-E and F-E$\flat$). At bar 9 this pattern is extended, suggesting that Nyman was indeed aware of its internal symmetry, with the entire tetrachord inverted at the major third (as seen in Ex. 2.2). The resulting eight-note, two-bar phrase is then repeated three times, again with very little rhythmic variation.

The Divertimento therefore resembles the *Canzona* in its emphasis on direct melodic motion, repeated rhythmic patterns and established formal structures. All three movements of the Divertimento are constructed around pre-existing forms: a stately March based on a dotted rhythm, the aforementioned Siciliano employing a characteristic iambic pattern in compound metre, and a brisk Scherzo in alternating duple and triple time-signatures. Nyman described each one as '[diverging] a little ... from [eighteenth-century] forms' (Nyman 1964b). He even modelled the March on the opening movement of Mahler's Second Symphony, although the resemblance is more in terms of Nyman's use of certain rhythmic and melodic gestures rather than the wholesale adoption of Mahler's large-scale symphonic trajectory. In incorporating something of Mahler's language, Nyman displays an early example of implicit and indirect references to precursor models not dissimilar to the types of borrowing identified by Kevin Korsyn in his analysis of nineteenth-century music (see Chapter 4). Nyman's willingness to utilize formal and stylistic elements from the historical past is already an important feature. One could say that his approach in these early works is broadly 'intertextual' in the manner with which certain formal and stylistic aspects of the musical language of composers such as Mahler and Bartók are brought to bear on Nyman's own style, although he does not employ direct reference or quotation.

## Wardour Castle

Despite some fleeting allusions to twelve-note techniques in his student compositions, Nyman's exposure at the time to serialism and its methods was very limited. The Academy was not generally recognized as a hotbed of avant-garde activity during the early 1960s, and it is unlikely that serial composition was taken seriously there. According to composer Christopher Hobbs, writing about the place towards the close of the decade:

> Outside the Academy it was 1968. Inside, little seemed to have changed since 1945, which was where the music history course ended each year, on the basis that the premiere of *Peter Grimes* in that year had ushered in an era of modernism with which serious music students need hardly concern themselves. (Hobbs 1981, p. 2)

When Nyman was finally formally introduced to serial techniques during a composition Summer School at Wardour Castle, Wiltshire in 1964, the pressure placed upon him to adopt these methods resulted in a complete creative impasse. His reaction to serialism was to remain silent as a composer for a decade, as documented in various biographical accounts (Schwartz 1996).

While it is true that Nyman's early works displayed significant promise, the relatively small corpus of works suggests that he had not yet set his sights solely on becoming a composer. Neither was he at the time totally opposed in principle to twelve-note methods, though he clearly experienced difficulties both aesthetically and creatively with the kind of post-Webernian form of total serial organization then favoured by the European avant-garde. He was, to be sure, prodigiously talented in any number of music-related areas and could equally turn his hand to musicology or performance. Therefore the idea that a promising compositional career had been unceremoniously forced onto the procrustean bed of modernist dogma is misleading. It is not altogether surprising that Nyman decided instead to develop further his musicological interests during the late 1960s and early 1970s. Nevertheless, he did not cease composing entirely, as attested by the experimental *Bell Set No. 1* (possibly composed as early as 1971) and a series of number pieces inspired by the 'machine' music of John White (see Chapter 3). Also of particular importance – given the direction his music took from 1977 – was Nyman's attempt to combine musical quotation with tape music. He recalled later that '[at] the time [1972] I had one of the first English synthesizers. I therefore decided to create a short soundtrack partly using synthesized sounds, partly using revamped fragments from Mozart mixed in with 1930s dance music' (Rivière and Caux 1987, p. 74).

Nyman's experiences at Wardour Castle were instructive in many ways. He found the concept of serial composition exciting but could not bring himself to write using these methods. Nyman has commented retrospectively that he had not been 'strong enough ... to resist [serialism] and ... still use tonal chord sequences' (Nyman, 2000), but this seems a rather harsh self-criticism. The pressure to conform with – and adapt to – a post-war serial ideology was difficult to resist, and any composer deviating from the norm would risk having their work branded as regressive or 'backward'. Thus after some abortive attempts Nyman decided to opt out entirely and set his sights instead on musicological research (Schwarz 1996, p. 196). What followed may have been a knee-jerk reaction to the prevailing modernist dogma, but Nyman subsequently spent three years researching and editing Baroque music at the King's College, London.

## Baroque musicology and ethnomusicology

Nyman's studies at King's with Thurston Dart from 1964 to 1967 provided him with a specialized range of editorial, critical and analytical skills. These newly acquired musicological techniques and the resulting broadening of intellectual horizons were not gained in and for themselves. Wherever Nyman's musical pursuits took him, his compositional instincts invariably followed. Although he may have composed little during this time, his forays into the areas of editorial musicology, analysis, ethnomusicology, publishing and even film production fed back into, and regenerated, his later creative work.

Nyman's immediate interest was focused on rounds, canons and catches in English seventeenth-century music. He may well have been encouraged in this direction by Dart himself who was a leading scholar on Baroque music in general and Henry Purcell in particular. Dart had completed several editions of Purcell's sacred and secular works and published an article on his chamber music leading up to the composer's tercentenary year in 1959 (Dart 1957; 1959a; 1959b). As a sign of the esteem with which he held his young protégé, Dart presented Nyman on his twenty-first birthday with the *Musica Britannica* edition of the second volume of John Bull's keyboard works, to which Nyman later returned when composing his String Quartet No. 1 (Dart 1963).[3]

It is worth noting that what especially drew Nyman towards Baroque music were those elements considered anathema by modernist composers of the time. Tonality, melody and consonance were all essential ingredients in the formation of a Baroque musical language, but it also possessed elements that had little in common with later tonal practice. Purcell's use of circular, repeating forms resulted in the absence of large-scale harmonic goal-orientation, which provided Nyman with a different perspective on tonality. This spurred him on to study non-directed tonal motion in Baroque music. His proposed doctoral thesis was to be a study of seventeenth-century 'Systems Music', and it may not have been entirely coincidental that in turning his back on the European avant-garde and seeking affirmation in the repetitive patterns of certain lesser-known formal models of the past, Nyman was also unwittingly aligning himself with the a-teleological structures of American minimal music.[4] These associations manifested themselves not through minimalism however, but rather when Nyman embarked on a brief foray into folksong collecting in Romania in 1965.

## Romania

Nyman soon realized his mentor's musical interests extended well beyond Baroque. At King's College Dart implemented an innovative honours degree entirely in the study of non-Western music, one of the first of its kind in Britain. The importance bestowed by Dart upon folk traditions and music cultures of the world motivated him to secure a residency for Nyman in Romania during 1965–66, supported by a bursary from the British Council. He was also keen to see his pupil broadening his cultural and musical horizons. Nyman recalls,

> I told him that I had never been out of England for any length of time, so he thought it would be a good idea if I studied abroad. Where? The British Council offered scholarships to East Europe and he knew that the Romanian quota was not filled. Why not Romania then? What could I study there that was relevant to the [seventeenth-

---

3  See Chapter 8 for a discussion of this work.

4  For a discussion of this concept, see Mertens 1988, pp. 16–17.

century] bawdy songs I was then editing? It doesn't matter – what about folk music? (Nyman 1971h, p. 872)

Dart may have believed that Nyman's experiences in Eastern Europe would resurrect his flagging desire to compose. Whatever the case, his first taste of social and cultural life beyond London was revealing and rewarding. Nyman later recalled, 'from a personal point of view it was the best year of my life ... I fell in love with the environment, the villages, the music ...' (Jeffries 1990, p. 93). His aim was to collect and record folk songs and melodies, and some of them provided melodic material for his String Quartet No. 3, composed some twenty-five years later.

While undertaking ethnomusicological research in Romania, Nyman came across similar censorious attitudes to the ones that had driven him away from contemporary music in the first place. The implementation of ideological values by modernist composers in order to legitimate a post-war, avant-garde approach was also being used in folk music. Its proponents wished to 'cleanse' any unwanted elements from the indigenous tradition so that folk music could be elevated and appreciated in the same way as European art music. Having approached ethnomusicology with an inquisitive and open mind, Nyman instinctively veered away from the learned and contrived delivery of the 'official' tradition to more authentic and instinctive modes of expression, interpretation and performance. As with Purcell's repetitive chaconnes and ground basses, certain 'unofficial' folk forms encountered by Nyman in Romania shared common conceptual and aesthetic ideas with the post-experimental American scene that he was to embrace a few years later. In an interview with Meyer, he recalls,

> My attitude to [Romanian folk] music was somewhat unconventional, in any case compared with the standards of the professional [folk] collectors ... my musical perception was similar to how it was ten years later, when I knew about minimalism and Cage. I came across a music band that played with many mistakes. I found this very exciting, but I was the only one to do so. I discovered some funeral songs that seemed to be at first sight incredibly different but then I noticed how they were all built according to the same musical model. So this was therefore a reference to minimalism, but who had any clue already about minimalism in 1965? Obviously, I had an instinct then that I still have today, but my perception in the meantime has been coloured by other experiences. (Meyer 1989, p. 51)

## Nyman as critic

Rather than guiding him back to composition, Nyman's Romanian sojourn confirmed that all music could be subjected to similar forms of ideological control and state censorship. This revelation was important to Nyman. In viewing music as a socially and culturally constructed phenomenon, this led him to identify composition as a form of critique of the 'material' aspect of music. One way of highlighting a critique of musical language was through quotation, borrowing, allusion, rearrangement and re-composition. The pressure to adopt modernist principles or the need to apply acceptable ethnomusicological criteria pointed to a general malaise, where the perpetuation of certain kinds of scientifically rationalized and theoretically verified 'truths' about musical meaning actively denied or suppressed other existing forms. Nyman's ability to move across and shift between the tectonic plates of musical fact and constructed fiction, or identify officially approved or discouraged musical practices later helped him define his own compositional voice.

However, unable or unwilling at the time to harness these thoughts in any creative way, Nyman returned from Romania to the safe haven of Baroque editorial musicology. A direct offshoot of his doctoral research was the production of a new edition in 1967 of Purcell's Catches for Stainer and Bell, complete with hitherto suppressed bawdy lyrics; and he also edited Handel's Concerti Grossi op. 6 for Eulenburg Editions.[5] With his doctoral dissertation incomplete, Nyman was under increasing pressure to secure some form of regular income. He took up several short-term positions with various music publishers until invited in July 1968 to contribute an article for *The Spectator*, then under the editorship of the future British Chancellor of the Exchequer, Nigel Lawson. 'Blocks of Granite', on the music of Olivier Messiaen, duly appeared in the 12 July issue, the first of some forty regular contributions made by Nyman between 1968 and 1970. He also contributed articles for *The Listener* and, a little later, *The New Statesman*. Table 2.1 provides a list in chronological order of Nyman's writings and compositions during this time, with dates and sources. The left column includes the number of articles published, while the right side provides a list of compositions, steadily increasing from 1976 onwards up to the completion of *The Draughtsman's Contract*.

Over one hundred short articles on a wide range of music-related subjects were produced during 1968–78. Many of these featured twentieth-century works (representing some seventy contemporary composers) with an emphasis on first performances and new recordings. Nyman's views on new music formed themselves into a book-length study published in 1974 (though completed some two years previously), called *Experimental Music: Cage and Beyond*. Soon thereafter Nyman renewed his interest in composition, tentatively at first, but from 1976 with increased purpose. He continued to write about music by contributing a series of important articles to *Studio International*, elaborating on the post-experimental aesthetic discussed in the final chapters of his book. But as his list of compositions expanded and his work gained in popularity, Nyman's writings became less frequent.

These critical texts are essential in providing valuable information about the kinds of music Nyman heard, the opinions he formed about them and their impact on his own compositional development. Read against this background and that of Nyman's self-proclaimed 'rebirth' as a composer in 1977,[6] Nyman's texts display many of the aesthetic factors that eventually gave shape to his creative persona. They provide a clear indication of the music he heard, reviewed, understood and appreciated. While

---

5  He later wrote an article on these seventeenth-century drinking songs (Nyman 1969).

6  Nyman uses this term in Anderson 1983, p. 261 and elsewhere.

## Table 2.1    Nyman's writings and compositions, 1968–82

| Year | Number of publications (books, articles, reviews, interviews, papers) | Selected list of works |
|---|---|---|
| 1968 | *Spectator* (13), *Listener* (3), *Tempo* (1) | – |
| 1969 | *Spectator* (24), *Listener* (2), *Music & Musicians* (2), *Tempo* (1) | – |
| 1970 | *Spectator* (5), *New Statesman* (4), *Listener* (2), *Tempo* (1) | – |
| 1971 | *New Statesman* (14), *Music & Musicians* (2), *London Magazine* (2), *Musical Times* (1) | – |
| 1972 | *New Statesman* (3), *Music & Musicians* (3), *Art & Artists* (1) | – |
| 1973 | *Listener* (8), *Musical Times* (1), *Tempo* (1) | *Bell Set No.1* |
| 1974 | *Experimental Music: Cage and Beyond* (book), *Music & Musicians* (2), *Listener* (2) | – |
| 1975 | 'Experimental Music and the American Vernacular Tradition' (paper at Keele Univ.), *Listener* (2) | *1–100* |
| 1976 | 'Against Intellectual Complexity in Music', *Studio International* (8), *Listener* (2) | *The Otherwise Very Beautiful Blue Danube Waltz, Il Campiello, 1st Waltz in D, 2nd Waltz in F* |
| 1977 | *Listener* (6), *Studio International* (2), *Contact* (1) | *In Re Don Giovanni, A Walk Through H* |
| 1978 | '*A Walk Through H*: The Musical Score' (*Catalogue of the BFI*) | *Vertical Features Remake* |
| 1979 | – | *Bird List Song, The Masterwork/ Award-Winning Fishknife* |
| 1980 | – | *The Falls, A Handsom, Smooth, Smart, Clear Stroke, A Neat Slice of Time, Birdwork, Melody Lists in 3 & 8, Plotting for the Shopkeeper* |
| 1981 | – | *Act of God, Five Orchestral Pieces Opus Tree, M-Work, Bird Anthem, Real Slow Drag* |
| 1982 | – | *The Draughtsman's Contract* |

he was prepared to write about a wide range of musical forms and styles, he was nevertheless unafraid to present his own opinions about them. Such firmly held views eventually fed back into compositions he wrote from the mid-1970s onwards. By discussing music already in existence, the critic constantly addresses her/his subject from an intertextual perspective, drawing out influences, comparing and contrasting works, performances or recordings, or placing a particular composer in context. In adopting some of these elements in his later musical language, intertextual elements form part of both the creative and critical dimension in any study of Nyman's music.

# Chapter 3

# Texts in Context

Nyman could not have chosen a better time to become a critic. Contemporary music in England generally and London in particular was flourishing. Otto Karolyi wrote that 'during the 1960s Great Britain and, above all, London, became one of the leading centres of music. The doors were opened, as it were, and the possibilities of experimentation seemed boundless' (Karolyi 1994, p. 103). Nyman's writings often display a shared sense of enthusiasm and excitement at being part of a thriving cultural environment, such as the statement made in 1969, that 'music is alive and flourishing in considerable opulence in London; there's an unprecedented "we never close" atmosphere about [the place] at the moment ...' (Nyman 1968a, p. 74).

The beginnings of a New English Musical Renaissance had already taken hold with the emergence of a group of composers whose music Nyman had previously encountered at Wardour Castle. Goehr, Birtwistle and Maxwell Davies – all in their thirties and dubbed the 'Manchester School' – combined a knowledge and understanding of twelve-note concepts with an interest in medieval forms and music theatre. Goehr's *Naboth's Vineyard*, Birtwistle's *Punch and Judy* and Maxwell Davies's *Eight Songs for a Mad King* were all given first performances between 1968 and 1969, all three receiving favourable reviews by Nyman in *Spectator*, *Listener* and *Tempo* magazines respectively. Although reluctant to imitate their work, Nyman was nevertheless content to proselytize, and he became directly involved with one of the 'triumvirate' when asked to provide a libretto to Birtwistle's opera *Down by the Greenwood Side*, also performed in 1969.[1] Nyman's anti-establishment spirit brought him closer to Birtwistle than the other two, and their paths were to cross again in 1976 when, as musical director of the National Theatre, Birtwistle invited Nyman to provide music for a staged production of Goldoni's *Il Campiello* (see Chapter 6). Birtwistle and Maxwell Davies were also influenced by mediaeval and renaissance techniques of quoting and paraphrasing pre-existing chants or popular melodies. Such features distinguished their work from the mainly modernist concerns of continental European composers of the time, such as Boulez, Stockhausen and Xenakis, and alerted Nyman to the possibility of borrowing and reusing musical material.

## Cultural and musical context

Further impetus was provided to the new music scene in London by the presence of many leading European lights. Boulez was appointed guest conductor of the BBC

---

1  For Nyman's summary of this opera see Nyman 1971g, pp. 120–21.

Symphony Orchestra in 1964, and together with the corporation's music controller William Glock 'put together programmes that would contradict every accepted notion of programme-building, and would illuminate the twentieth-century repertory as never before' (Kenyon 1981, p. 317). But the main focus was on Karlheinz Stockhausen, the leading proponent of the European avant-garde at this time, who had acquired something of a cult status in England.

The controversy and interest surrounding Stockhausen's music extended beyond the fringes of contemporary music to the areas of rock and jazz. John Lennon's experimental 'Revolution 9', which appeared on The Beatles' so-called *White Album* (recorded in June 1968 and released later that year), may have been indirectly influenced by Stockhausen's *Hymnen* in its cut and paste collage of taped musical fragments (Macdonald 1995, pp. 233–4). Paul McCartney also attended performances of music by Stockhausen and Luciano Berio around this time (Kozinn 1995, p. 136). The Beatles clearly occupied a different cultural space to that of Stockhausen or other members of the musical avant-garde, but the erosion of genre distinctions and consequent blurring of categories between high art and popular music were merely examples of much wider cultural transformations taking place during the late 1960s. In more general terms, this period witnessed a gradual loosening up of certain aesthetic, theoretic and philosophic certainties previously championed by modernism and canonized in the avant-garde compositions and writings of composers such as Boulez and Luigi Nono. These figures represented to Nyman and others the continuation of an increasingly abstract, autonomous, exclusive and ultimately self-perpetuating system governed by its own internal, self-regulating set of principles and methodologies.

A postmodern reading would view serial composition as a kind of meta-narrative discourse, claiming aesthetic and epistemological high-ground over other forms of musical production.[2] Nyman's writings similarly engage with the issue of musical modernism across four key areas. First of all his writings provide a critique of the theories and practices of the avant-garde movement. Secondly, Nyman questions the legitimacy of the European avant-garde by adopting the experimental aesthetic advocated in America by John Cage, in England by Cardew, and later by the American minimalists. Thirdly, he investigates the methods of the post-experimental school of English composers of the mid-1970s, who made valuable use of intertextual signifiers such as musical quotation, parody and pastiche. Finally, Nyman advocates a more explicit intertextuality, lying at the intersection between high art and popular culture and which he defined as a form of 'vernacular' music. Taken together these musical codes and practices amount to a rejection of modernism and move towards the kind of postmodernism that typifies Nyman's early mature style.

---

2  For a detailed discussion of this term see Lyotard 1984, pp. 31–7.

## The avant-garde and modernism

Nyman's critique and ultimate rejection of the European avant-garde is most visibly demonstrated in his writings on Stockhausen and Boulez. The sheer proliferation of works produced by Stockhausen during the 1960s may explain his ubiquity in Nyman reviews from 1968 to 1971. Stockhausen simply could not be ignored, and any radical or controversial musical innovation would almost inevitably come about through, or by means of, his compositions. Nyman's fascination with Stockhausen may have been motivated by the fact that Cardew, who at this time became increasingly influential, had worked with Stockhausen in Cologne a decade or so earlier.

Certainly Cardew's subsequent reflections on his time spent working with Stockhausen were less than complimentary (Cardew 1961a; 1961b). Nevertheless, Stockhausen appears initially at least in Nyman's writings as a credible alternative to the rigorous formalism of Darmstadt serialism: a kind of European version of John Cage. Indeed, both Cage and Stockhausen had attracted earlier comparison with their shared views on indeterminacy and chance; both having been famously placed together inside the cockpit of a plane in a photographic montage (see Revill 1992). Stockhausen's use of 'group' or 'moment-form' suggested a composer exploring processes that eschewed conventional organizational principles, advocated new modes of listening, and even appeared to weaken or challenge the authority of the composer. Some of Nyman's statements regarding Stockhausen's *Kontakte* could be mistaken for a discussion of Cage-style indeterminacy: '[Moment-form is] totally dependent on new perceptions of musical time … [both] the creation of individual sound events … and in the overall form [exist] only "now", at this moment in a theoretically endless sequence' (Nyman 1968b, p. 269). Stockhausen's restructuring of temporal elements resulted in a more intense focusing on sound 'in isolation', a notion that is supported in Nyman's appraisal in 1968 of *Aus den sieben Tagen*, in which he comments on 'the extent to which Stockhausen is now directly involved in sonic, rather than theoretical, material' (Nyman 1968c, p. 810). He may even have believed at this time that Stockhausen's brand of structural indeterminacy signalled a kind of postmodernist 'death of the composer as individual genius', and a relinquishment of control *à la* Cage.[3] In addition, Stockhausen's music deliberately broke free of genre and boundary distinctions, integrated music with movement, theatre and ritual, and brought it back into contact with certain spiritual and transcendental elements.

Whatever the case, a review of *Kurzwellen* some two years later captures the uneasy paradox of freedom and control that lay at the very heart of Stockhausen's compositional aesthetic. Nyman observes that on the surface *Kurzwellen* appears to have been composed indeterminately, allowing for a significant degree of freedom in performance. In reality, however, it is still under the control of the composer who continues to assume the role of musical master and genius. In summarizing *Kurzwellen*, Nyman concludes, 'Stockhausen is definitely *the composer*' and the aesthetic principles at work in his compositions are no different to those of any other

---

3   On the death of authorship see Barthes 1977, p. 142.

post-Enlightenment composer engaged with individuating and reifying the concept of the musical 'idea'. Drawing comparison with Cage in order to position himself on the other side of the fence to Stockhausen, Nyman argues,

> Cage really does give you as near total freedom as you can have. The concept of development is alien to Cage, but what else [other] than 'development' in the [Beethovenian] sense would you call the way all the performers seem to pounce [in *Kurzwellen*] with undeniable relish, on the drum signal of the BBC World Service? (Nyman 1971a, p. 282)

Stockhausen abdicated certain responsibilities in the area of musical notation in the full knowledge that music's mechanical form of reproduction – its existence as 'recording' – was indeed indelibly fixed, and he continued to assume complete control over this aspect. In fact Stockhausen's concept of open form served more transcendental, spiritual and mystical ends. Each moment could contain within itself the seeds of a kind of elemental temporality. Intrinsic organic relationships between the whole and its parts were preserved, while vertical 'clusters' – the building blocks of moment-form – ultimately served to bring about an absolute unity of form and content, of structure and material. Therefore the presence and power of the individual 'genius' lay undiminished in the figure of Stockhausen despite suggestions to the contrary.

Nyman's comments on Boulez provide further evidence of his increasing disaffection with European modernism. They focus on the nature of 'intellectualism' in music, and are discussed in a book review entitled 'Boulez's Law' (Nyman 1971b). Nyman's initial discussion centres round Boulez's codification of avant-garde techniques in his book *Boulez on Music Today*. Written in 1963 when Boulez had already severed his early association with Cage and his admiration of Stockhausen had appreciably cooled, Boulez's Adornoesque polemic on 'various fetishes ... [that] arise from a profound lack of intellectualism', is a two-pronged attack on the spiritual indulgence of Stockhausen on the one hand and the Dada excesses of Cage on the other (Boulez 1971, p. 22).

Laws underpinning such compositional procedures as enumerated by Boulez in this theoretical treatise aim to preserve the sacrosanct self-sufficiency of the modernist work. By constructing a musical grammar forming a syntactical basis for 'linguistic' competence in avant-garde techniques, Boulez sets out the terms of modernism's own self-legitimacy: an undisputed form of scientific knowledge and methodological practice that banishes all other 'discourses' from its rarefied atmosphere. Modernism's rejection of familiar 'found' objects and referential units of meaning are described by Nyman as 'those old forbidden fruits ... scattered along [Boulez's] path to technical self-knowledge – recognizable pulse, tonal chords, in effect everything modern music seems to lack ... as their imagery is too strong, too specific for this patently artificial system to sustain' (Nyman 1971b, p. 466). He then draws comparisons between Boulez and Stockhausen in order to suggest that their similarities ultimately outweigh their differences:

In the final analysis Stockhausen has not really renounced the kind of techniques proposed in [Boulez's] book, since even a piece like *Kurzwellen*, with its plus and minus notation and short-wave radios, attempts to extract the maximum amount of differentiation from its material – which is the story of the self-same European 'masterpiece' tradition [that] Boulez ... attempts to defend. (Ibid., p. 467)

In addition to modernist meta-narratives of technical self-mastery and knowledge, autonomy, individual genius, the canonization of works and the dissemination of an abstract, formalized system, Nyman later attacks another sacred cow, namely the championing of intellectual ideals. Intellectualism in avant-garde theory is often defined through straightforward binary oppositions between complexity and simplicity (Nyman 1993a, p. 206). Nyman's critique of musical complexity is based on the premise that avant-garde intellectual value-judgements tacitly measure 'simplicity' only in relation to its opposite form: simple musical structures are defined through more complex structures. This hierarchical aesthetic ensures that in modern music 'simplified moments are either set against other moments of greater complexity, or they fulfil a complex role in the total structure of the work' (ibid., p. 206). In music falling outside the modernist domain however, simplicity is regarded as an absolute, 'something approaching a constant', existing in and for itself. In some examples of musical modernism, such as Stockhausen's *Mantra* (1971), Nyman even argues that the concomitant values of complexity and intellectualism no longer measure up: '*Mantra* demonstrates ... that musical value is not necessarily commensurate with impressive technical apparatus, elaborate formal structures and acres of notes' (Nyman 1971c, p. 343). Having rejected the main tenets of modernism in his writings Nyman replaced them with an alternative set of principles: he soon embraced the experimental, anti-aesthetic approach of Cage, American minimalism, and English experimental music.

## American and English experimental music

Nyman's own reservation about the direction taken by post-1945 European modernism was largely confirmed through the radical reformulation and reconfiguration of music's very purpose and existence in the writings and ideas of Cage. The term coined by Cage to describe this new movement, though not without reservation, was 'experimental' (Cage 1961, p. 7). In essence, the experimental ethos questioned all established notions relating to composition, performance and its reception. Silence assumed a central role in the experimental aesthetic, and as an absolute and impersonal measurement of time was used in addition to – or even sometimes instead of – sound. Sound was divested of all its layers of historical weight and significance in order to revisit a natural state (Cage) or recover a kind of lost innocence (Satie). Experimental music drew attention to the fact that notation essentially consisted of a series of directions given shape through a series of enacted and premeditated gestures or responses by a performer. Nyman observed in Cardew's *The Great Learning*

(1968–71), for example, that 'one is made intensely aware, as if for the first time, of the physical intension of sound' (Nyman 1972b, p. 132). The absence of fixed meanings extended also to the reception of the work where multiple interpretations and responses were encouraged instead of an emphasis on unitary focus.

Cage anticipated that the principles underlying his counter-aesthetic would pose a threat to orthodox modernism when he famously predicted in 1957,

> A parting of ways ... [the avant-garde composer] may complicate his musical technique towards an approximation of ... new possibilities and awareness ... or [the experimental composer] ... may give up the desire to control sound ... and set about discovering means to let sounds be themselves rather than vehicles for man-made theories or expressions of human sentiments. (Cage 1961, p. 10)

Indeed it was Cage's emancipation of sound from intention that caused a major fracture between the European and American avant-garde. Cage's use of chance operations, indeterminacy and graphic notation resulted in a series of unforeseen outcomes, described by Landy as the process of 'infiltrating purposelessness into music' (Landy 1991, p. 4). In fact, degrees of 'non-intention' were filtering through to European modernism, where composers such as Stockhausen, Berio and Lutoslawski adapted experimental techniques to suit their own formal, textural or notational requirements. Indeed American experimentalism's use of abstract or hidden processes often masked any clear differences between the two. Definitions such as '[that] in which the innovative component of any aspect of a given piece takes priority above more general technical craftsmanship expected of any art work' could equally be applied to European avant-garde or American experimental music, where emphasis was also given to the importance of originality and invention (ibid., p. 7). Cage's general avoidance until the late 1960s of any explicit symbolic representation in his compositions, 'so that sounds may be heard, as much as possible for what they are, not for what they mean' also resulted in works where the modernist ideals of abstraction and intellectualism were often brought to the surface (Cage, in Nyman 1999, p. 36). American experimentalism may therefore have set itself up in opposition to modernism's perceived ivory-tower elitism and exclusivity but shared with it a common drive towards innovation. As Alastair Williams summarizes:

> Many of the art forms that arose during the 1960s, such as chance music and pop art, are frequently understood as reactions against the determinist, technological modernism of the 1950s ... the situation is, however, more complex than this interpretation indicates: the pop avant-garde and experimental art may challenge the divide between elitist and mass art, but they are still very much at one with the notion of the new and of technological advancement. (Williams 1997, p. 125)

While innovation and the critique of the forms of production linked both experimental and avant-garde approaches, many crucial differences separated them, particularly in terms of their cultural and social value. After its post-1945 inception the European avant-garde became officially recognized and institutionalized, receiving state sponsorship and support, while the experimental movement was granted very little funding or publicly endorsed in any way. Nyman identified in 1972 an irreconcilable gulf existing between the established, patronized forms of high modernism and the alternative, unofficial and unrecognized 'experimental', when he stated that these 'two nations' of contemporary music

> ... don't mix ... and their roles and rewards are mightily different. Avant-garde means fame, festivals, commissions, and acceptance by the establishment and their audiences; experimental means a ghetto, repressive tolerance, a small but totally dedicated following, and earning your living some other way. (Nyman 1972c p. 434)

This stark socio-political prognosis of experimental music's cultural economy – neglected, ridiculed and marginalized – ultimately led post-experimental composers such as Nyman to establish a more direct interface with its public through the self-conscious fusion of pop and avant-garde sensibilities.

By the late 1960s the American movement had established itself in England largely through the endeavours of Cardew, who had come into contact with Cage while working with Stockhausen in 1958. Nyman became involved with this movement early on, initially as critic, then as performer and later as editor and composer. His book on the subject provides for the first time a detailed definition of the term 'experimental' (Nyman 1999, pp. 1–30). Out of the standard division of music into the three categories of composition, performance and listening, Nyman forms a cosmology of experimental music and its relationships (see Figure 3.1).

Using Cage's famous silent piece *4'33"* as the archetypical expression of experimentalism Nyman explains the movement's principal aims. From the point of view of performance and reception *4'33"* is designed to adapt to the contextual and environmental conditions of the moment in which it is realized. This idea is unlike most compositions belonging to the Western classical tradition where the composer's imprint is indelibly fixed upon the work.[4] Along with the unique and unpredictable moment invested in each performance, Cage also introduces the idea of temporal freedom and flexibility in music, where pieces vary in length, content and duration.

Simplifying musical directions or dispensing with them altogether enabled performers without any specialized knowledge of notational practices to perform experimental pieces. 'Making sounds' was no longer the performer's only *sine qua non*, but she or he could also 'make silences', movements, actions and other gestures. Performers became part-composers part-realizers through such activities, and the hitherto unquestioned authority of the composer was devolved. The performer's role in experimental music was to recreate anew, rather than to render as faithfully as possible, the composer's creative and expressive intentions. A performer reacted in an experimental environment to unpredictable situations arising from any given performing context, intentionally or unintentionally built into the piece. Again using

---

4  Paradoxically *4'33"* has also retained a sense of identity by becoming a work and being 'authored' by Cage.

**Figure 3.1 Nyman's 'cosmology' of experimental music**

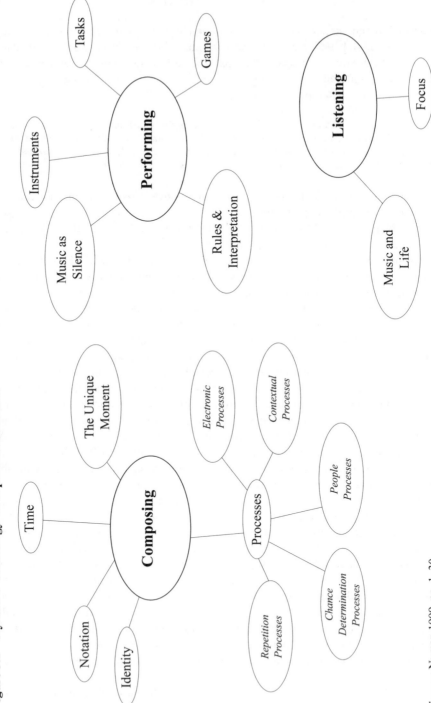

*Source:* Nyman 1999, pp. 1–30.

Cardew's *The Great Learning* as an example, Nyman summarized these differences by saying that due to the 'incorruptible latitude of the score ... each participant ideally fulfils the roles of performer, listener, critic and composer' (Nyman 1972b, p. 131).

In emancipating the role of the performer, Cardew and others were encouraged to establish the Scratch Orchestra. Cage had already thought up this concept when he suggested that 'art instead of being an object made by one person is a process set in motion by a group of people. Art's socialized' (in Nyman 1999, p. 130). 'Paragraph 2' from Cardew's *The Great Learning* provides an example of this kind of socialized music making. All performers read from the same set of directions. A group of percussionists play through a series of twenty-six rhythmic patterns in any order. At the same time a vocal group sing a set of pitches in written order where the duration of each set is regulated by a single breath, thereby creating an ever-increasing series of overlapping lines between each group. The emphasis therefore shifts towards 'group rather than individual music' and the performance itself as a form of process.

Group composition of this kind sparked interest in experimental music from polytechnic-affiliated fine arts departments rather than from traditional university or conservatoire establishments. Indeed some of Nyman's early pieces were written in order to suit the kind of creative and collective – but not necessarily technically accomplished – music-making practised and performed at polytechnics. Art colleges had been for many years a nurturing ground for blues and rock musicians, who engaged with sound – as with their art work – in a direct and more tactile manner.[5] Nyman and other classically trained composers later adopted the pragmatic approach of pop culture by forming their own 'bands' or ensembles rather than relying on state-supported orchestras or ensembles, shaping and sculpting their own distinctive sound. Many composers and performers associated with the movement went on to teach at various polytechnics during the 1970s as shown in Table 3.1.

Table 3.1   **Composers and musicians working in art colleges, 1965–75**

| Composer, performer | Institution |
| --- | --- |
| Gavin Bryars | Portsmouth College of Art, Leicester Polytechnic |
| Cornelius Cardew | Morley College of Art, Maidstone College of Art |
| Michael Nyman | Trent Polytechnic, Maidstone College of Art, Goldsmith's College |
| Michael Parsons | Portsmouth College of Art |
| John Tilbury | South West Essex Technical College, Kingston, Portsmouth, Falmouth |
| John White | Leicester Polytechnic |

*Source*: Nyman 1976c, pp. 282–3

---

5   For an account of art's impact on pop see Frith and Horn 1987.

If the role of the performer had been radically altered in experimental music, Cage's critique of sound and silence also re-engaged the audience in fundamentally new ways. Cage believed that each individual's perception of, and response to, the musical object to be unique and based on a complex interactive grid of constantly shifting contexts, surroundings and circumstances. From this supposition, Cage advocated a 'new mode of listening', concentrating on the 'activity' rather than the 'purpose' of sounds (Cage 1961, p. 10). Setting up a situation where the audience aurally reconstructed the music from basic materials presented to them was taken up and further developed by a subsequent generation of American minimalist composers.

Another aspect that brought the experimental tradition and musical minimalism closer together was the use of musical process, as shown in Figure 3.1. Although a broad range of processes are listed by Nyman in *Experimental Music*, including chance-determined procedures adopted by Cage and those utilizing electronic technologies, three types are particularly interesting because they are adopted by Nyman in his own pre-minimal, experimental compositions. These three types are people, contextual and repetition processes respectively. People processes allow performers to 'move through given or suggested material, each at his own speed', reading from the same part but responding to it in a different way, the effect of which has been described by Parsons as that of '"unity" becoming "multiplicity"' (Parsons, in Nyman 1999, p. 6). Nyman cites Morton Feldman's *Piece for Four Pianos* (1957) and Rzewski's *Les Moutons de Panurge* (1968) as examples of people processes. Contextual processes involve making decisions based on performing outcomes, on 'actions dependent on unpredictable conditions and on variables which arise from within the musical continuity' (ibid., p. 6). Some overlap exists between these two methods, and works such as Cardew's *The Great Learning* exhibit a tendency to use both. The third, which provides an important connection between American experimental music, minimalism and the English experimental movement, involves 'extended repetition', where the same or a similar recurring pattern becomes the focus of a piece, out of which 'unforeseen' elements often arise (ibid., p. 8). Pieces of this nature include Terry Riley's *In C* (1964) or John White's 'machine' compositions.

## American minimalism

Nyman's writings display a respect for experimental music but do not convey the same level of enthusiasm with which he greeted the emerging generation of American composers of the late 1960s, whose works were still largely unfamiliar to British audiences at the time. While various terms were applied to early incarnations of this form (including 'pulse', 'systems', 'static' and 'hypnotic' music), Nyman was one of the first to coin the term 'minimal' music, in a *Spectator* review in October 1968 (Schwarz 1996, p. 8).[6] Although the term had previously been applied to various

---

6  Nyman preferred the adjective 'minimal' to the epithet 'minimalist', and continued to use it in his book *Experimental Music*.

types of modern art, 'minimalism' in relation to music was uncommon. Nyman may have been thinking of some of Cage's theatre music when he first referred to a performance by Nam June Paik at the ICA as a 'minimal-happening' (Nyman 1968d, p. 518; Schwarz 1996, p. 12). Indeed it was not uncommon during the late 1960s for it to be applied to forerunners of the genre, such as La Monte Young's extended drones, George Brecht's isolated 'events' or Feldman's enigmatic soundworld (Strickland 1993, pp. 240–44).

In any case, Nyman's familiarity with the founder members of this movement was established in 1970 when he first interviewed Reich, and then organized the Steve Reich Ensemble's first appearance at London's ICA Nash House, which took place in March 1971 (Potter 2000, p. 198). Glass's music was also performed for the first time in England in 1971 (Nyman 1976e, p. 64). Buoyed by the freshness and originality of what he heard, Nyman contributed some important early articles, interviews and analytical essays on the movement, even performing with Reich's ensemble on their return to England in 1972 (Nyman 1971d; 1972a; Schwarz 1996, p. 196).

The impact of minimalist music – particularly that of Steve Reich – on Nyman was as profound as it was immediate. Reviewing a recording of Reich's *Four Organs* and *Phase Patterns* in 1971 (the disc was not released in Britain until the following year), Nyman's enthusiasm spills onto the page, as though eager to document a decisive musico-historical moment: 'you will hear a new classical music of unprecedented vitality and strength of purpose, a music that extends beyond the frontiers of the Cage–Stockhausen era' (Nyman 1971e, 248). Minimalism's emphasis on new modes of listening owed something to Cage, where the listener plotted a path through the overlapping, multi-layered tapestry of repeating patterns or would concentrate on the music's resulting psycho-acoustic effects. But the differences in many ways outweighed these similarities. Nyman observes that 'one generation after Cage, [the minimalists] have replaced silence by a completely unbroken continuum, improvisation and indeterminacy by freedoms within severely circumscribed limits, and the multi-sensory experience with a completely new experience of time' (ibid., p. 248).

Reich's early tape pieces *It's Gonna Rain* and *Come Out* (1965–66) both made use of recording technology in order to advance and evolve certain compositional methods. Unlike European avant-garde electronic music, which viewed technology as an accurate and reliable means of realizing pre-established compositional theories, Reich's early pieces demonstrate how technology could directly influence and transform creativity. Reich explains in an interview with Nyman: 'what tape did for me basically was on the one hand to realize certain musical ideas that at first had to come out of machines, and on the other to make some instrumental music possible that I never would have got to by looking at any Western or non-Western music' (Nyman 1971d, p. 230).

While Reich's initial interests may have centred round the nature of human engagement and its imprecision in imitating machines, the musical results were anathema to both American experimental music and the European avant-garde.

Regular pulsation, unitary focus, determinacy and consonance brought minimalism much closer at least on the surface level to rock and pop music. Yet minimalism was not a form of popular music. In allowing pattern and process to become the 'object' of the work, and by developing the idea of constructing compositions according to predetermined modular schemes or additive and subtractive methods, minimalism represented an almost extreme extension of modernism's obsession with structure and formalism by abnegating the subjectivity of the material and the personality of the individual from the creative process (Ritzel 1993). Reich's belief that musical processes should run along entirely by themselves according to a machine-like logic also suggested a highly formalist approach. Neither entirely modern nor postmodern, but maybe closer to Hal Foster's term 'antimodernist', minimalism stood at the intersection between the two periods (Foster et al. 2004). As Potter states, '[minimalism's] hard-line stance of negation suggests that it operates as an alternative ... [but one] that is decidedly modernist in its stance' (Potter 2000, pp. 9–10).

## Decay music

Soon after meeting up with Reich and possibly due to some encouragement from him, Nyman sought to combine some of the principles governing experimental and minimalist approaches in his own music under the title 'Decay' music. The term had previously been used in Cardew's comments about John White's *Tuba and Cello Machine*, where 'all Machine music [represents] a *decay process* anyway [my emphasis]' (Nyman 1976a, p. 234). As a first attempt at this new aesthetic Nyman composed *Bell Set No. 1*, which was premiered at the Cockpit Theatre, London in 1973. The score was subsequently published in the Experimental Music Catalogue's *Anthology of Rhythmic Music*.

Written for 'any combination of pitched or non-pitched highly resonant metal percussion instruments', *Bell Set* is based on a series of four simultaneously sounding rhythmic structures, each one initially comprising three durations. Example 3.1 presents the opening patterns of the first rhythmic part. Rhythms belonging to parts two, three and four are derived from, or 'systematically related' to, the three-quaver cell (1+1+1) first heard in part one (Nyman 1976a, p. 236).

In all the other parts the middle value is augmented to create varied patterns where player two plays quaver, crotchet, quaver (1+2+1), player three quaver, dotted-quaver, quaver (1+3+1), and player four quaver, minim, quaver (1+4+1). This simple process of rhythmic expansion also generates separate transformations along each part. Player one's second rhythmic cell augments the two outer durations creating crotchet, quaver, crotchet (or 2+1+2), until the outer values become thirty times the original statement (or 30+1+30). Player two gradually increases the combined rhythmic values of each unit, so that they become 3, 4, 5 ... 43. Player three has by far the greatest rhythmic expansion. Each unit maintains a symmetrical shape across

**Example 3.1** *Rhythmic patterns in* Bell Set No. 1 *(first rhythmic part)*

its forty-two units, while gradually augmenting the combined values by adding two in each case (3 becomes 5, then 7, and so on), so that by the final unit 1+3+1 has become 28+22+3+22+28. The fourth part's rhythmic process unfolds in a similar way to the second part, but due to an increased value in the opening pattern, it ends with a combined rhythmic total of 49 quaver beats. As the distinguishing element in each part, the middle value is therefore left unaltered throughout.

Nyman has described the process applied to *Bell Set* as a 'developing rather than permutative system', where 'four independent, but systematically related, sets of … rhythmic patterns are superimposed (each set [containing] short figures to be repeated a number of times, all but one beat in each figure one unit longer than the previous one)' (Nyman 1976a, p. 236). Although the general impression is one of rhythmic expansion across each part, Nyman has observed that the perceived effect is different. Rather than the expected effect of gradual decay across the entire time-span, 'instead, predominantly fast motion, suddenly and unexpectedly at a given point some seven minutes into the piece, becomes slow', due in part to the 'more complex, unpredictable phenomenon' caused by the contrapuntal movement of simultaneously moving parts (ibid., p. 236).

The complete absence of any melodic or harmonic material in *Bell Set* clearly signifies a radical departure from the early student compositions analysed in the previous chapter. Nyman may have had in mind Reich's recent *Four Organs* when he composed it. Both works are ostensibly for four players (in *Bell Set* the number is stated only as a minimum requirement and *Four Organs* also includes a 'metronomic' fifth part for maracas). Both build into four individual parts a gradual process of deceleration on a macro-structural level, resulting in a slowing down of rhythmic movement while the process expands. Nyman has in addition drawn attention to the differences between the two pieces, where despite the '"logic" of numerical or other systems', *Bell Set* allows the 'uncontrollable force' of sound to rise to the surface. As a result, '*Four Organs* sounds seamless; the additive system of *Bell Set* is numerically seamless, but the music leaps' (Nyman 1976a, p. 243).

Parallels may also be drawn between Nyman's working methods and other composers. Glass's additive rhythmic technique is suggested in the irregularly augmenting units (in particular Glass's early minimalist exercise, *One + One*). Cage too inevitably casts his shadow over the work. The American's first important works were written for percussion ensemble, emancipating him decisively from the strictures imposed by Western concepts of harmonic syntax and structure. *Bell Set* likewise releases Nyman from the syntactical neo-classical straightjacket of his earlier student style. Furthermore, the piece may have been planned as the first in a series of rhythmic exercises following Cage's set of *Construction* compositions. *Bell Set* was originally recorded along with *1–100* for release on Brian Eno's newly established Obscure Records in 1976,[7] and together they represent a general shift from within the post-experimental music aesthetic where popular culture and art music are brought closer together. Eno's early experiments in combining delay-processing systems with sustained sounds and repeated patterns resulted in a technologically grounded form of minimalism. His background as an art student and rock musician also enabled him to explore on a more instinctive and tactile level the timbral colouristic potentialities of electronically generated sounds while at the same time allowing personal creative and expressive choices to hold sway over the dictates of an overarching system or process. In recording *Discreet Music*, for example, Eno was concerned in making:

> [Something] that wasn't uncomfortable ... music you don't have to concentrate on [...] if you want to focus on another level, there's a set of ideas that are interesting in terms of systems working like Steve Reich's piece 'It's Gonna Rain'. And to stop it being monotonous – and, I suppose, completely ignorable – I did make changes during the

---

7   Michael Nyman: *Decay Music*, Obscure Records (OBS 6, 1976).

piece. This touching up is very much a philistine idea in the experimental composer's terms; it's wanting to entertain. But I think that borderline area is a very interesting one. (Eno 1975a)[8]

Another composer working along similar lines to Eno was the American Harold Budd. His 1976 recording of *The Pavilion of Dreams*, produced by Eno, also featured performances by Nyman and Gavin Bryars.[9] Eno's aim in establishing Obscure Records was to open up the market to an audience which he had identified was gradually moving away from the standard pop single format towards an engagement with more extended and less dramatic musical structures:

> People are listening to music in a lot of different ways and for a lot of different reasons … [they] are quite capable of sitting and listening to an uninterrupted 25 minute piece of music which doesn't have lyrics and doesn't have all the things that were thought to be necessary to sell a record … people are moving into a listening pattern that is far less dramatic and assaulting, they are capable of listening to pieces that go on for a time on a fairly level plateau and then fade out and disappear, i.e. that don't have some big climax at the end. (Eno 1975b)

The detached, cool objectivity of Nyman's *Bell Set* complements Eno's vision of a post-experimental style, creating 'a kind of endlessness, of something happening in the background and not disturbing whatever else is happening'. The sonorities on the original recording are somewhat reminiscent of the Promenade Theatre Orchestra's delicate chimes, of 'tinkling toy pianos [and] soothing psalteries' (Nyman 1971f, p. 28). In a more recent version by the Czech-based Agon Orchestra, the rather innocent clock-like contraptions of sounding bells, triangles, gongs, cymbals and tam-tams are replaced by an array of ready-made instruments created out of industrial scrap iron, pipes, cables and metal strings resembling some kind of futuristic post-apocalyptic machine.[10]

## English post-experimental music

The non-referential, abstract nature of material in *Bell Set* in fact situates it within the 'experimental' rather than 'minimalist' tradition. But a 'collective-indeterminate' approach – Nyman's so-called 'people process' – already suggests an interest in more openly 'vernacular' works of the period such as Riley's *In C*, Rzewski's *Les Moutons de Panurge* or White's *Photo-Finish Machine*, where each player works their way through the material independently. Nyman adopts a similar procedure in the other composition included on the *Decay Music* recording, *1–100* (see Example 3.2).

---

8  See Brian Eno's *Discreet Music* (EEG 23, 1975).
9  See Harold Budd's *The Pavilion of Dreams* (EEG 30, 1978).
10  *Graphic scores and concepts*: Agon Orchestra conducted by Petr Kofron (Audio Ego 01-2).

**Example 3.2**    1-100

This piece draws even further on features associated with the English post-experimental movement during the first half of the 1970s. Significantly the final chapter of Nyman's book on experimental music does not end with American minimalism but with a survey of English post-experimental music. This movement adopted in equal measure elements associated with both American experimental and minimal music in that the freedom of the former was combined with the rigour and discipline of the latter.

In 1971 Nyman characterized the experimental movement as being represented by 'three mutually inclusive characteristics … the systemic, the Sibelian and the stolen' (Nyman 1971i, p. 599). The first owed a debt to the American minimalists, the second concentrated on the 'dense … slow and dark hued' textures characteristic of the European symphonic tradition and the third on a more intertextual approach

**Example 3.2**  *concluded*

borrowing from pre-existing material. Composers such as Hobbs, Brian Dennis and Michael Parsons echoed in some of their works the gradual processes of Reich or Glass, writing music 'whose structure and … note-to-note procedure [is] determined by *a priori* numerical systems' (Anderson 1983, p. 168). Others fused systems with fallibility. White's 'machine' pieces in particular provided a 'model of a new tonal determinacy' according to Nyman, where 'sounds tend towards a sort of ragged consonance, the procedures usually involve much repetition with changes happening almost imperceptibly over large spans of time' (Nyman 1971f, p. 27). The degree of randomness built into White's rigid, machine-like structures set the English school apart from its American counterpart, resulting in 'gentle, casual, slow, unassertive' music whose 'systems are totally fallible [in] bringing about unexpected solutions' (Nyman 1976b, 186–8). The English model displayed a more relaxed approach to systems while at the same time referring more openly to past music and pre-existing materials. Thus in White's music both 'system and sentimentality' come into play, occasionally resulting in compositions that call to mind the humour of Satie (Nyman 1977, p. 8).

Some of these features are heard in Nyman's *1–100* for four or more pianos, composed in late 1975. Unlike *Bell Set*, which generates temporal decay through rhythmic augmentation, *1–100* creates a similar effect by using the physical character of the piano and the tension or sustaining quality of its strings. Furthermore, whereas *Bell Set*'s indeterminate pitch structure lacks any clear harmonic reference, *1–100* adopts a harmonic process commonly found in Baroque music. Originally planned as the soundtrack to accompany a Peter Greenaway film, *1–100* anticipated later working methods by employing a pre-determined numerical grid, allowing both sound and image to exist relatively independently of one another while at the same time adhering to a common structural plan. Although the music was not eventually used in Greenaway's film, Nyman clearly considered it to be of sufficient musical interest for it to be reproduced as a concert piece.

The composition in fact possesses an unswerving internal logic and independence. Its 100-chord number sequence forms a structural grid from which a Baroque-style harmonic process gradually unfolds (see Ex. 3.2). The pattern's cyclical movement is characterized by an oblique motion in the bass, rising up a perfect fourth then falling by a perfect or diminished fifth interval, and usually harmonized by major or minor chords, or permutations thereof. The use of alternative fifths intervals allows the chord sequence to either remain within a previously established harmonic region or shift across into related ones. By the point at which the twenty-first chord is heard, Nyman has effectively constructed a completely chromatic set of major or minor triads. Within this basic guiding principle he appears to select freely from the choice of chords at his disposal; indeed one of the most interesting features of the piece is the manner in which fixed and free elements cohabitate. For example, while some minor harmonizations initially appear towards the beginning and middle of each ten-chord cycle, suggesting a standardized pattern (see chords 3–6, 12–15, 22–5), they are not generated through any built-in process. Indeed only one minor triad verticalization is sounded between chord sequences 70–79, namely the first, an F minor ninth. While certain progressions explore diatonic, flat-side or sharp-side regions, any sense of tonal stability is simultaneously undermined by the inexorable progress of the bass line. This sense of suspended animation is confirmed in the final chord: an unresolved dominant seventh on D.

Nyman's intention was therefore not to bring the whole sequence back full circle to the opening C major chord. The open-ended nature of the piece is only halted by a gradual descent in pitch and register, from the top range of the piano to its lowest depths. However, a progressive 'enrichment' of the opening sequence of basic major and minor triads, with or without sevenths, may be traced throughout the cycle: 11–20 first introduce dominant sevenths, major and minor ninths then follow, and dominant ninths and added sixths are added later. One can hear in the unfolding process a kind of evolutionary progress of the sequence as used during the Baroque, Classical and Romantic periods, and even onto its more contemporary appearance in jazz (as exemplified in the final set of combined dominant and major ninths).

In truth, by such time as the more extended triadic patterns have been introduced (around a quarter of the way through the cycle) it is likely that the chords themselves would only be partially recognizable amidst the polytonal haze, given that each player is to proceed independently through the sequence having determined that their previously struck chord has died out. *1–100* is another example of a 'people process', one where each performer must remain steadfastly independent of the other. The process brings to the surface generic fluctuations, alterations and irregularities within the sustaining mechanism of the piano. Central to the physics of the piano's sound is the notion that the length of decay will increase as its pitches become lower, creating increasingly protracted lengths of time between each attack. Other factors built into this 'physiological' process include the structure of the harmonic series arising from each chord, the instrument's attack and decay time, microtonal fluctuations in frequency, and the vibration or 'beat' of each string when 'two different frequencies are sounded together' (Pierce 1983, p. 96).

In addition, the decay curves of individual partials in a particular piano tone in themselves produce 'irregular vibrations', some of which 'may even increase in intensity before starting to decay'. The piano's 'inharmonicity' also provides it with a defining and characteristic timbre. Such fractional deviations in tone production are thus embedded in the work's process. In his study of the physics of sound, Pierce has pointed out how differences in extremes of instrumental register result in highly varied acoustic experiences: '[in] high-frequency partials or overtones the chief musical impression is derived from the fundamental ... clearly toward the low end of the piano keyboard musical pitch is conveyed by salient harmonics or partials, not by the fundamental' (Pierce 1983, p. 94). Such features are 'built into' this piece by Nyman.

Unlike *Bell Set No. 1*, *1–100* re-engages with a relic from the past whose harmonic origins may be traced to the musical syntax of the Baroque era. The sequence itself is generic, though Nyman appears to have had in mind the music of Vivaldi when he wrote it. In this sense it signals the beginning of a more conscious engagement with musical intertexts (see Rivière and Caux 1987, p. 75). Paradoxically, the musical process employed does not always draw attention to either the inherent logic or the intertextual resonance of the harmonic sequence. The chord progression is subjected to its own process of de-familiarization as homophony gradually transforms into a polytonal polyphony and the defining characteristics of each harmonic construction become increasingly blurred. Through the application of a minimalist aesthetic – setting up a process and allowing it to run its course – *1–100* ends up occasionally evoking the modernist sound world from which it ostensibly attempts to escape. In fact, in terms of its instrumentation and notation (though not in terms of sound) it lies closer to Feldman's *Piece for Four Pianos*, where each player reads through the same score in his own time, creating 'a freely unravelling multiple canon suggestive of a free kind of phasing' (Potter 2000, p. 6). In Nyman's 'decay' aesthetic, tonality gradually fades into the background, but in other compositions from this time he is keen to preserve a clearer sense of tonal identity and provide explicit references to the past.


## Vernacular intertexts

Alongside the employment of English post-experimental and American minimalist techniques, Nyman began to adopt an increasingly pluralist and eclectic approach. His writings again provide evidence of this in the emphasis he places upon music belonging outside the Western art music tradition. Reviews of concerts and recordings appear in the areas of rock and pop, folk, early music (and performance practice), ethnic (now 'World Music') and Eastern music. Together these genres constitute a colourful and diverse patchwork of styles and traditions, a musical vernacular or *lingua franca* partly brought about by the increased globalization of culture and mass communications. Evidence of this is to be found in the appropriation of diverse cultural references in pop and rock music, for example. The Beatles and other pop groups had made use of Indian sounds and structures in their songs, and the progressive rock movement made multifarious references to Baroque, classical or folk idioms.

Dart had encouraged Nyman to take an interest in world music during his studies at King's College. Receptive to the proliferation of styles within the cultural dynamic of the late 1960s, Nyman identified with the qualities of a musical vernacular, such as the emphasis on active and collective composition and participation, a direct engagement with timbre and colour and an intuitive, spontaneous and unimpeded approach to creativity and performance. These approaches were often absent from the abstract concepts of the avant-garde aesthetic. Pop music in particular provided alternative modes of creation and reception, motivating some contemporary composers to revisit the basic materials from which sounds were produced. Nyman points out, for example, that 'the basic expressive needs that pop caters for, and which Webern and Stockhausen outgrew, have always been tied up with melody and rhythm [and] it is interesting to note that even the straight avant-garde, after years in the desert of post-Webern abstraction, is beginning to renew itself at the well of regular pulse and tonality.' In another article Nyman claims triumphantly that 'melody rides again' in the compositions of the English experimental school (Nyman 1970a, p. 574; Nyman 1971f). An early allusion to popular culture is also found in a short experimental film produced by Nyman in 1968 called *Love, Love, Love*, with its clear reference to The Beatles' song 'All You Need is Love'.[11]

For Nyman, as with certain types of rock music (such as that of Procol Harum, The Nice and ELP), the vernacular style included well-known works from high

---

11 In a later interview Nyman acknowledges the lyrical and melodic influence of Beatles songs on some of his music (Meyer 1989, p. 53).

Baroque to late Romanticism. 'Popular classics' such as Handel's 'Hallelujah Chorus' or Tchaikovsky's *1812* overture made up the repertoire of the unique Portsmouth Sinfonia, an eclectic and eccentric collection of trained and amateur musicians who placed passion and enthusiasm above technical accomplishment and precision, imbuing their music with an altogether different kind of 'social reality'. Many other composers belonging to the post-Cardew school combined old and new or high and low references in their music. For example, Hobbs's 25-minute orchestral work *The Arnold-Wolff-Ferrari Orchestra Book* consisted of '250 particles from the works of some ninety composers, which were chosen and then juxtaposed by random means' (Hobbs, in Anderson 1983, p. 205). Hobbs also sometimes 'cannibalized' his earlier works for fresh material – a practice adopted later by Nyman on a much wider scale. White represented the same musical material in a variety of different guises in his 'symphonies'. Bryars' music also reflected at this time an interest in simultaneously combining both high and low aspects of cultural performance. He borrowed the Dada term 'ready-made' to describe some of his compositions, and in *Jesus' Blood Never Failed Me Yet* incorporated a recording of an old tramp tenderly singing a sweetly melancholic religious song while providing an increasingly elaborate accompaniment and orchestration to the endlessly repeated melody.

Nyman's writings on vernacular music provide perhaps the clearest indication of an aesthetic shift away from modernism towards alternative expressive models, a middle-ground lying on the cusp between high art and popular culture. He reiterated this idea somewhat later: 'I don't think we should write music that is removed from the musical vernacular – the music that's around [us] and on the airwaves' (Nyman 1991, p. 23). These forms often employ tonal inflections, harmonic consonance, modality, pulse and repetition. Vernacular styles show an insouciant disregard towards stylistic development and the evolutionary approach championed by Enlightenment ideals and foisted upon the creative artist in the name of historical progress.

Nyman addresses this theme in a paper given at a conference on American Music at Keele University in 1975, where he challenges prevailing notions of music history by sifting through 'unofficial histories' and hidden narratives of Western art music in order to uncover examples of unconventional or unorthodox tonal writing. He encounters them in the compositions of Anthony Philip Heinrich (1781–1861). A Bohemian by birth, Heinrich moved to the United States where he became known as the 'Beethoven of America'. In his use of musical references and self-quotation Heinrich was out of step with then current Romantic ideals of unbridled individualism and self-expression. Nyman puts forward a case for him as the founder of an alternative music history of experimental music (somewhat modernist in its reference to the origins and evolution of this movement) where music is characterized by '[no] progress, no climax, no discernable logic, no development, [and] growth by accumulation [and] succession rather than progression' (Nyman 1975b, p. 152).

A similar approach has been adopted in Eno's reconsideration of popular music's function, where the relationship between centre and periphery, culture and subculture has been reversed:

My view of the history of music is that the things which seem to be at a tangent, to be peripheral, have in fact been the mainstream. You find this particularly in rock music. I'm trying to argue against the idea of a pure line. It's a mistake to think there is a logical progression from one condition to the next. (Eno 1975a)

Likewise, in other reviews Nyman has continued to champion the cause of composers who played against current conventions, eschewed unity for diversity, and consistently eluded simplistic stylistic and historical categorization; composers such as Michael Praetorius in the early seventeenth century, C.P.E. Bach in the eighteenth, and Satie, Lord Berners, Varèse and Cage in the twentieth. Another article by Nyman dating from this time goes as far as to question the very position granted to purportedly great works – or 'high peaks' of art, as he calls them – stating,

It all depends on what vantage point you view [them] from ... [to] me, the quartet attributed to Benjamin Franklin, in which all the strings are retuned to enable every note to be played on an open string, is a peak. So, too, is Cage's *String Quartet* of 1949, whose quiescence beautifully defuses the explosiveness of the high peak tradition. (Nyman 1975a, p. 480)

## Texts and references

Anthony Philip Heinrich's compositions are understood by Nyman to be deliberate 'misreadings' of traditional harmonic principles and procedures. He cites Heinrich's *Divertimento* for piano (c.1820) as an example of the composer setting up 'a chain of highly idiosyncratic waltzes, which succeed each other with no regard for the tonal, thematic or structural logic of [then] contemporary European models' (Nyman 1975b, p. 149). As a prominent vernacular form during the nineteenth century, the waltz became one of the primary means by which post-experimental composers revisited consonance, tonality and repetition. Hobbs, in his *Czerny's 100 Bouquet Valses for the Piano by Lanner and Strauss arranged for such as cannot reach an octave*, wrote a piece consisting of 'looped fragments from assorted Victorian piano pieces, arranged and played in a cycle of keys' (Hobbs, in Anderson 1983, p. 205). Howard Skempton in particular emphasized the graceful simplicity and subtlety of this form in an early piano piece called simply *Waltz*. Nyman described it as 'the first experimental tonal piece to be conceived in terms of a connected melodic and harmonic sequence – a new tonal "language"' (Nyman 1999, pp. 167–8). Other examples include White's *Gothic Waltz* and Ivan Hume-Carter's *Ross and Cromarty Waltzes*, composed for the latter's eponymous orchestra and written so that 'anyone with little or even no [musical] knowledge could participate in the performance of [these] waltzes – after all you would only need to know how to play four or less notes' (Nyman 1999, pp. 169–70). Also working in the context of a post-Scratch Orchestra tradition was the Majorca Orchestra established by James Lampard and Robert Mortimer.

Nyman later applied a parallel performance practice to his own group, the Foster's Social Orchestra, established by him in 1976 when he was lecturer in the Fine Art Department at Trent Polytechnic. Nyman had observed in Hume-Carter's compositions a '[gentle re-emphasis] ... from a very innocent standpoint [of] the division of harmonic music into melody and accompaniment' thus allowing him 'to divide the roles of student players initially into more expert (tunes) and less expert (accompaniments)' (Nyman 1976c, p. 283). Taking its name from 'a collection of simple arrangements' by the mid-nineteenth-century American composer Stephen Foster (ibid., p. 283), two arrangements by this orchestra have been included on the soundtrack recording to the film *Ravenous*, co-written with Damon Albarn in 1999.[12] The first, called 'Noises Off' opens with a simple four-bar melody in D major, repeated with some minor melodic and harmonic variations. A brief contrasting third section in the relative minor key is followed finally by a return of the opening tune. The texture is clearly separated throughout into a melodic line played on violins supported by a countermelody on clarinet. Additional instruments (such as a trombone) provide a harmonic bass line. While this basic texture provides sufficient variety in the opening two sections, a sudden shift to the more 'demanding' passage in B minor during the third half, and its subsequent movement back to the tonic via A major, distils the musical content into an almost skeletal structure comprising merely of melody and bass; what was therefore a three- or four-part texture is reduced to two-part movement.

Of more immediate effect is the music's actual sound. Here, one is aware of a palpable sense of struggle and control with the technical limitations of each player and the laboured contortions required in order to produce any realistically plausible sound. This is 'minimal' music stripped bare of aesthetic or conceptual meaning but executed with humble conviction and simple purpose. Though far from technically accomplished or polished, it reflects a nineteenth-century social musical practice out of which emerged the American vernacular tradition that influenced such diverse figures as Philip Sousa and Charles Ives. In his discussion of Ives's formative musical experiences, for example, Wilfrid Mellers argues that in such contexts 'the only criterion of "correctness" is the music's truth to experience' (Mellers 1987, p. 40). Ives's father actively encouraged musical experimentation and described the out-of-tune singing of a local stonemason called old John as that of a 'supreme musician ... look into his face and hear the music of the ages ... don't pay too much attention to the sounds ... if you do, you may miss the music' (ibid., p. 40).

Unlike the cerebral post-experimental aesthetic of *Decay Music*, Nyman's other compositions of this period draw upon a direct vernacular language by making clear use of tonality, harmonic and rhythmic repetition, and simple melodic lines. Written for Foster's Social Orchestra in 1974[13] the one-page score for the *First Waltz in D* separates out two musical strands into melody and accompaniment, as seen in Example 3.3.

---

12 Michael Nyman and Damon Albarn: *Ravenous* (EMI Soundtracks, 522 3702).

13 The date provided in the Chester Music catalogue is 1976.

**Example 3.3**   *Nyman's* First Waltz in D

Nyman's *First Waltz* consists of a continuously repeating tonic-subdominant progression in D major while all melodic instruments gradually play their way through a series of seventeen two-bar units varying from one to five pitches. The melody encompasses in total nine pitches spread across the tessitura of a minor tenth, from B to D. Rhythmic interest is maintained throughout by the frequent addition of a tied note across many of the two-bar repeated segments, occasionally creating a sense of three against two. As with Riley's *In C*, each module is repeated at the discretion of the performer, resulting in a multi-layered polyphonic effect created out of single melodic lines. Each unit is also built out of the preceding set of pitches in such a way that the melody gradually develops out of, but slowly away from, its original form. *Second Waltz in F* expands on these principles, as seen in Example 3.4.

The two-bar harmonic sequence of the *First Waltz* is extended here to a four-bar pattern consisting of F major, B♭ major, G major and C major chords (or I-IV-ii$^{\#3}$-V). Against this sequence is heard an 84-bar melody divided into twenty-one four-bar units. The melodic span of an octave and minor sixth employing eleven discrete

**Example 3.4**   *Nyman's* Second Waltz in F

*continued*

pitches is wider than the previous example, possibly reflecting the progress achieved by the orchestra's players during the intervening period. This line works differently, however, by moving away from the opening pitches of the melody before returning back to them, creating a greater sense of closure.

In a version of the *Second Waltz* on the 1981 Michael Nyman album (called simply *Waltz*) lines weave in and out of the texture, overlaid with chromatic freeform improvisations from jazz saxophonists Evan Parker and Peter Brotzmann.[14]

---

14   Michael Nyman, 1981 (Piano Records, Sheet 005).

**Example 3.4**   *concluded*

Parker's work was predominantly with the London Musicians' Cooperative, but he also made appearances with Cardew's improvisation group AMM throughout the late 1960s (Prévost 2001, p. 27; Anderson 1983, p. 164). While Parker's angular extemporizations are designed to offset the four-square motion of the accompaniment, Nyman's melody lists interlock in such a way as to create a series of 'resulting patterns' – patterns accidentally created out of the combination of two or more lines – similar in effect to those encountered in Reich's early phase pieces. Unlike Reich's minimal compositions, Nyman's tunes float above a solid and unswerving harmonic structure that would sound equally at home in a classical work or chord sequence 'vamped' in a pop song. The overall impression is of intertextual poly-stylistic eclecticism where musical references are drawn from a vast pool. According to Nigel Osborne, '[we] are plunged into the gloom of a Cretan taverna; is it the squawking and squealing of karamusas and bouzoukis? No, it is a waltz; the needle is stuck on the 'hook' of a Bacharach chorus' (Osborne 1983, p. 40).

The manner in which vernacular styles were reintroduced by Nyman and others during the mid-1970s suggests a more decisive break with modernism than that of experimental or early minimalist music. In its 'reclamation of traditional techniques through pastiche and quotation' Alastair Williams has identified the postmodernism of the following decades as reacting 'strongly against the core of high modernism which rejects the past in favour of a technological future' (Williams 1997, p. 125). Susan McClary in her discussion of musical postmodernism has also identified a general trend since 'the watershed years of the 1960s [in which] many composers have come to believe that music should be "com-posed" – literally, put together – from elements recognizable to a substantial community of listeners, that it should participate in a public arena where interpretation is actively provoked' (McClary 2000, p. 141). These 'recognizable elements' – tonal signs and signifiers across a wide vernacular topography – are, according to McClary, at the same time 'decentred' through mechanized repetition and re-presentation. The effect is one where the listener becomes increasingly aware of the manner in which the expressive gestures of postmodern styles have been 'constructed' or 'deconstructed' from the 'rhetorical devices that still persuade us of their unmediated authenticity in classical concerts or movies' (ibid., pp. 143–4). Nyman's reconstruction of Baroque or classical sequences work in the same way, alerting the listener to the fact that what is being heard is, in fact, 'not' classical.

Nyman's own purpose in writing waltzes may have been to bring about a satisfactorily practical solution to certain conceptual and aesthetic problems relating to post-experimental music. The music of Reich, Glass and Riley demanded an almost devotional loyalty and technical mastery from its performers. Nyman's waltzes on the other hand could easily be learned by non-readers and adequately performed by any group of amateur players in the Scratch Orchestra, Portsmouth Sinfonia, art school tradition.

Another piece to exploit this form with an almost Dada sense of deliberation was *The Otherwise Very Beautiful Blue Danube Waltz* (1976). During this time White, Bryars and fellow composers Dave Smith and Ben Mason had established the Garden Furniture Music Ensemble, whose aim was to promote experimental music to a wider audience by performing it in unconventional venues and spaces, such as theatre foyers. Nyman's own *Blue Danube Waltz* was given its premiere by the composer in similar circumstances, in the foyer of the National Theatre on 14 June 1976, with both Smith and Mason participating (the other two players being John Lewis and Orlando Gough). The premiere took place some four months before Nyman's music for the company's *Il Campiello* production was due for performance there.[15]

The piece's title is taken from a passage in Arnold Schoenberg's essay 'Brahms the Progressive', where he admonishes Johann Strauss' use of 'slightly varied repetitions ... in the otherwise very beautiful *Blue Danube Waltz*' (Schoenberg 1984, p. 399). Schoenberg's comments suggest that he is rather dismissive of the somewhat formulaic and predictable nature of Strauss's waltz, though acknowledging at the same time its 'simple beauty'. Nyman's use of Schoenberg's quotation, however, pays homage to the work's 'otherness' by breaking down and rebuilding each musical fragment from the found source. Unlike the process used in *In Re Don Giovanni*, this affects the overall structure of the original. In this case, Nyman's composition has been constructed out of Strauss's well-known waltz, *An der schönen, blauen Donau* op. 314.

---

15  See Chapter 6 for a more detailed account.

An interest in music as 'material' or a source upon which a composer could draw was inspired by Cage's notion that music could 'permit any sound, from any part of musical history, from *any* musical history, to be heard in them' (Nyman 1970b, p. 617). In *The Otherwise Very Beautiful Blue Danube Waltz* the music is generated from the opening thirty-two bars of Strauss's waltz but re-presented through the application of a 'people' process used by Frederic Rzewski in *Les Moutons de Panurge* (1969). The Rzewski piece utilizes a logical system by which the original musical material is gradually and inexorably composed out through successive additions of each pitch along a melodic chain, a process that resembles Glass's additive cycles (Adlington 2004, p. 42). In Rzewski's piece, a single 65-note melody is supplied with each note played in the sequence 1, 1-2, 1-2-3 … 1-2-3-4 until the entire phrase is completed. The process is then reversed, allowing every player to return back to his or her original starting place. Rzewski advises any performers who loose their way during the reconstruction of this process to 'stay lost … [do] not try to find your way back to the fold' (Nyman 1999, p. 158). Unlike Nyman's waltz, the melodic line for *Panurge* is entirely 'abstract' and is largely based on patterns derived from transposed Dorian or Mixolydian modes.

In Nyman's composition, Strauss's 32-bar sequence generates larger contiguous blocks of ninety-six beats, resulting in a piece of some 528 bars. Consequently *The Otherwise Very Beautiful Blue Danube Waltz* possesses a greater degree of fallibility during performance due to the fact that, the longer a process will take to complete, the higher the risk will be of Rzewski's 'sheep' wandering astray. This occurs to humorous effect in the only existing recording of the work (taken from the first performance at the National Theatre) where one 'stray' pianist is left stranded, playing the final 32-bar segment on his own to end the performance, while all the other pianists have completed their process.[16] Its effect in performance, according to Nyman, encourages one's focus to shift away from the rigid structural process to the way in which superimposed parts accidentally move out of phase with each other, creating (as with *1–100*) a free blurring of tonal harmonies despite the harmonic patterns remaining resolutely fixed.

## Beyond Cage

To negotiate a path through Nyman's writings and early experimental works towards the early mature style of his compositions in the late 1970s is therefore possible. Gradual disillusionment with the principles underlying the European avant-garde, a respect and admiration for Cage and the American 'experimental' tradition, a sense of breakthrough that first accompanied his exposure to the music of Reich (which dated back to his first hearing of *Come Out* in 1968), a thorough intellectual and working knowledge of the English experimental movement, an enthusiasm for vernacular

---

16   Recent English Experimental Music (Audio Arts Magazine, vol. 3, no. 2).

musical forms (such as rock, folk and world music) and an interest in quotation and allusion: all were important landmarks along a musical route that led Nyman beyond Cage and the post-experimental tradition to a post-minimal language. Surveying his writings as a whole, the dynamics of pluralism and an alternative musical aesthetics is reflected in the broad range of music encompassed by them. Nyman perceived a hubristic elitism in musical modernism and an obsession with abstraction for its own sake. He sought inspiration elsewhere, and in a variety of sources.

Nyman's style during the mid 1970s lies somewhere between the slightly older generation of American minimalists, his own contemporaries within the English post-experimental scene, and the younger generation of composers (such as Eno and Hassell) whose works suggested a new art-rock or new wave style. The difference between minimalism and rock music was that the former still advanced some form of critique of the work whereas the latter was unashamedly omnivorous in its heterogeneous appropriation of old and new, high and low. Nyman himself described the difference between the two as that between 'systems' and 'intuitive' music, where 'the ear rather than the process is the initial and final arbiter' (Nyman 1977). Eno also stated that 'experimental music involves too much intellect and not enough sensuality ... [in experimental music] the process is supposed to be interesting in itself. I don't go for that. I think if something doesn't jolt your sense, forget it. It's got to be seductive' (Eno 1975b). Eno's emphasis primarily on the way in which music made sense 'as sound' is largely absent in Nyman's early post-experimental compositions, but he was nevertheless drawn to its qualities. In a discussion of a Budd recording, he once noted the way in which the music existed 'on a single plane, with the focus just on the simple input, on primary colours, on anti-abstraction and on *genuine* anti-illusion' (Nyman 1976d, p. 72).

Although the basic technical elements of Nyman's style had been established through these works – repetition, consonance, a free approach to process and implicit or explicit reference to pre-existing materials – the means by which they could be effectively communicated had yet to be discovered. Nyman was of course aware that in addition to constructing their own processes and formal structures, Reich, Glass and Riley had also created distinctive and clearly identifiable soundworlds, through establishing unique instrumental and vocal ensembles or through performing their own music. Nyman marked his own individual sonic imprint for the first time when he composed *In Re Don Giovanni*. This soundworld was developed largely in tandem with the important series of soundtracks composed for Greenaway's films during the late 1970s and early 1980s.

Paradoxically, the immediacy and individuality of Nyman's sound existed in a dichotomous relationship with his use of pre-existing music, a fact that was made even more obvious in his deliberate attempt to clothe old music in almost punk rock fabric. If the latter provided a mark of individuality, the former appeared to contradict this notion by clouding the issue of authorship. Part of the music's appeal revolved around patterns of discourse set up by these oppositions. Nyman's music would often give the impression of speaking in more than one voice. It appeared to possess what

Russian literary theorist M.M. Bakhtin described as 'heteroglossia': an engagement both with the 'given' language (Western classical music in this case) and its 'other' (the unofficial vernacular or popular 'tongue') (Bakhtin 1981). Thus the heteroglot nature of Nyman's music sets up a dialogic relationship between musical texts, each one referring back to a previous musical utterance.

Such terms are frequently encountered in intertextual discussions of language or literary works, but their application to music is less common.[17] Nyman's willingness to borrow and quote was in addition a sign of growing confidence rather than creative insecurity. Once the Nyman sound crystallized in the early 1980s, any musical material could be poured into this mould in the knowledge that it would form a clearly identifiable sonic imprint. Nyman's intertextual orientation partly served as a means to realize his newfound soundworld, while a scholarly approach to musical material meant that he could reanimate pre-existing material by applying various analytical, editorial, critical and aesthetic approaches to it. Thus a broad range of intertextual methods and applications evolved from this approach, many of which will be examined during the second half of this book. The analytical and critical skills employed by intertextuality belong primarily to the study of literature, poetry and art, however. Before applying some of these intertextual principles to music examples in general, and to Nyman's works in particular, it is first necessary to examine the term as employed generally in the fields of art, literary criticism and music.

---

[17]   See, however, Sutcliffe 2003, pp. 145–216.

# Chapter 4

# Mapping Intertextuality in Nyman

Intertextuality has its origins both in the structuralism of Saussure and the dialogic approach of Bakhtin. Nevertheless, the dialectical struggle between language as a universal form, and one that exists as a specific set of utterances, preoccupied artists long before Saussure's division of the two in his *Course in General Linguistics* (1916). While composers of the Baroque and Classical eras believed that they partook of a common musical language, as examined in Chapter 1, Saussure's distinction between 'langue' and 'parole' enabled language to be analysed as an object existing in a single moment in time (something one suspects would have been strangely unfamiliar to the eighteenth-century musician). Saussure's binary opposition also drew attention to the fact that language could only be understood in terms of itself, *through* language. Extended to other forms of communication (such as art and music), any explanations of musical or artistic meaning could not be extended beyond the boundaries of any linguistic interrogation of those forms. In effect, nothing could exist outside the 'text' because everything was ultimately contained within it.

In music, as in language, a composer's command and control over a given set of codes and utterances became a kind of litmus test for musical competence: those who could 'speak the language' were more likely to be understood and valued by their peers and by the extended community of knowledgeable performers, critics and musicologists of the age. Moreover, those who could develop language through original and innovative means were elevated still further. If one merely echoed or reflected an already spoken language (or worse still, aped a dead one) accusations of insincerity and lack of originality would inevitably follow.

At the same time one could also argue that to speak the language of one's own is to adapt the language of others. Both possess a shared set of rules and practices. The language of intertextuality – a language that describes the relationship between texts past and present – may clear some interpretative space for a more balanced and critical understanding of Nyman's use of quotation and appropriation. If Nyman's work appears to function outside conventional boundaries of composer/composition, how can we best describe and understand it?

Certain terms used in literary criticism provide a useful basis from which Nyman's work may be examined. Originally intended for application in literary or philosophical texts, these terms form interesting parallels with music and literary forms. Gérard Genette's use of the term 'bricoleur' to describe someone who 'creates a structure out of a previous structure by rearranging elements which are already arranged within the objects of his or her study' has a certain resonance with Nyman's approach (Allen 2000, p. 96). A bricoleur does not produce an exact copy of the original, but rather he or she re-presents the previous structure's content and form, and by doing so reconfigures its signifying potential. Part of the problem in identifying Nyman as 'the author' of a composition such as *In Re Don Giovanni* lies in the fact that he is, in effect, doing the job of a literary critic or music analyst by rearranging the 'original' work 'into the terms of [critical analysis]' (ibid., p. 96). To some critics, this may not qualify as 'proper' composition, but, as shown in Chapters 3 and 4, Nyman's formative experiences as editor, musicologist, ethnomusicologist, critic, analyst and performer have all fed back into his understanding of the role of a 'composer': one that lies closer to the notion of putting things together, and of selecting and combining objects. For such a process to be effective, however, the analysis and recomposition of an existing work has to emerge from within an already identifiable and fully formed musical language, as was the case with Nyman.

A term such as bricoleur emerges in discussions on intertextual theory and criticism when signs and their relationships are understood to provide the standard currency of cultural exchange. The intertextual domain therefore yields a rich resource in exploring and explaining Nyman's compositional methods and approach. An intertextual reading of *In Re Don Giovanni* might conclude that it is on one level dialogic – a conversation or negotiation of ideas between Mozart and Nyman – or on another level entirely heteroglossic, representing the plurality of eighteenth- and twentieth-century voices carried within Mozart and Nyman. Another reading would interpret Nyman's aims here as 'amplifying' a 'hypotext': the hypotext in this case being a Mozart aria (and Nyman's own composition would function as the 'hypertext' in this instance). Genette identified the hypotext as something that emerged in any situation where two texts became united. By analogy Nyman therefore applies to the Mozart hypotext a three-way process of 'extension, contamination and expansion'. He repeats the original 15-bar phrase eight times, gradually adding layers of material (extension and expansion), but by including elements of non-classical instrumentation and performance practice Nyman also creates a 'contamination' of the original (Allen 2000, p. 110). The idea of 'amplifying' a hypotext seems especially appropriate given that Nyman's ensemble literally 'amplifies' the precursor piece, creating at the same time a very basic difference between 'original' and 'copy'. As seen later in *Drowning by Numbers*, Nyman adopts a 'metatextual' approach too, where the metatext – in this case the second movement of Mozart's Sinfonia Concertante K. 364 – 'takes up the relation of "commentary" to another text' (ibid., p. 102).

## Contexts

How then can intertextual theories illuminate Nyman's working methods? Firstly, these theories often engage with, and seek to describe, examples of artistic production in contemporary society. They view artistic production as essentially interrelated and interdependent, emphasizing correspondences between – as opposed to within – texts. Identifying connective threads in art can be traced to the etymology of the word 'text', which comes from the Latin *texere* 'to weave'.

Like a 'tissue of quotations', a web or texture, texts are infinitely adaptable (Barthes 1977, p. 146). They do not exist in isolation, but are rather woven together from the 'material' of language. Kristeva described texts as being 'constructed as a mosaic of quotations; any text is the absorption and transfiguration of another' (Kristeva 1980, p. 39). 'Text' is often preferred in literary theory to the more imposing description 'work'. The former implies that any authorial decision or action will be followed by a re-action and response. Texts are open and extroversive whereas 'the work' suggests closure, finality and completion. Texts set off chain reactions of signification between other texts while the work's main purpose is to mark out its own sense of self-presence by becoming distinct from any other. Barthes preferred the term 'text' to 'work' because it illuminated the necessarily provisional and relational nature of writing: '[the] plural of the Text depends ... not on the ambiguity of its contents but on what might be called the stereographic plurality of its weave of signifiers' (Barthes 1977, p. 159). The text's ambivalence and heterogeneity is not deemed a weakness, but rather brings with it a positive force. Eagleton summarized its meaning thus,

[all] literary texts are woven out of other literary texts, not in the conventional sense that they bear the traces of 'influence', but in the more radical sense that every word, phrase or segment is a reworking of other writings which precede or surround the original work. There is no such thing as the 'first' literary work: all literature is 'intertextual'. (Eagleton 1983, p. 138)

Robert Worby once described Nyman's music as a 'classic example of intertextuality, of meaning being generated through an interconnecting weave rather than a straight linear thread' (Worby, in Nyman 2002, p. 16). His comments draw attention to the fact that Nyman's music does not always follow a direct narrative path but is made up of multi-narrative layers.[1] The 'text as [a] weave' also appropriately describes Nyman's stylistic approach. Minimalism's musical processes are designed to generate patterns that in turn generate textural layers. They often quite literally create a musical 'weave'.[2]

John Frow's use of the term *intra*textuality may also help illuminate a general intertextual shift between Nyman's early and later music.[3] Frow uses *intra*textuality to explain the point at which a text departs from 'hypogrammatical' conventions and clichés in order to establish its own network of internal correspondences. The text thus forms its own *intra*textual matrix – a set of semantic co-ordinates plotted across a larger *inter*textual field. While Nyman's earlier compositions are more thoroughly *inter*textual – referring to pre-existing texts by other composers – his later works adopt a more *intra*textual or inter-referential approach, where ideas are borrowed

---

1   See, for example, Nyman's chamber opera *The Man who Mistook his Wife for a Hat*, discussed in Chapter 7.

2   A visual representation of the kind of textural weave heard in minimalist music has been included on the cover of the first recording of Steve Reich's *Drumming*, which features a detail from his wife Beryl Korot's oil on hand-woven canvas *The Babel Text* (Elektra Nonesuch 979 170-2).

3   For a summary of Frow see Allen 2000, pp. 130–31.

or developed from his own earlier compositions.[4] As shown later in this chapter, intertextuality may also take on explicit or implicit forms, or become absolute or referential.

Intertextuality should not be understood as merely a method of mapping influence on other works. Michael Klein distinguishes between the two by arguing that '[the latter] implies intent or a historical placement of the work in its time or origin ... [the former] implies a more general notion of crossing texts that may involve historical reversal' (Klein 2005, p. 4). Although both types are historically driven, influence is unidirectional and goal-orientated while an intertextual enquiry is multidirectional, or, in Klein's description, 'dynamically bilateral' (ibid., p. 11). Cage's writings also view history as a site for discursive negotiations between past, present and future agencies. His anecdote about musical influence – '[when] I once asked Arragon, the historian, how history was written ... [he] said, "You have to invent it"' – suggests that history is as much reconstructed in the present as it is inherited from the past (Cage 1993, p. 237). Cage would often quote painter Willem de Kooning's words to support this idea: '[the] past does not influence me; I influence it' (Cage 1961, p. 67).

## Analysis and intertextuality

Before applying a number of methodological approaches to Nyman's music, it is first necessary to survey the range of studies that have drawn to a greater or lesser extent on certain intertextual precepts. These developments have taken place largely in the area of analytical theory, but they have also found currency in related areas, such as parody and collage.

Though lagging behind linguistically informed musicological disciplines such as structuralism and semiology, intertextuality has nevertheless been applied to a diverse range of music historical and stylistic areas, from the motets of the early fifteenth century to dance culture in the early twenty-first (Allsen 1993; Rietveld 1995). Some studies have made use of particular methods and concepts developed by theorists such as Harold Bloom and Barthes (McCreless 1988; Korsyn 1991). Others, in employing an open – or extroversive – form of semiology in their methodologies come close to evoking an intertextual approach without necessarily embracing intertextual concepts or adopting its terminology.

Published in 1991, Kevin Korsyn's intertextual analysis of Brahms's piano music was one of the first musicological studies to explore this area. Defining intertextuality as 'a model for analysing compositions as relational events rather than as closed and static entities', Korsyn sets out to apply Harold Bloom's 'anxiety of influence' to musical works (Korsyn 1991, p. 8). According to Bloom, 'influence becomes something poets actively resist, rather than something they passively receive, and

---

4 The relationship between intertextuality and inter-referentiality will form the basis of the analysis of another Nyman opera, *Facing Goya*, in Chapter 10.

poetry becomes a psychic battlefield, an Oedipal struggle against one's poetic fathers, in which poems seek to repress and exclude other poems' (ibid., p. 8). Intertexts thus emerge from a subconscious Oedipal battle between a 'precursor' text as poetic 'father' and its intertextual 'ephebe'. The latter attempts to shed all traces of influence in order to assert 'his' textual independence and superiority from the 'father' text. Influence is thus characterized by Bloom as a form of patriarchal anxiety. Korsyn establishes a similar model for musical influence, stating

> [the] meaning of a composition can only be another composition, a composition not [in] itself, and *not* the meaning of the other piece, but the *otherness* of the other piece, manifested not only through the presence of the precursor-piece, but also through the precise figurations of its absence. (Ibid., p. 14)

He illustrates this theory by demonstrating how Brahms's Romanze op. 118 no. 5 actively and creatively misreads Chopin's Berceuse op. 57, composing out and completing thematic, rhythmic, structural and even expressive potentialities only hinted at in the earlier work. In doing so, however, Korsyn's analysis only serves to illuminate the internal coherence and self-sufficiency of Brahms's own music rather than establish its (dis)connection with another work along an intertextual chain. If a meta-discourse or overarching concept does inform Korsyn's analysis, then it is one which seeks to demonstrate the way 'great' works of art engage with historical precursors only to mark themselves off from the past. Composers such as Brahms were thus compelled to clear out autonomous creative spaces for themselves in the increasingly overpopulated pantheon inhabited by great composers of the past, such as Bach, Beethoven or Chopin. Thus in its attempt to transcend the corrupt power of influence, Brahms's music displays an almost fearful sense of historical self-awareness and self-consciousness, by suppressing its power.

In mapping out a series of 'defence mechanisms' for musical intertexts, Korsyn's theory forms a kind of hermetic seal around the work. Brahms's appropriation of a precursor model is revealed by Korsyn only in order to show how the composer strives *beyond* it – how Brahms adopts the traces of Chopin's musical ideas to ensure closure within his own work. By pursuing untapped pathways only hitherto implied by the precursor text, the new work establishes its own unique identity so that it may ultimately be elevated to the status of a canonical 'text'. Klein summarized this dichotomy when he stated that 'for all their richly detailed comparisons ... Korsyn's analyses à la Bloom only underscore our idea of the great artwork as univocal utterance of the great composer' (Klein 2005, p. 18).

If Korsyn's theoretical strategies appear to contravene the spirit of any intertextual enquiry, his adoption of Bloom's theory of creative misreading is nevertheless relevant to a body of work where associations with precursor models are masked or repressed. Robert Hatten has applied the twin concepts of style and strategy as a means of also highlighting 'relevant intertextual relationships' in the music of Beethoven (see Allen 2000, p. 175). Both Korsyn and Hatten have chosen as the focus of their analysis what Barthes would describe as 'readerly' or 'classic' texts. According to Barthes, readerly (or lisible) texts elevate their status to that of 'the work', emphasizing and upholding the idea of stable meaning or doxa (Allen 2000, p. 79). Writerly (or scriptible) texts, on the contrary, revel in the para-doxa of multiple meanings. A semiotic network of references and associations suggested in Nyman's compositions resembles a form of 'writerly' text. His music encourages the listener to become a producer of textual meanings rather than a passive bystander (Barthes 1974, p. 4). Meaning is thus shaped by the listener during the here-and-now of performance rather than structured and analysed retrospectively. Intertexts situate the reader at the centre of textual meaning. Graham Allen also draws attention to the role of the listener when he states that 'texts presuppose inter-texts, which the reader [or listener] must then actualize within a semiotic reading of the text' (Allen 2000, p. 125).

Korsyn's form of latent or implicit intertextuality is arguably of only limited use in the study of Nyman's music. While there are certainly examples of indirect appropriation in his music, Nyman's intertextual methods often encourage and sometimes force the listener to identify with a precursor work. This approach became more common in certain forms of twentieth-century music, where more explicit relationships have been drawn within and between texts. It is not without significance that intertextual theories emerged during the 1960s as a viable theoretical alternative to structuralist poetics, when parody, pastiche, allusion, collage and quotation were at the same time being instilled into contemporary artistic practice.[5] David Beard and Ken Gloag have commented on this exchange between theory and practice, pointing out that 'the inherent intertextuality of music has been enlarged upon as compositional practice' (Beard and Gloag 2005, p. 96). In general, then, composers became less concerned about suppressing musical influences or closing out the past. Jann Pasler has also identified a greater shift in composers' attitudes and response towards the music of the past, commenting that they now

> [tend] not to diffuse the power of their sources nor try to subjugate them through distortion or commentary [but] seem to accept each source on its own terms, revel in the association with this music, and delight in the coexistence they have tried to create. (Pasler 1993, p. 18)

A symbiotic relationship between literary theory and artistic practice can be traced back to developments in early modernism, where 'self-consciously intertextual [forms of] writing' (Allen 2000, p. 50) were adopted not only in the novels of Joyce, Kafka and Proust, but also in the music of Satie, Stravinsky and Ives. Linda Hutcheon has observed that from 'Pound and Eliot through to contemporary performance artists and Post-Modern architects, intertextuality and auto-representation have come to dominate critical attention' (Hutcheon 1985, p. 2).

Joseph Straus's intertextual study of music from the first half of the twentieth century, like Korsyn, also draws on Bloomian methodology. According to Straus,

---

5　For a detailed exposition on quotation and collage during the second half of the twentieth century see Watkins 1994, pp. 377–442.

composers during this time 'wilfully reinterpret traditional elements in accordance with their own musical concerns' (Straus 1990, p. 16). He sets out to examine conflicts that have arisen in the music of Schoenberg, Berg, Bartók and Stravinsky 'between traditional elements and the post-tonal context that subsumes them' (Straus 1991, p. 431). These 'misreadings' manifest themselves in, for example, localized references to tonality within a serial context, in the continued use of traditional tonal designs (such as sonata form), or in the adoption of large-scale harmonic structures. Straus proposes eight intertextual stratagems for the music of this period. Some are generic, such as the generalization of a thematic idea from one work to another without necessarily quoting the original. Some are more text-specific, such as the magnification and intensification of an idea from an existing work ('motivicization') or the reordering of previous material either synchronically ('compression') or diachronically ('fragmentation'). Others serve to illuminate the manner in which a subsidiary idea belonging to an earlier work may acquire a more central function in a later composition, or where a previously central idea acquires a subsidiary function later on. The traditional purpose and function of tonal forms are also neutralized or 'immobilized' primarily by means of symmetrical structures (Straus 1990, p. 17).

Parallels may be drawn here between Straus's intertextual typology of early modernist music and the structuralist concept of *vraisemblance*. This term was adopted in literary theory in order to describe a 'semblance of reality' imposed upon a novel by its author. According to Jonathon Culler, the concept of *vraisemblance* provides a basis for any intertextual approach, given that any work will borrow from the past in order to evoke a sense of realism. Modernism's appropriation of parody and irony is one example, where 'one work takes another as its basis or point of departure and must be assimilated in relation to it' (Culler 1975, p. 140). Klein has also written about the appearance of tonal references in modernist – specifically serial – compositions by drawing on the Freudian concept of 'the uncanny' (*das unheimliche*). Freud's definition of the uncanny as 'something … once known to us, but has been repressed and forgotten [that] in a later mental stage any reappearance … seems new and terrifying' may, in the context of an atonal composition suggest that tonal appearances act as 'ghostly [reminders]' (Klein 2005, pp. 78–9).

Straus and Klein's observations about parody have more in common with Nyman's music than Korsyn's implicit intertextuality. Though rarely parodic in the narrow, prescriptive sense, Nyman's music conforms to Linda Hutcheon's wider and more neutral definition of the term, as examined in more detail later. The notion that quotation is used ironically by Nyman has been questioned by Beirens, for example, who argues that 'Nyman's attitude towards historical material is too diverse and too intelligently worked out, to be merely categorized as ironic' (Beirens 2005, p. 414). Of more interest is the manner with which a dialogue is established between elements of Nyman's own musical language and the pre-existing material he employs. A closer historical precursor in this sense might be Gustav Mahler. Musical signs are constantly transferred within and between his works, as demonstrated in Samuels's analysis of his Sixth Symphony (Samuels 1995).

Samuels's analysis concentrates for the most part on identifying introversive (i.e. structural) musical features, such as motivic, thematic and rhythmic ideas. This often yields rich layers of intertextual associations embedded in Mahler's works in general. Some may take on specific examples, such as the manner in which a motivic idea from the first movement of the Sixth Symphony is 'written into' the slow movement (Andante), while others suggest the voices of other composers. More generally, the character and formation of typically Mahlerian traits recur in his use of distinctive rhythmic patterns. These generic features range across his entire oeuvre and Samuels describes them as 'idiolectic': '"[a] vocabulary" of gestures which are distinctively Mahlerian' (ibid., p. 34). From this observation, Samuels is led on to certain features of Mahler's music that form 'an intertextual motivic "nexus"', or 'a specific intertextual web of cross-references' (ibid., pp. 50–53). Such features include intervallic patterns that shape aspects of melodic construction across a whole range of works and genres, including the Third, Fifth and Sixth Symphonies, or Mahler's fondness of playing with established formal and structural archetypes.

Furthermore, in the fourth movement of the Sixth Symphony, Samuels sees Mahler as engaging in a self-reflexive commentary on the actual 'history of sonata form writing' (ibid., p. 70). Not surprisingly, Mahler's work has become a fertile site for postmodern readings. Unlike the implicit intertextual strategies adopted by nineteenth-century composers in the studies of Korsyn and Straus, Mahler's self-consciously explicit approach to quotation and reference lies much closer in spirit to Nyman's methods. It is not without significance that Nyman cited Mahler's music as an important early influence due to its rich allusions and expressive qualities (Nyman 2000).


## Quotation and modernism

My necessarily brief and selective survey of intertextual applications suggests that these approaches adopt one of two basic formulations. The first is *implicit* in nature, and relates to the subconscious movement of generic and schematic types from one text to another (Korsyn, Straus). The second is more *explicit*, and deals with the notion that intertextuality often rises to the surface of a composition, or can even become the subject of the work itself (Samuels). Of the latter type, overt allusions or quotations are therefore predominant. Hutcheon has used the terms 'manifest or secret' to describe these two intertextual states (Hutcheon 1985, p. 21). A similar distinction has been made in Michael Riffaterre's work, where determinate (or obligatory) and aleatory intertextuality set out the conditions upon which a theory of intertextual perception is formalized. Summarizing the difference between implicit and explicit types, Allen explains that in order to 'locate a necessary intertextual relation between a text and an inter-text' one is either directed by the text itself 'to the appropriate intertext, or [by] deciding arbitrarily, lacking direct textual evidence, that a particular intertextual relation is the significant and interpretively informing one' (Allen 2000, p. 140). Textual references are therefore either intentional or not, and recognized or ignored by the listener.

A more overt form of intertextuality has thus emerged through the use of quotation. Although Stravinsky, Ives, Satie and others made use of this technique in the first half of the twentieth century, the new pluralism of the 1960s resulted in composers engaging directly with the methods and techniques of quotation, often in order to evoke tonality by way of disruption and fragmentation (see Meyer 1967, pp. 172–85). Avant-garde composers such as Stockhausen, Berio and Mauricio Kagel developed openly intertextual techniques where tonal references were directly stated or implied, while in America, Cage also made use of other composers' music as material in *HPSCHD* (a collaboration with Lejaren Hiller, 1969), *Cheap Imitation* (1969), *Apartment House 1776* (1976), and later in his series of *Europeras*, from the entire operatic repertory. Cage's adoption of more consciously intertextual methods in his music occurred at a time when Nyman was also becoming aware of its possibilities. In addition, Stockhausen superimposed a whole host of recordings of national anthems in his tape collage *Hymnen* (1967), although both Cage and James Tenney had already made use of pre-existing recordings in their *Credo in US* (1942) and *Blue Suede* (1961) respectively. In all the above examples, tonality is heard merely as a musical trace, rising occasionally to the surface before being pulled under by washes of saturated chromaticism or subjected to musique concrète-style techniques of splicing, vary-speeding and juxtaposition.

In Stockhausen's *Hymnen*, fragments from national anthems are heard against a 'continuous backdrop of radiophonic and electronic sounds' resulting, according to Maconie, in a 'deliberate distressing and distortion of [familiar] musical objects' (Maconie 1998, pp. 8–9). Hutcheon's description of this work as 'a productive-creative approach to tradition' suggests that Stockhausen is again attempting to transcend the original material's utilitarian purpose (Hutcheon 1985, p. 7). Stockhausen appropriates techniques of allusion and quotation into an otherwise avant-garde, modernist aesthetic. Cage's approach is on the contrary not so much to assimilate and transmute the original text but to preserve its spirit by deconstructing its grammatical structure: to use 'Words / without syntax, each word / polymorphic' (Cage 1985, p. 7). The following generation of composers, including Alfred Schnittke, Arvo Pärt, David Del Tredici, William Bolcom and Louis Andriessen all made varied use of collage and quotation in their music during the late 1960s and 1970s.

In Andriessen's case, his intertextual model was probably the third movement of Berio's *Sinfonia*, a work 'about influence' that became influential in its own right. Unlike the Bloomian 'anxiety' prevalent in nineteenth-century compositions, in his 'In ruhig fliessender Bewegung', Berio draws musical influences out into the open using techniques that resemble psychoanalytical 'free association'. At the centre of the movement's intertextual referents is the third movement Scherzo from Mahler's Second Symphony. As previously noted, Mahler was fond of quoting and adapting his own music and that of other composers in his works. In the Scherzo, Mahler refers to Bruckner, Beethoven and Schumann, although Osmond-Smith has been careful to add that 'whether or not these should be regarded as conscious quotations is difficult to determine' (Osmond-Smith 1985, p. 43). The material from Mahler's symphony forms a kind of ground plan for Berio's composition, though the latter goes much further in adding layers of textual references through quotations from a wide range of sources.

Berio reanimates the dramatic design of Mahler's Scherzo by overlaying at key moments the gestural qualities of specific quotes. The effect is one of 'constant [fluctuations] in harmonic density' (ibid., p. 48) but unlike the role of the Scherzo, they do not follow any structural or even narrative logic. They function rather as localized variations or colorations, springing forth from the melodic and harmonic syntax of the Mahlerian 'metatext'. Berio imparts logic to the movement's intertextual design by grouping quotations together by genre (such as Concerto), type (Scherzo), medium (Ballet and Opera), and even programmatic association (the elements, such as water) (ibid., pp. 48–53). Berio's quotes create a sense of dense textual pluralism, a multiplicity of authorial voices, evoking by way of their 'parallel semantic proliferation ... the labyrinthine "stratification" of Joyce's *Finnegans Wake*' (ibid., p. 53). Even seemingly subliminal connections between spoken text and musical text are synchronized, such as when the word 'earth' elicits Stravinsky's 'Danse de la terre', or references to a Valéry poem about the sea triggers a quote from Debussy's *La Mer*.

Strangely enough, and despite its heterogeneous qualities, 'In ruhig fliessender Bewegung' is nevertheless immediately recognizable as Berio's composition. It still communicates a sense of ontological existence, an in-itself-ness. Out of the dense *pasticcio* of quotations, Berio's eclectic originality still shines through. Nevertheless, his direct use of quotation lies closer to Nyman's intertextual approach, one in which quotation also plays an important role.

Intertextuality has thus appeared both in postmodern theory and practice, in analytical method and compositional approach, but how can these principles and procedures form part of a general survey of intertextuality in Nyman's music? The notion of an abstract (or non-specific) intertextuality will be contrasted in the following description with examples of referential (or specific) types in order to highlight the multiple layers of signification at work in many of Nyman's compositions. His use of self-reference and self-quotation provides another level of intertextual engagement, as seen later in the analysis of the third and fourth string quartets, and in particular the opera *Facing Goya*.

**Intertextual definitions**

Musical references in Nyman's music may be hidden or overt, implicit or explicit, premeditated or unintended. In mapping out an intertextual model for the study of Nyman's music, one is also in effect mapping out many of the salient features of his musical language. Nyman has occasionally employed the term 'intertextuality' in describing his own work. In a set of liner notes accompanying his soundtracks to Greenaway's films, he defines it as the 'the fortuitous and deliberate connections and disconnections between the four scores ...' (Nyman 1989a). From these examples of 'recyclings and reworkings' Nyman extrapolates a set of nine common characteristics that form in essence an inventory of techniques for any intertextual study of his music (see Table 4.1).

**Table 4.1   Inventory of intertextual types in the
Nyman–Greenaway soundtracks**

1.  Music based on [the] pre-existing music [of other composers] (1)

2.  Music used in more than one film

3.  Music composed before the start of filming

4.  Music recorded over a pre-existing recording

5.  Use of pre-existing music (2) [composed for a previous occasion by Nyman]

6.  Death music

7.  Vocal music

8.  Instrumental versions of vocal music

9.  Waltzes

*Note*:  The numbering system adopted in this inventory follows the one used by Nyman.

*Source*: Nyman 1989a

The first type describes the process of elaborating upon pre-existing music by another composer, and as such may be an example of 'single-piece' intertextuality, where one pre-existing source serves as a basis for a whole series of movements, as in the soundtrack to *Drowning by Numbers* (1988). This work shares much in common with an earlier soundtrack by Nyman, to Greenaway's film *The Falls* (1980), which is more accurately a 'single-fragment' intertext (though other unrelated pieces of music such as *Bird List* (1979) are also used in it). Both examples demonstrate a thoroughgoing and comprehensive engagement with the source (or sources). According to Beirens' three categories of intertextual types, *The Falls* is an example of 'defamiliarization', in which the original material is taken out of its original context and 'different solutions [are applied to modify or reduce] the borrowed material into a form that is suitable for ... use in a new composition' (Beirens 2005, p. 424). *Drowning by Numbers* advances this idea further, towards a form of intertextual 'deconstruction'. Here the original is dismantled in such a way that its relationship with the source becomes at times highly ambiguous. In other examples, a single passage or movement may not form the compositional basis for a work but is instead juxtaposed with other material.

Such single event intertexts may include isolated references, as the one of Purcell's funeral music for Queen Mary in the *Trombone Concerto* (1995), or Nyman's own self-quotation of the opening chord progression from *And Do They Do* (1986) at the end of *MGV* (1993).

At the opposite end lies the 'multi-piece' intertext, where a number of compositions furnish material for a single work. *The Draughtsman's Contract* (1982) is a well-known example, where ground basses have been taken from various Purcell pieces, but there are many others. Schumann songs are used in the opera *The Man who Mistook his Wife for a Hat* (1986), and the String Quartet No. 1 (1985) combines quotations from Bull, Schoenberg and Alex North's 1965 hit for The Righteous Brothers, 'Unchained Melody'. The latter example should more correctly be described as 'multi-authored' intertextuality, in contrast with the single-authored examples described so far, though self-evidently any act of borrowing or appropriating is multi-authored, inevitably involving Nyman and another composer (or composers), unless of course he is quoting himself.

In Nyman's nine-fold inventory of intertextual uses, the fifth type in fact refers to the quotation and adaptation of his own material from one piece to the next. Although any intertextual analysis is bound by outside factors or influences, Nyman's self-quotations are interesting precisely because they create an associative chain from one opus to another. The term adopted to describe this form of intertextuality will be 'inter-referential', instead of the potentially misleading term *intra*textual (see previous chapter), which is ambiguous because it normally refers to connections *within* texts rather than between them. If one were to think of Nyman's entire oeuvre as one large text, however – and there is good reason to believe that Nyman would view it rather in the way that Sterne's *Tristram Shandy* or Cervantes's *Don Quixote* become a repository for everything their authors wish to write about – then any specific example of inter-referentiality is, globally speaking, *intra*textual. An analogy with Saussure's distinction between 'parole' (words) and 'langue' (language as it exists *in toto*) is relevant here since the nature of Nyman's musical inter-referentiality reflects on the level of 'musical speech' the general and universal nature of his musical language. One may therefore encounter examples of single-authored multi-piece intertextuality: a composition that borrows musical materials from previous compositions for which Nyman, as far as can be ascertained, is the sole author. The *Concerto for Harpsichord* (1995) is one such example, which borrows from *Tango for Tim* (1994), itself based on music from the slightly earlier soundtrack to the film *A La Folie* (1994).

Other forms of inter-referentiality emerge when a third-party enters – such as a film director – and decides to reuse a piece of music intended for another project. One may therefore hear the track 'Fish Beach' from Nyman's *Drowning by Numbers* in scenes from *The Cook, The Thief, His Wife and Her Lover*, or piano pieces originally composed by Nyman for Michael Winterbottom's film *Wonderland* (1999) reappearing in his film *9 Songs* (2004). The latter example is interesting because, while the role of Nyman's film music is on the whole non-diegetic (that is, it remains part of the film's soundtrack and is not played or heard by the characters themselves), Nyman's physical appearance in *9 Songs* (playing at his sixtieth-birthday concert) allows him to become part of the 'diegetic' nine songs that punctuate the film's structural narrative.[6]

Media, technology, sound recording and film have also generated new intertextual constructions in Nyman's music. Punk rock band The Flying Lizards' single 'Hands to Take' was composed by superimposing a new text (a vocal line) onto a pre-existing multi-track recording of Nyman's *Bird List* song. A different situation may occur as a result of a film process, where an original recording used as a guide for editing a sequence of shots has to be faithfully reproduced according to tempo, gesture and rhythm. The original music (which often cannot be used for copyright purposes) provides the scene with its overall duration and pacing, but is now replaced by a recording expected to accompany a scene that accompanied the original recording. The reproduction of the original literally becomes a copy in this case, a shadow or simulacrum of the original – completely erased but still 'present' by its absence.

### Intertextual types and categories

Intertextual examples in Nyman's music will now be divided according to either their abstract or referential functionality. Abstract forms refer to type rather than detail and are represented by global and generic features. Referential forms on the contrary reflect detail rather than type and usually indicate that a source lies (or refers) outside Nyman's music to another composer and composition. Abstract forms may be further subdivided into two varieties: general and specific. The former provides a series of common traits found in his compositions, while specific abstract intertextual features are generic but may still be isolated according to a particular type. Character and function of these types will now be outlined.

*General (non-specific) functions of abstract intertextuality*

General intertextual functions in Nyman's music may be divided according to rhythm, harmony, melody, form and sound. The most salient rhythmic principle upon which Nyman's music is based is unsurprisingly repetition. It occurs both in terms of bar-by-bar repetition (sometimes referred to as 'musematic' repetition) and 'discursively', from section to section. Rhythmic patterns reinforce metre by articulating strong and weak divisions of the beat. Although metric ambiguity is an important generative feature of Nyman's music, very rarely does one experience any sense of metric disorientation through a complete absence of any regular pulse or beat.

---

6  There are other diegetic moments, such as when the kitchen boy Pup sings Nyman's setting of the Miserere in *The Cook*, or when 'Bees in Trees' is heard either coming out of a radio or played on a hi-fi system in *Drowning by Numbers*.

Harmonic patterns are either built up from common-tone chords of an essentially triadic nature, sometimes employing added sixths, sevenths, ninths and occasionally polytonal harmonies, or are based on chords that do not conform to conventional (i.e. tonal) sequences, employing triadic sequences that emphasize distant chords within a conventional key scheme established by the circle-of-fifths progression. Patterns often emphasize chords a tritone apart, such as in Part Five of the *Masterwork Samples* (a suite of pieces that formed the music to a performance sculpture by Paul Richards and Bruce McLean called *The Masterwork/Award-Winning Fishknife*, 1979) where a sequence is heard using $A^\flat$-Dm-F$^\sharp$-C.[7] In this example, two sets of tritones are outlined, separated by two major third intervals. In such cases a particular chord sequence may form the basis for melodic overlay and variation. These are often built on short, cell-like ideas, which are combined to create larger units. A feature of Nyman's melodic shaping is his preference for stepwise contiguity. His melodic lines often set out from close intervals and gradually extend the intervallic gamut outwards in a fan-like pattern. Chords may be presented successively (in the form of melodic lines) or simultaneously. Indeed a strong connection exists between both elements. Extending and/or subtracting harmonic, melodic and rhythmic units or employing principles of augmentation and diminution is also a common feature.

In terms of form, Nyman's music may be reduced initially to either singular or diverse types. Singular is meant here to describe the relatively small-scale, self-contained compositions that inhabit a particular sound world from beginning to end. Although changes may take place in any one or all of the following harmonic, rhythmic and melodic domains, and the work may even become sectionalized, the overall impression is one of singularity and unity. Many of Nyman's early compositions fit into this description, as do most of the cues supplied by him for various film soundtracks. Diverse forms are often larger-scale (i.e. operatic or orchestral) compositions, which make use of greater contrasts and juxtaposition of ideas. Terms such as 'grid-like' have been used to describe these larger blocks of material.

Nyman's sound also draws upon generic references to instrumental types and their construction. Its use of string quartet, flute, trombone and horn signifies 'classical' music, while saxophones situate themselves across both jazz and pop divisions. The bass guitar supplies Nyman's soundworld with its most direct rock reference, but sound production is additionally affected by the adopted performing practice of any given situation. This is particularly the case when using piano and voices, both of which belong to the classical and pop worlds respectively. In writing *The Kiss*, for example, Nyman deliberately set out to contrast the classically 'read' voice with the 'unread' vocal sound of pop production (Nyman 1988a). Piano and bass guitar often play loud, accented, detached, repeated notes, imparting a sense of rhythmic energy and propulsion reminiscent of rock music.

---

7   This sequence supplies a tritone variation on the circle-of-fourths pattern first heard in *1–100*.

*Specific functions of abstract intertextuality*

A significant number of generic forms appear from one work to the next. Dance patterns have interested Nyman since his student compositions in the early 1960s. Tangos feature in various contexts, but Nyman's extensive use of the waltz is one notable example of generic intertextuality, as seen in its inclusion as the ninth element in his nine-fold inventory (see Table 4.1). Some of Nyman's waltzes are also inter-referential (*Anohito Te Waltz* is based on 'Sheep 'n' Tides', for example). Early waltzes adhere to normative patterns, but later Nyman develops and expands his treatment of the form's rhythmic and metric character. An unorthodox waltz is heard in *The Piano* soundtrack in 'Here to There' (itself paraphrasing the Scottish folk-melody 'Gloomy Winter's Noo Awa'), where a metric structure alternates 4 bars of 3/4 with two of 5/4. His theme song for the children's cartoon animation 'Titch' also makes use of a waltz figure. Table 4.2 provides a list of waltzes in Nyman's music.[8]

**Table 4.2   Nyman's waltzes**

| | |
|---|---|
| *First Waltz in D* (1974) | 'Fish Beach' (1988) |
| *Second Waltz in F* (1976) | 'Book Depository' (1988) |
| *The Otherwise Very Beautiful Blue Danube Waltz* (1976) | 'Here to There' (1993) |
| *92 (or 86) Added Sixths for Molly* (1977) | 'Anohito No Waltz' (1993) |
| *Melody Lists in 3 and 8* (1980) | 'The Master, the gunner, the boatswain and I' from *Noises, Sounds and Sweet Airs* (1994) |
| 'Disposition of the Linen' (1982) | 'Waltzing the Bird' (1994) |
| 'Delft Waltz' (1985) | *The Waltz Song* (1995) |
| 'Sheep 'n' Tides' (1988) | 'Titch' (1997) |
| 'Bees in Trees' (1988) | |

In constructing melodic and rhythmic figures Nyman often draws upon a pool of individual types and topics. These are not so much overt quotations or references as flexible units that can be endlessly transformed or varied according to content and context. An idea which plays a subsidiary role in one work may therefore assume a more central role in another, its features magnified and potentialities explored in

---

8  Doubts could be raised as to whether *Added Sixths* and 'Fish Beach' are indeed waltzes, if only on account of their slow tempi, and 'The Master, the gunner ...' may be more correctly described as a sea shanty.

greater depth. Variations existing *between* Nyman's compositions often reflect the variations applied *within* them. Contextual differences arising from a comparison between two related works may become more significant than the fact that they are associated intertextually.

Variations upon variations appear in Nyman's music, creating a seemingly endless fractal spiral of connections and inter-connections. Such examples might include the rapid, ascending scale-like figure heard in the piano part in *Love is Certainly, at Least Alphabetically Speaking* (1983) (see Ex. 4.1).

**Example 4.1**    *Ascending scale figure in* Love is Certainly, at Least Alphabetically
            Speaking

This figure appears later in a work for piano trio, *Time Will Pronounce* (1992), but this time plays a less important role. It also appears during the penultimate section of the opera *Facing Goya* (2000) though it is not heard before this moment. The intertextual spectrum therefore includes at one end 'direct' (referential) quotation or repetition, but as more and more melodic, rhythmic or harmonic transformations, variations and alterations are applied, ideas increasingly assume a character of their own, eventually becoming unrelated to that of the prototype (which may in any case be a prototype of a prototype). Themes of image and reproduction, of hidden original forms and conspicuous simulacra are therefore important aspects of Nyman's compositional approach.

Another essential generic part of Nyman's rhythmic inventory is syncopation. Sometimes syncopation appears to be incorporated into the musical process where it is foregrounded to such an extent that it forms the 'subject' of the music: the music is as much about syncopation and its rhythmic and psycho-acoustic properties and effects as anything else. In other contexts it does not so much form a structural role but is rather accentual and 'dialectal'. Syncopation first appears in the openly vernacular early scores (the Waltzes in D and F) in dialectal form in order to play across the accompaniment's rhythmic and metric predictability. But its potential as a device for generating larger musical structures is first used in 'An Eye for Optical Theory' from *The Draughtsman's Contract*. In 'Stroking' from *Making a Splash* (1984) Nyman alternates straight and syncopated versions of the four-note sequence D–G–C–A, derived from a Monteverdi madrigal. He overlays this repeating bass line with a melodic idea that is subjected to increasingly more complex rhythmic augmentations and diminutions while fluctuating insistently between G and D major. A six-note figure, consisting of B♭–D–A♭–C–G♭–F at the end of *Plotting for the Shopkeeper* (1982) functions in a similar way.

Examples of generic 'accentual' syncopated figures in Nyman's music typically oscillate between the tonic and its upper auxiliary note, or between the tonic and mediant. The established intervallic relationship is subsequently varied through extension. This pattern is already evident in the opening line from the Second Waltz in F (see Ex. 3.4) and is also heard around halfway through the *Masterwork Samples*, as seen in Example 4.2a. In this case the syncopated line may be traced to the Bartók-like 3+3+2 pattern previously established in the bass. It reappears in a melodic line heard towards the end of 'Secondary Treat' from the *Michael Nyman* LP (1981). This syncopated pattern is used to very different ends in the viola line of 'To the Edge of the Earth' from *The Piano* soundtrack (in Example 4.2b), and also in the aria 'How Do I Know You Know' from Act 1, scene 2 of *Facing Goya* (see Example 4.2c).

**Example 4.2a**   *Theme from the* Masterwork Samples

**Example 4.2b**   The Piano*: 'To the Edge of the Earth'*

**Example 4.2c**   Facing Goya*: 'How Do I Know You Know'*

A significant number of what might be described as 'generic' harmonic patterns are also developed in Nyman's music. Only a systematic harmonic analysis of all chord progressions and their recurrence would establish the exact nature of these connections and deviations, a task beyond the scope of this present study. However, many chord progressions are reused in Nyman and the nature of their reuse may vary widely. The use of the F-D♭-A♭-C sequence from *Bird Anthem* in *A Neat Slice of Time* (1980) is a relatively straightforward example of Nyman reusing a specific 'abstract' quotation.

In other examples, subtle changes are introduced along a connecting chain suggesting a process of enrichment or refinement of the original version. 'If', from *The Diary of Anne Frank* (1995), is one such example. Its opening chord sequence

is indirectly derived from another four-chord sequence, which forms the basis of
the main section of Nyman's Saxophone Concerto *Where the Bee Dances* (1991).[9]
Example 4.3a from the Saxophone Concerto uses a sequence consisting of an
F major seventh, G dominant seventh, C major ninth and A minor seventh chord
pattern formed underneath a simple melodic descent from E to C via D over a pedal
C. Unlike other Nyman sequences, which possess a tendency towards harmonic
openness, this sequence suggests closure due to the V-I implication of its final two
chords (though for this to be the case the bass would need to move from E to A and
the key to be A minor not C major).[10] Other versions of this sequence may be traced to
a variety of sources. A more basic three-chord variation of this pattern appears at the
beginning of *Love is Certainly, at Least Alphabetically Speaking* (1983), presented in
Example 4.3b.[11] In the same year Nyman composed a soundtrack to Michael Eaton's
film *Frozen Music* (1983) in which the sequence accompanies a distinctive, almost
pentatonic, melodic line. In this case harmonic motion towards the tonic is at its
strongest in the film score, where Nyman may have felt that the musical language
required more direct treatment.

The original progression may have been taken from the second half of the eight-
chord sequence that opens the *Masterwork Samples*, forming a ground plan for a
series of melodic variations. This sequence, consisting of $Am^7$-$Dm^7$-$G^7$-$Cmaj^7$,
is elaborated upon in the third section. In fact its circle-of-fourth or fifths motion
is reminiscent of the prototypical chord sequence of *1–100*, and to that of a more
general 'referential' intertext: the Baroque sequence. It also shares common features
with the opening sequence of 'Time Lapse', from *A Zed and Two Noughts* (1985),
taken from Biber's *Requiem*. The Biber quote thus becomes a specific instance of a
generic type. In 'If', Nyman wishes to draw out connections between the generic and
the specific by including a quote from 'Time Lapse', as seen in Example 4.4.

**Examples 4.3a and b**    Where the Bee Dances*: chord sequence* / Love is
                           Certainly, at Least Alphabetically Speaking*: chord*
                           *sequence*

---

9    The opening of this concerto borrows from another source, the rather aptly titled 'Where the Bee
Sucks' from *Prospero's Books* (1991). Nyman has noted that the sequence originates in the soundtrack to
*Frozen Music* (see below).

10   Beirens suggests that Nyman prefers 'closed harmonic formulas', but his compositions employ at
least as many examples of 'open' patterns (Beirens 2005, p. 408).

11   This also provides the chord structure for the song 'Why' from *The Diary of Anne Frank*.

**Example 4.4**  *'If' from* The Diary of Anne Frank

Two quite specific points about Nyman's musical language can be drawn from these observations. First, that he often constructs pieces from self-contained patterns flexible enough to be applied to a variety of different contexts. Secondly, these syntactical patterns form part of a series of generic or expressive codes (dynamic, energetic, static, reflective and so on) upon which Nyman draws at various points. A corollary to this, however, is that a certain neutrality and objectivity remains in these musical ideas which allows Nyman to rework them in a variety of contexts. Music originally devised for a Japanese computer game such as *Enemy Zero* may also provide musical accompaniment to a 1929 silent movie (*Man with a Movie Camera*). This suggests that the musical sign as a whole can possess a degree of arbitrariness, a quality that has been utilized by Nyman in his film music in particular.

Both abstract and referential elements are often seen to cohabit in Nyman's music. His score for *Basic Black* adopts a favourite generic sequence, the doo-wop sequence (I-VI-IV-V). The doo-wop pattern has a strange hybrid dual paternity in that it belongs generically to rock 'n' roll but specifically to a cadential sequence from Mozart's Sinfonia Concertante K. 364, and may be heard in a distilled version in a musical 'quote' from *The Falls* soundtrack, *89-90-91-92* (1980). Its descending submediant formula has been frequently used in pop songs, ranging from Ben E. King's 'Stand by Me' to David Bowie's 'Ashes to Ashes' (Moore 1992, p. 89). The pattern became so popular in 1950s America that it generated a whole popular music genre called doo-wop. In addition, *Basic Black* demonstrates a capacity to generate a series of second and third-generation 'texts'. Its distinctive opening chord sequence consists of four minor seventh chords Gm⁷-Em⁷-F♯⁷-Bm⁷. This pattern serves as a harmonic basis for a second-generation appearance in *The Kiss* (1985). It forms a third-generation variation in the opera *Vital Statistics* (1987), and a fourth-generation appearance in *Facing Goya* (2000). Goya himself reappears as a cloned human in the final act of the opera, strangely mirroring Nyman's genetic musical modifications. Meanwhile a new harmonic progression is introduced at the end of *The Kiss*, which also forms a second-generation version in *Vital Statistics* and third-generation variations in *Facing Goya*.[12] In some cases, Nyman's aim is only to supply a straightforward arrangement of an existing score, such as *Taking a Line for a Second Walk* (1986) providing a two-piano adaptation of the ballet score *Basic Black*. Nyman has taken this idea further by creating an entire orchestral part from *Taking a Line for a Second Walk*

---

12   This harmonic pattern will be discussed in more detail in Chapter 9.

for the Saxophone Quartet Concerto (2001). Arrangement in this sense ought to be differentiated from transcription, where creative changes are inevitably forced upon a new work as a result of performing practicalities and artistic concerns (such as in the case of *Zoo Caprices* and *A Zed and Two Noughts*).

*Referential intertextuality*

Nyman's oeuvre in certain respects functions as a kind of family network or – to use Leipsitz's term in a somewhat different context – 'families of resemblance'; Nyman has also used the expression 'musical family tree' to describe relationships between his compositions (Leipsitz 1997; Nyman 1988a). The unity of Nyman's entire output is tied to the concept of the work as a family of associations. Within this unity, external factors – outside, referential texts – are admitted and employed. Indeed the transformation of this body of work is replenished and reanimated through the use of specifically 'referential' intertexts.

Without wishing to extend the analogy too far, the family tree idea is applied by Nyman in the following way. 'Paternal' forms are established through the admittance of other composers' works into a kind of family network of compositions. Because they enter from outside the internal network, they are effectively extrinsic and passive until they impose themselves upon it. Once active and intrinsic, they play a formative and subsequently developmental part in the network's function. Such paternal forms have included Monteverdi, Bull, Biber, Purcell, Mozart, Chopin, Schumann, Wagner, Brahms, Schoenberg and Webern.

Some of these allusions are of a peripheral nature, and remain generally passive by either informing only part of a work, or being transformed in such a way by Nyman that the original's context and function is no longer relevant or important. A four-note sequence possibly derived from Monteverdi's eighth book of madrigals appearing in the *Water Dances* suggests a type rather than a stylistic feature. Likewise the subtle integration of a Chopin chord sequence in the opening to 'Corona', from the *Six Celan Songs* suggests that Nyman sometimes wishes to further obscure traces of the original.

At the same time, and of equal importance, are texts that spawn other texts. They provide the means by which a text may be reproduced in another, and the pattern replicated *ad infinitum*. These 'maternal' texts directly generate other pieces. Some serve to endlessly animate and expand the process, while the lifespan of other musical ideas is seen to be short by comparison. Incidental features of a both generic and referential type characterize certain periods in Nyman's output. One feature in Nyman's style during the early 1990s was the use of an ascending phrase first employed in *La Traversée de Paris* ('L'Arche de La Défense'). This melodic type often sets off from an initial downbeat, reaching up to, and sometimes beyond, an octave. A syncopated effect is often added to the phrase by tying the first note of both the third and fourth semi-quaver groups to its preceding note, as heard in the opening theme from the String Quartet No. 3 (1990) (see Ex. 4.5).

**Example 4.5**  *String Quartet No. 3 (opening)*

In this example it assumes a central thematic role, but on other occasions its function is subsidiary, such as a horn passage at bar 143 of *For John Cage* (1992). In the latter example, the ascending theme appears within a dynamic, rhythmic context, while in the third quartet it is lyrical and inward-looking. The theme's potential, a paradox given its rising trajectory, is often used to signify introversion and self-doubt, as heard in 'Outside Looking In' from the film *Carrington* (1994). Its appearance in the latter's soundtrack came at director Christopher Frampton's request, allowing Nyman to simply reproduce it and also continue the recomposing process as the film cues demanded.

References also appear accidentally in Nyman's music, but may nevertheless serve to reinforce the character of the original source, such as the unconscious allusions to Jerry Goldsmith's theme from Star Trek's *The Next Generation* in *Gattaca* ('Not the Only One', 'It must be the light') or Queen's song 'We are the Champions' in *Wonderland* ('Franklyn'). Clearly unintentional (and therefore closer in nature to forms of implicit intertextuality discussed earlier in this chapter), messages on the forum section of the official Nyman website (http://www.michaelnyman.com/forum/) have drawn attention to some of these chance occurrences. If the identification of ostensibly unintentional quotations is highly arbitrary, of more importance to the present study is Nyman's use of intentional intertextualities in his compositions.

In analysing explicit examples of quotation in Nyman's music it is necessary to locate the intertext both within and outside its immediate context. Beirens has described these aspects as 'intra- and extra-musical' (Beirens 2005, p. 414). Intra-musical refers to the quotation's function within a particular composition, whereby 'a "dialogue" emerges between the original material and the way it has been processed, modified, juxtaposed with other material and integrated into a formal structure' (ibid., p. 415). Extra-musical function indicates the nature of the quotation's relationship with the original source by means of identification, meaning and association (ibid, pp. 414–15). The nature of the text's interaction with its intertexts is crucial to any understanding of Nyman's musical language. While the use of collage and juxtaposition sets up a conflict between the primary source and its new location, Nyman's quotes are on the whole embedded within his own musical language. His use of past styles clearly connect with his own form of post-minimalism – the use of ostinati, tonally-derived chord progressions, recognizable melodic shapes and variation forms – all belong to the music both of Nyman himself and of those from whom he quotes. Thus the challenge of any composer wishing to employ quotation in any integrated way in his or her music is 'to provide a new musical context for the "borrowed" material that takes at least some of these associations into account and/or uses it to articulate some musical or extra-musical meaning' (ibid., p. 403). With this in mind, the aim of the following series of case studies is to uncover, examine and contextualize the variety and uses of borrowed material in Nyman's oeuvre, starting with a body of compositions in which these references have been made explicit: the soundtracks to Peter Greenaway's films.

# Chapter 5

# Parallel Universes: The Nyman–Greenaway Soundtracks

Spanning a period of over fifteen years, Nyman's collaboration with Peter Greenaway marks a defining point in his development as a composer. In a medium where long-term association is unusual, their creative partnership during the course of over a dozen film projects has done nothing short of redefining the symbiotic relationship between sound and image in film. De Gaetano has compared their achievements with that of Eisenstein and Prokofiev, Hitchcock and Herrmann, or Fellini and Rota (De Gaetano 1994, p. 17). The techniques adopted by Nyman from film music have assisted him in the general formation of his compositional style. Indeed the adaptability of Nyman's music in Greenaway's films illuminates the purpose, function and meaning of his music in general. The importance of creating a distinct sound world, of pacing and structuring time and of using material resourcefully: these features have evolved alongside Nyman's film projects. Likewise, Nyman's classical music upbringing has enabled him to view the film medium as the *Gesamtkunstwerk* of the late twentieth century. An intuitive sense of the 'operatic' in Nyman's music has often encouraged Greenaway to cut film sequences to the speed, tempo, length and sometimes even the mood of the soundtrack.

Greenaway and Nyman's collaboration was based on a sharing of common aims and interests and a mutual respect for and understanding of each other's work. Nyman demonstrated a keen interest in film since his student days, and evidence of Greenaway's musical knowledge is seen in its application in his films. For example, he assigns a more important functional role to music than is common and also makes use of musical techniques when picture editing. Denham has described his work in this area as 'so diligently rhythmic as to create an almost musical resonance' (Denham 1993, p. 11). Nyman's music is at the same time highly evocative and strongly visual in nature.

Commonalities in their aesthetic aims and working methods may be seen in the juxtaposition of old and new elements. De Gaetano has described this as a combination of 'richness, opulence, overabundance of Baroque imagery on the one hand, and the formalist processes of minimalism on the other' (De Gaetano 1994, p. 19). Nyman's soundtracks animate Greenaway's images and at the same time provide his films with a parallel musical universe. The music's energy often generates a sense of momentum and movement. Its referential tone deepens the verbal and visual message or underscores the required sense of detachment. Its 'systemic' construction allows it to be disassembled in the short early 'structuralist' films, while its neo-Baroque features allow it to be transmuted from the seventeenth century to the present day (ibid., p. 23).

The combination of these two extremes has led Ritzel to distinguish between Greenaway's increasingly ornate neo-Baroque structures and features on the one hand, and Nyman's stripped-down minimalism on the other (Ritzel 1993). Nyman's music nevertheless provides Greenaway's self-conscious designs with an affective and expressive quality. Greenaway often presents Nyman's music in its most direct and unadorned form in his films. By contrast, the soundtrack recordings indicate a refined level of engagement with musical material which is not always evident when shown with images.

Music's clear divisions, modular cycles and repetitions are analogous to Greenaway's picture representations. Brown has suggested that the music 'strongly contributes to the sense of a series of superimposed frames coming out vertically from the screen that one has in most Greenaway films, the creation of these frames depending as much on a creative process of sorts on the part of the viewer/listener as it does on the director/composer creative process' (Brown 1994, pp. 181–2). Nyman's music appears to go beyond what Ritzel has described as 'a kind of forceful presence in the film's background' (Ritzel 1993). It provides a key element in the film's multi-narrative network, imbuing Greenaway's films with an architectural sense of space, complexifying and enriching its visual and verbal imagery with additional layers of cultural connotation (De Gaetano 1994, p. 23). This chapter will provide a description of the working methods and general aesthetic approach of Nyman and Greenaway, before isolating and contextualizing examples of quotation, borrowing and the recomposition of pre-existing material in the soundtracks themselves.

**Background**

Greenaway and Nyman first met in their early twenties and immediately started to share an interest in French and Italian New Wave cinema. At the time Greenaway had invested in a Bolex camera and set up a small cinema screen in his London house where they would watch films by Godard, Resnais and Truffaut. Unlike conventional cinema, these films did not try to create an illusion of reality but instead emphasized the fact that film was something literally 'com-posed', assembled from edited sequences of scenes, dialogue, camera shots, sound effects and musical fragments.

Greenaway adopted these ideas in his early, short, experimental films, playing games with the medium in order to draw its construction to the surface. In the alphabetical *H is for House*, *Water Wrackets* and *26 Bathrooms*, words play a structural rather than a dialogical role. A voiceover reads out detached 'statements of fact' reminiscent of natural history documentaries. Often referred to as the 'voice of God' because of its inseparable unity with the filmic image, its seriousness and sobriety signified for Greenaway the myth of indisputable authority and unqualified truth. Greenaway's self-legitimating inventories of linguistic devices have also included acronyms, abbreviations and other forms of literary contraction and rationalization.

Greenaway also evokes at the same time in his early films the pastoral landscape paintings of Constable or Turner, either by setting them against the backdrop of the English countryside (*H is for House* or, later, *The Draughtsman's Contract*) or making landscapes the subject of the film (*Vertical Features Remake*). He therefore plays on the dichotomy between reality and our attempts to describe and possess it through language. His films suggest that language seeks to colonize reality by applying its own rationalized systems of classification, categorization and identification. He deconstructs language by showing how it ends up skewing reality, merely providing an image of what it sees 'in words'. These 'formalistic narrative games' provide a link between music and other cinematographic elements in Greenaway's early films. Although he eventually adjusted his methods in order to work within the conventions of 'dominant cinema', his later films maintained a link with these processes.

Nyman's first foray into film was not in fact as a composer but as cameraman and director, coinciding with Greenaway's early projects produced during the late 1960s. In 1968 Nyman produced a short 5-minute film shot at a Legalise Cannabis rally at Speaker's Corner in London's Hyde Park, which he called *Love Love Love*. As suggested by its title, the soundtrack consisted of The Beatles' 1967 song 'All You Need is Love'. It may not seem altogether surprising, given his musical background, that Nyman decided to make the film the exact length of the song, but this was nevertheless an unorthodox, back-to-front method of working. A film composer is normally required to shape the music to fit the film and not *vice versa*. Nyman's approach is one of choreographing the film to music, allowing the latter's sense of time and motion to dictate the pacing and editing of the film.

Having no editing experience Nyman turned to Greenaway for assistance. This was effectively their first collaboration, although other projects dating from around the time, such as a children's cartoon series *Ganglion*, were also planned. Though it goes unmentioned in accounts of Greenaway's films, Nyman also supplied music for a short film called *Tree* (1966). The music was later rearranged for the Michael Nyman Band into *Five Orchestral Pieces Opus Tree* (1981). Apart from the deliberate wordplay on the film's title (a technique borrowed from Greenaway) *Opus Tree* also plays on the title of the musical work on which it is based, Webern's *Five Orchestral Pieces* op. 10. Nyman's interest in referring to, and making use of, previous styles and forms is already apparent in this early work, though he does not make any direct thematic or harmonic reference. *Opus Tree* could be seen as an attempt by Nyman to recover something from the legacy handed down to him by the twelve-note tradition. Other minimalists before him, such as La Monte Young and Terry Riley, admired Webern's use of chromatic stasis, fixed registers, colours and textures.

The work (at least in its later version) sets out to redefine the chromatic and textural implications in Webern's music, ostensibly taking as its model the opening of the third piece in the set. In the original work Webern creates a shimmering effect by including repeating rhythms, trills and tremolandos in the mandolin, guitar, celesta, harp, glockenspiel and percussion parts, while at the same time introducing a seven-note phrase in longer note values divided between solo violin and horn. The textural character of the original is maintained in Nyman's free recomposition but the harmonic language is based on chromatically shifting seventh chords and unfolding triadic patterns. Its repetitive structures evoke Reich, but the floating, dreamy soundscape is closer in spirit to Eno or Budd. Whether these changes were made to the piece at a later date is uncertain, but the 1979 recording from New York's Kitchen archives suggests that Nyman was already treading a minimalist path at an early stage in his career.[1] 'Initial Treat', taken from *Opus Tree*, is included on the 1981 *Michael Nyman* LP, and also plays on the film's title.

Nyman's association with Greenaway during the 1970s moved in parallel with his non-film projects, the most important being his work for the National Theatre's production of Goldoni's *Il Campiello*. He was asked in October 1976 by Birtwistle (the theatre's music director) to provide music for this play, which was set in seventeenth-century Venice. Nyman used some gondoliers' songs he had found in the British Museum, 'which had been collected in the eighteenth century and arranged [for] voice and piano or piano solo' (Anderson 1983, p. 263). These sources were intended as 'raw materials' for a more experienced composer such as Nino Rota to come along and arrange, but in the end Nyman undertook the task himself. When the production ended in February 1977, Nyman kept the ensemble together and built up a repertory for it based on a concert suite from the play, arrangements 'of grand opera arias and other popular classics for unusual instruments' in the tradition of the Scratch Orchestra and Portsmouth Sinfonia, and Nyman's own compositions, starting with *In Re Don Giovanni* (ibid., p. 263).

A strong emphasis on 'arrangement as composition' that characterized the Campiello Band's performances naturally led Nyman to further explore its potential in his later 'arrangements' of Purcell, Mozart and others. But it was as much the rough and untutored sound of the band, created by combining medieval and renaissance instruments such as shawms, sackbuts and rebecs with folk and popular ones – banjos and saxophones – that gave it a distinctly 'bizarre' quality. One such example is an arrangement of 'Il Miserere' from Verdi's *Il Trovatore*.[2] Nyman assigns the operatic duet between Leonora and the Troubadour line to a shawm and rebec while adding a banjo part to replicate the string ensemble's pizzicatos at various points. Despite remaining totally faithful to the original, the unusual instrumentation has 'an element of bizarrery about it' (ibid., 263). Although the Campiello Band gradually lost its more antiquated instruments, the colourful patchwork quality of the ensemble's sound was kept, and utilized further in Greenaway's *A Walk Through H*, a journey presented in an art gallery through a series of interconnected drawings of maps, and is still noticeable in his epic non-narrative film *The Falls*.

---

1  'Five Orchestral Pieces for [*sic*] Opus Tree', in *From the Kitchen Archives: New Music New York 1979* (OMM0015).

2  A recording is included on a CD accompanying Volume 11 of the *Leonardo Music Journal*, 2001.

## Music and image

A key element in understanding the Nyman–Greenaway collaboration lies in the unique relationship formed between sound and image in their work. The role of film music traditionally has been to enhance and heighten the film's visual and emotive qualities. Nyman and Greenaway established a radical alternative approach where music existed separately and autonomously from the visual narrative. Nyman has commented on how he would often start writing the music before Greenaway had made the film, thereby allowing him the freedom to 'work independently of the film's immediate content by creating sound structures which precisely parallel (but do not ... reproduce) the visual structures' (Nyman et al 1978, p. 91). This unconventional approach acknowledges music's independence while at the same time recognizing its power to affect and influence the film's images and narrative, reinforcing Nyman's view that '[music] doesn't merely support what is going on: quite often the character of a scene exists only because of the music' (Simon 1982, p. 226). Allowing ideas to co-exist rather than become dependent on each another or subservient to a master narrative has been adopted later in Nyman's collaborations with choreographer Shobana Jeyasingh, pop musician Damon Albarn, his work with the Orquesta Andaluzi de Tetouan, and the 'Sangam' project.

In his critique of the film medium, Fredric Jameson also acknowledges an independent role for music, pointing out, '[movie] music in any case ... acquires its own autonomy within the modernist loosening of forms, and often develops a formal power not inferior to the visual image itself' (Jameson 1992, p. 209). Nyman has also stated that 'sound has a fundamental tendency towards autonomy' (Nyman et al. 1978 p. 92). Unlike conventional film music, Nyman's soundtracks 'never functioned as a background to the plot [and] it had nothing to do with the interplay between the actors' (Nyman in Haglund 1994). This view, clearly shared by both composer and director, partly came out of Nyman's belief that music should never be composed as an adjunct to a film. His attitude towards film composition is essentially the same as when composing concert music. He may in this respect be seen to be imposing a classical sensibility onto film composition, where music's autonomy has always been sought and maintained. In fact, Nyman does not so much transfer a set of values from one medium to another but rather considers all music to be 'classical' in its own right.

The independent coexistence of sound and image in Greenaway's films clearly alters and influences their meaning. De Gaetano explains that the 'figurative and musical discourses represent independent paths that meet in the audiovisual film dimension', creating in literary terms a metonymic association between image and sound, rather than a symbolic one (De Gaetano 1994, p. 18). The two forms are not inextricably linked but rather provide different approaches to a given context. De Gaetano claims that Nyman's music therefore 'proposes independent discourses which are parallel to images', but adds that the 'blending of the two forms of art, of the two different ways of thinking and composing music and images, however, places music in a subordinate position compared to images' (ibid., p. 18). This abstract approach allows for a degree of indeterminacy between music and action; both director and composer follow an agreed set of guidelines but work independently of one another.

Despite the formalist parallelism between music and image, De Gaetano also points out that the 'structuralist prerogatives of the collaboration between the director and musician [are often] overcome by a final "logic"', as seen in the evolution of *A Walk Through H*, where the structural model gives way to the director's intuitive judgment. In such cases 'the final relationship between music and images goes beyond any pre-determined plan' (ibid., p. 24). While these decisions may obscure or eliminate the structural progression of a film, there nevertheless remains a residual structural trace. Sometimes the logic overriding formal concerns only draws these devices closer to the surface. In the laboratory sequence in *A Zed and Two Noughts*, for example, the music eventually chosen by Greenaway at Nyman's suggestion parallels and punctuates the pulsing and flickering fluorescent lights. Nyman's music is deliberately combined with the visual in such a way as to enable it to function on its own terms (Rivière and Caux 1987, p. 89). Music in Greenaway's films therefore always begins 'as an independent piece, with a continuing history and life of its own, whatever the negotiations with the images it accompanies – images often still unfilmed when the writing of the music began' (Woods 1996, p. 129).

The relationship between Nyman's music and Greenaway's images may be summarized according to the following six types. While this list is not intended to be exhaustive, many of the music's main functions are covered here.

1. Coexisting function. The music works independently but in parallel with the narration, dialogue or action. It does not so much accompany the narrative but rather co-exists alongside it. In *The Cook, The Thief, His Wife and Her Lover*, for example, the relationship between image and music was initially intended to be built around the six locations represented in the film, with each being ascribed its own colour, aura and design. Eventually, these formal processes were not adhered to rigorously in each instance.

2. Primary function. In the case of *The Cook*, the music's impact, rather than being coexistent with the images, is at times 'to be found in the operatic sense and theatricality of the film' (De Gaetano 1994, p. 27). Heard at its most potent during the scene of the funeral procession, where the rhythmic uniformity of the music provides the pacing for the choreographed movement, Nyman's music assumes a primary function. Such scenes are as much about the performance of music as of anything else. The music influences and dictates the film's shooting, editing and presentation.

3. Prefatory function. In such cases the music serves to preface, anticipate, punctuate or emphasize the film's structure. In *The Falls* or *Act of God* a specific chord sequence is employed to signal the beginning of a new list, category, number or character. As a result the music may undergo almost imperceptible

variations due to the length of time separating each repetition. 'Bird Anthem', the prefatory music in *Act of God*, for example, is subjected to a series of changes in time signature and tempo during the course of the film. Nyman's music for *The Draughtsman's Contract* also prefaces the twelve drawings undertaken during the film. Music simultaneously parallels and prefaces scenes in this way, or becomes a way of musically identifying a particular character or situation.

4.  Commentary function. The opposite of type 3 above, music used in this way appears after words or actions have been completed, as a kind of non-literary commentary device. It is used extensively in *A Zed and Two Noughts* and is combined with its coexisting function in *Death in the Seine* (1989), where, after a brief history of each death and conjecture as to what caused it, music accompanies each toe-to-head shot of dead corpses.

5.  Diegetic function. There are only a few examples in Greenaway's films where Nyman's music is performed 'on screen' and heard by the other characters, the most obvious being the kitchen boy Pup or Flavia the cabaret singer, both from *The Cook, The Thief, His Wife and Her Lover*. Greenaway may have avoided using music diegetically because of its overt realism. Nyman's music is often heard diegetically in other films, such as Michael Winterbottom's *The Claim*, *Nine Songs* or, famously, in Jane Campion's *The Piano*.[3]

6.  Subsidiary function. Allowing music to revert to mere accompaniment would have contradicted Greenaway and Nyman's aesthetic approach, but there are examples where music relinquishes its structural role and starts to resemble the film music archetype. 'Fish Beach' is used very effectively in this way, gently punctuating the dialogue between the three Cissies in *Drowning by Numbers* or the trysts of the wife and her lover in *The Cook*.

## Film and intertextuality

As already noted, Greenaway's methods of using Nyman's music is by no means arbitrary, although the relative autonomy of the music allows it to function independently and therefore cross between film contexts. This basic intertextual quality is further emphasized in both Greenaway and Nyman's shared enthusiasm for reference, quotation and allusion. Indeed the act of 'stealing' or borrowing from literary, artistic or musical sources is alluded to at the beginning of *A Walk Through H*, where a voiceover reports that two of the ninety-two drawings 'were stolen', before adding hurriedly, 'though not by me'.

Greenaway's intertextuality is often highly eclectic and multidimensional. It makes multiple references to art, literature and characters from other films. Sometimes even locations from other films reappear, rather in the same way that a piece of music may be transferred from one film situation to another. Many films evoke a painterly and

---

3  Music's diegetic function in *The Piano* will be the subject of Chapter 9.

illustrative nature by including a whole range of art historical references. In *Drowning by Numbers* scenes and characters from the paintings of Brueghel, Mantagna and Velásquez are brought to mind, echoing the film title's pun on 'painting by numbers'. Vermeer's paintings weave an intertextual thread throughout *A Zed and Two Noughts*, while the aviary associations in *The Falls* are probably meant as a kind of parodic homage to Hitchcock's famous film *The Birds* (1963).

Nyman has described music's function in Greenaway's films as 'on the one hand complete in itself [but] on the other hand a source of raw material, rich and open, which can be reheard or reworked' (Rivière and Caux 1987, p. 79). The Greenaway collaborations indicate the extent to which Nyman's music can be transferred or translated from one context to another. Some of these relationships are highlighted in the intertextual 'family tree' included in Figure 5.1. Each film soundtrack is based on pre-existing works. The 'Vivaldi' sequence written for *1–100* and partially used in *A Walk Through H* is generic rather than specific.[4]

On the other hand quotations from Purcell and Mozart provide a specific context or set of contexts for Nyman's quotation, though in both cases a generic trace still exists. In Purcell's case Nyman adopts a Baroque 'type' (the ground bass) commonly found in seventeenth-century music, and the cadential formula from Mozart is common to both classical and pop music. Nyman adopts Cage's idea (inspired by de Kooning's comments, see Chapter 4) that recent history is brought to bear on the past, and that Mozart may be heard and reinterpreted through the filter of late twentieth-century popular music. In this respect it is interesting to note how certain sequences of a more generic nature find their way into a variety of musical contexts while specific varieties, such as Purcell's own ground basses, are less interchangeable and adaptable.

The level of association existing between and within these soundtracks is multifarious. Any attempt to provide a thorough and authoritative list of connections between all Nyman's works would be almost impossible, given the level of conscious and unconscious appropriation established between them. Some significant connections have been drawn in Figure 5.1, but these only relate to the film soundtracks themselves and do not include offshoots – works that are otherwise unrelated to either Greenaway's films or the film medium in general.[5] Some precursor pieces, such as the music for Lucinda Childs's dance *Childs Play*, are also left out despite generating parts of *A Zed and Two Noughts*. In this case the referential intertext is derived solely from the Biber quotation, whose solo violin transcription was used later in *Death in the Seine*.

Some films display a more eclectic intertextuality. *The Cook* provides room for both Purcell and Mozart, though clearly not at the same time. Many of the lesser-known films are veritable repositories for fragments and 'cuttings' from a variety of works. *Death in the Seine* includes the aforementioned sections from Biber, some Purcell and also music from *La Traversée de Paris*, which later spawned

---

4  Vivaldi's name is referred to in an interview by Nyman in Rivière and Caux 1987, p. 75.

5  In the case of *Prospero's Books*, this would lead to an entirely new set of intertextual 'branches'.

**Figure 5.1    Intertextual references in the Nyman–Greenaway soundtracks**

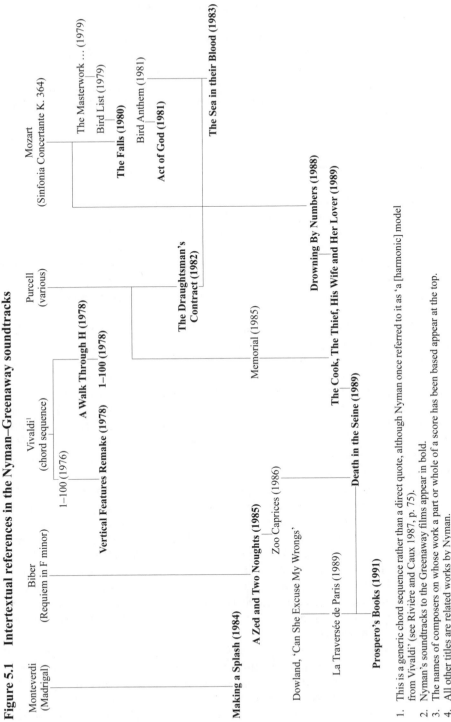

1.   This is a generic chord sequence rather than a direct quote, although Nyman once referred to it as 'a [harmonic] model from Vivaldi' (see Rivière and Caux 1987, p. 75).
2.   Nyman's soundtracks to the Greenaway films appear in bold.
3.   The names of composers on whose work a part or whole of a score has been based appear at the top.
4.   All other titles are related works by Nyman.

*Prospero's Books*. The musical family tree structure is only a broad-brush method of demonstrating interconnectivity and if misread or misunderstood could lead to misleading or erroneous conclusions. Of more interest from an intertextual viewpoint than merely tracing connections and associations is Nyman's treatment of these texts, not only from a purely technical perspective but also in terms of their relationships with Greenaway's images.

## The non-narrative films

Greenaway's films are generally divided into two broad phases. The first phase is often described as 'non-narrative' in function, covering a period from 1977 to 1982, and consisting of 'a number of short experimental … films' including *A Walk Through H*, *Vertical Features Remake*, *1–100*, *Act of God* and *The Falls* (Nyman 1989a). These films have in common an interest in representing 'reality' through listing, charting, reconstructing and reinterpreting facts and figures in a self-consciously faux-scientific manner. Traditional cinematic concepts of plot, dialogue, action and – by implication – narrative no longer apply, although Denham has pointed out that Greenaway derives his own narrative style from Borges and Alain Robbe-Grillet's 'literary itemization [where all] the features maintain a rigorous element of structuralism and a critique of the nature of systems' (Denham 1993, p. 17). Greenaway imposes rigorous structural and formal schemes upon these works only to subvert and deconstruct them, 'interrogating' the television documentary format in order to foreground the film's own construction (Denham 1993, p. 10; Lawrence 1997, p. 20). Greenaway continued to employ a broadly non-narrative approach in many subsequent productions, including *The Sea in Their Blood* (1983), *26 Bathrooms* (1985) and *Death in the Seine*, the latter lying somewhere between historical account, factual representation and fictional reconstruction.

The structural nature of these early films is demonstrated in their preoccupation with number sequences and lists. The music for *Vertical Features Remake* was composed according to a scheme of 11 times 11, the sequence 1–11, and the numerical progression 1–121, *The Falls* according to ninety-two variations on a four-bar sequence, and *A Walk Through H* based on ten cycles of ten ten-note chords. De Gaetano has claimed that in these films the music as much as any other element 'reveals the film's organization'. Whereas the degree of structural coexistence between sound and image is high in the non-narrative films, the role of music in the later work, though still essential to them, is not to such an extent part of the structural fabric of the film (De Gaetano 1994, p. 23).

Many characteristics of the early films are illustrated in *A Walk Through H* and *The Falls*. The former is an ornithologist's account of a journey through a series of maps exhibited in an art gallery. According to Peter Sainsbury, the film is 'an axiomatic metaphor [linking] cartography and consciousness' (in Nyman et al. 1978, p. 89) providing an unorthodox synthesis of film, photography, art, science documentary and travelogue. The maps represent an actual journey, though whether it is a physical or mental one is left open to question. Greenaway has described the film as 'a manifestation of a quest' (ibid., p. 90), though ultimately the journey itself rather than its destination provides a sense of purpose. Appearing to imitate a fact-based documentary, yet simultaneously self-consciously fictional, *A Walk Through H* deliberately plays against genre conventions and expectations. Greenaway removes any sense of authorship by retelling the story according to the fictional character Tulse Luper, who, like other names in the story, subsequently reappears in later Greenaway films. Luper represents both Nyman and Greenaway's alter egos in so far as he is 'an arch-cataloguer, a maker of lists, taking pleasure in accumulating more of the same yet resisting the essential minor differences' (ibid., p. 90). His cartographic representation of the journey implies that he has adopted for this undertaking an exact science. Maps are ostensibly intended to provide as far as possible a faithful rendering of a particular geographical area, but in *Walk* anomalies start to appear between the map's details and the 'narrative' account, until eventually 'the usual conventions of cartography start collapsing' (ibid., p. 91).

According to Sainsbury, Nyman's music for this film is 'at once structural and structuring, but also dramatically sympathetic to picture and to story' (ibid., p. 90). Greenaway and Nyman's structural approach adopts and adapts Cage and Merce Cunningham's music and dance collaborations of the 1940s and 1950s, starting with *Four Walls* (1944), where 'the dance-working of the structure and the musical-working of the structure were applied independently' (ibid., p. 91). While Nyman was free to compose within certain limits outlined by Greenaway, he nevertheless conceded that 'once the tape was out of my hands, the actual content of the music [entered] into a dialectical relationship with the film [...] sound and image [thus] have a more flexible relationship' (ibid., p. 92).

The music for *A Walk Through H* contains many intertextual features in Nyman's early style. A sequence of ten chords based on *1–100* is heard at the beginning, and like its precursor piece also starts on a C major chord. As with *1–100* this ten-chord pattern does not go full circle, ending three cycles short on an A major seventh. Neither does it directly replicate any sequence from *1–100* (the closest being chords 16–22 from the original). In all other respects the sequence is treated completely differently. A pulse-like effect created by the ten-beat repetitive cycle is strongly suggestive of American minimalism, though Nyman does not adopt either the additive rhythmic techniques of Glass nor the resulting patterns and processes of Reich.

Less typically American but nevertheless characteristic of early Nyman is the fourth section, called 'Wastes'. This was originally intended by Nyman for inclusion in the third part of the film and is based on a composition dedicated to Nyman's daughter Molly, called *92 (or 86) Added Sixths for Molly*.[6] Written for the Campiello Band prior to *Walk*, not only are the added sixths important, but also the rigorous application of alternating minor, major and dominant 13th chords, thus reflecting

---

6 One suspects that Nyman contracted the piece to thirty added sixths in order to satisfy the structural divisions of the film ($3 \times 10 = 30$).

Nyman's early interest in collecting musical categories.[7] The version used for *Walk* consists of two repetitions of seven eight-bar phrases, each phrase divided into two four-bar segments and each segment consisting of one added sixth. Fourteen added sixths are contained in the piece's two sections, totalling twenty-eight. Nyman achieved the requisite number of thirty added sixths by repeating the opening phrase, which consists of two additional sixths. The somewhat desultory impression gained from hearing the music is in fact misleading, as the methodical categorization of a chord type is undertaken as rigorously here as it is in later examples from *Drowning by Numbers*. Furthermore, Greenaway's treatment of Nyman's music in the final section 'Boundaries' is indicative of the importance he placed on music's ability to shape time in this film. The faster pacing of this movement is used to splice together sharp images of birds and maps. If music does not always set the tone then it often dictates the structure in Greenaway's non-narrative films.

*The Falls* relates the stories of 92 fictional characters, victims of a so-called VUE (a Violent Unknown Event), the effects of which causes them to turn into birds. Cage's influence on Greenaway is also to be found in this film's structure. The idea of structuring it according to ninety-two accounts came from Cage's lecture on 'Indeterminacy', although in Cage's version only ninety 'accounts' are heard (Cage 1961, pp. 260–73).

According to De Gaetano, Nyman's treatment of the Mozart sequence in *The Falls* functions as a kind of 'signature tune' to the ninety-two characters (De Gaetano 1994, p. 25). In the soundtrack it develops into a study in minimal variation, a musical exercise in accumulation with 'essential minor differences'. At Greenaway's request Nyman isolated a four-bar cadential passage from the second movement of Mozart's Sinfonia Concertante K. 364 and composed ninety-two different variations upon it. This short passage becomes a kind of meta-sequence for the film. Nyman expands the 'vertical' phase by, as he puts it, 'breaking the sequence down beat by beat and adding layers of new figuration' (Nyman 1989a). Aside from the Mozart references, Nyman's music is highly wrought and directly communicated, with the music for the opening titles initially taken from the *Masterwork Samples*. This subsequently became *Bird List*, which consisted of a soprano chanting bird names on a single high-pitched top A above a series of 4 dominant seventh chords.[8]

In this sense Nyman's method is different to Greenaway, a view shared by Heldt (1989) and Ritzel (1993). Nyman does not invent new musical classifications but rather deconstructs already received musical material by isolating it. Greenaway on the contrary builds up a rich network of associations through the use of highly arbitrary classifying systems, imbuing an inscrutable and sometimes contradictory world with its own strange sense of inverted order and logic. In truth, Greenaway imposes a structural limit on the classifying systems used in his films, as candidly pointed out by the skipping girl when she counts the stars at the beginning of *Drowning*

---

7  Nyman's interest in collecting and cataloguing items has also included bus tickets as a child, and later football programmes of matches featuring the team he supports, Queen's Park Rangers.

8  See Chapter 6 for a more detailed analysis of this chord sequence.

**Example 5.1** *Sequences 89-90-91-92 from* The Falls

*by Numbers*. Modelled on Rzewski's *Les Moutons de Panurge*[9] Nyman's layering technique in *The Falls* allows him to shift the musical focus away from the original without loosing sight of it completely. Greenaway's semiotic frame of reference in his films is always implied through the ineluctable linearity of language whereas Nyman's musical frame of reference is stated through the vertical simultaneity of his music.

The last four versions, 89–92, provide a useful reflection of the layering technique applied to Mozart's four-bar sequence, as seen in Example 5.1 (the transcription is taken from Nielsen 1992).

---

9  See Chapter 3 for a discussion of Rzewski's piece.

All six lines are heard in the very last variation; that is to say, Mozart's original melody and bass line, a repetitive rhythmic piano accompaniment similar in style to *In Re Don Giovanni* and reinforced with a melodic variation in the soprano saxophone; a variation of the bass line in the baritone saxophone and finally an alto saxophone line based on the second viola's part. Nyman gradually builds these layers up from 89 to 92 so that at 89 only the piano and baritone sax remain, at 90 all parts minus melody and bass are included, and at 91 all parts apart from the melody itself are present. This process resembles techniques of multi-track recording where parts are recorded over a harmonic and rhythmic template provided by the song's structure, and any number of parts may be selected, combined, muted, superimposed, edited or partially employed, thereby altering the vertical alignment of the music without affecting its overall form. Such methods have been developed in many pop forms, including the process of remixing pop songs or in specific genres such as dub reggae. Guitarist and composer Frank Zappa also adopted a highly individualized technique from the principle of multi-layering which he called 'resynchronization' or 'xenochrinicity', in which entirely new songs were created by superimposing independently recorded parts onto multi-track tape (Watson 1994, p. 303). Nyman has commented on the conscious way in which recording technology informs his compositional techniques:

> Recording on 24 tracks can be an advantage ... [instruments] recorded on different tracks give us a freedom to enhance the link between these ... instruments, as well as the chance to just use one of them. I use that as a kind of sign or musical effect in order to create variations or links between one aspect of the solo line and something which will appear later on in a multi-instrument piece (Caux and Rivière 1987, p. 79).

## The narrative features

The second Nyman–Greenaway phase consists of five feature films produced between 1982 and 1991: *The Draughtsman's Contract* (1982), *A Zed and Two Noughts* (1985), *Drowning by Numbers* (1988), *The Cook, The Thief, His Wife and Her Lover* (1989) and *Prospero's Books* (1991). Alongside the allusions and allegories of his earlier work Greenaway incorporates more conventional cinematic techniques based on what might broadly be described as a 'storyline', though one that is often made to appear self-reflexive. Narrative thus becomes a vehicle for examining the film medium and its conventions. A 'plot' in Greenaway's feature films provides a framework upon which formalist devices may be constructed and deconstructed. Formalism's emphasis on the elevation of the 'work' 'above any related or contextual factors' (Beard and Gloag 2005, p. 66) and concomitant claims of truth through detached objectivity and rigorous methodology is questioned in Greenaway's narrative games. His attitude towards formalism, then, is at best ambivalent. Greenaway employs such procedures in his films only to draw out the blind spots in their logical arguments and immanent structures.

### The Draughtsman's Contract

*The Draughtsman's Contract* is the first example where Nyman engages fully with an existing musical language and form rather than a mere idea or fragment; in this case his references are primarily Purcell's ground basses. His approach to Purcell's compositions is one of 'reconstruction, renovation, renarration, refocusing, revitalization, rearrangement – or just plain rewriting' (Nyman 1989b). Greenaway requested a soundtrack similar in construction to *In Re Don Giovanni*, but based instead on music appropriate to the Baroque parody period-drama setting of the film. The initial plan was to compose a ground bass for each one of two drawings undertaken by the draughtsman Neville, six ground basses being equivalent to twelve paintings in total. Although this plan was carried through by Nyman, Greenaway decided that there was not enough room to accommodate all twelve drawings with twelve pieces of music. The musical formula adopted by Nyman resembles the layering technique applied to Mozart's 'Catalogue' aria, but in this case it is refined, developed and extended in a series of seventeenth-century ground basses. Again choosing a musical device commonly used in seventeenth-century English music, Nyman subjects his adopted forms to a variety of elaborations and transformations, reflecting the fact that the ground bass was originally rooted in a tradition consisting of statement and variation. Indeed, the development of the ground bass reflects the progress of musical form in general in so far as it is based on the idea of composing variations upon existing ideas.

Early grounds were historically not so much based on a repeating lower part but on set harmonic formulae. Out of these chord patterns emerged the practice of fixing a melodic line, usually in the bass. Related forms, such as the passacaglia and chaconne subsequently developed where the bass formed a framework upon which harmonic variations could take place. A preference in the case of the former was seen for triple time movement in the minor mode, with a four-note pattern descending by step, while the latter would occasionally employ a major key and often, though not necessarily, a descending pattern.

The development of the English ground, where harmonic and rhythmic formulae formed the basis for elaboration, reflects a tradition where borrowing and exchanging ideas was common. Richard Hudson has pointed out that 'melodies for [grounds] could be drawn from the works of other composers', suggesting that the original spirit of the form was intertextual (Hudson 2006). Melodies previously stated above the ground formed the basis of new works, themselves becoming ground bass surrogates for further compositions. Later examples show that grounds were being constructed from entire textures, not merely from the bass. Nyman's research into Purcell and his contemporaries' music enabled him to incorporate these techniques into his own set of variations for this work.

Table 5.1 outlines the main intertextual references in *The Draughtsman's Contract*. Nyman has taken Purcell's basses from a variety of sources, reflecting their versatility in secular genres, from operas and odes to keyboard works. In most cases Nyman's

**Table 5.1    Intertextual references in *The Draughtsman's Contract***

| Title | Purcell reference |
|---|---|
| 1. 'Queen of the Night' | 'So when the glitt'ring Queen of the Night', from *The Yorkshire Feast Song* |
| 2. 'The Disposition of the Linen' | 'She Loves and She Confesses Too' (Secular Song, Z. 413) |
| 3. 'A Watery Death' | 'Chaconne' from Suite No. 2 in G minor |
| 4. 'The Garden is Becoming a Robe Room' | 'Here the deities approve' from *Welcome to all the Pleasures* (Ode) E minor ground in Henry Playford's collection, *Musick's Hand-Maid (Second Part)* |
| 5. 'Chasing Sheep is Best Left to Shepherds' | *King Arthur*, Act III scene 2, Prelude [as Cupid descends] |
| 6. 'An Eye for Optical Theory' | Ground in C minor (D221) (attributed to William Croft) |
| 7. 'Bravura in the Face of Grief' | 'The Plaint' from *The Fairy Queen*, Act V |

compositions are modelled on ground basses from single works. Where more than one bass has been used (such as in 'A Watery Death') both sources are kept separate and the divisions between the two made clear.[10]

Although Nyman set out to draw all his pre-existing sources from Purcell's music, in the case of 'An Eye for Optical Theory' he unwittingly chose a composition belonging to one of Purcell's lesser-known contemporaries, probably William Croft. In any case, Nyman's intention was not to reference any specific Purcell piece, hence the reason why he avoided using well-known examples, such as Dido's 'Lament'. His aim instead was to provide 'a memory of Purcell [but] not specific memories' (Nyman 1989b). All examples from the soundtrack are therefore meant to signify a kind of Baroque prototype. They acquire meaning not so much through what they are *per se*, but what is done to them rhythmically, structurally, texturally, melodically and sonically. In the case of 'An Eye for Optical Theory', Nyman dispenses with the harmonic straightjacket of the original, composing a series of melodic lines above a four-bar ground bass whose implied syncopations are drawn out and emphasized in the baritone saxophone part. While these lines are mainly built from variations of short two- or three-note fragments, some twenty bars before the end an extended tune emerges from the melodic weave, but even this is an amalgamation of the ground bass's syncopated quaver line and its walking bass 'shadow' in the piano part.

As with all Nyman's music for this film, the first piece, 'Bravura in the Face of Grief', was composed without recourse to Greenaway's images, although its sombre

---

10  Only the 'Chaconne' reference has been identified in this instance.

tone and dark qualities suggest that Nyman already possessed some indication of the film's subject matter. A sixteen-note ground bass slowly weaving its way down a whole octave from c to c' is the longest in the soundtrack, though Nyman does later employ a complete song-structure in 'Queen of the Night'. In this, as in certain other movements, Nyman takes the bass line merely as a starting point, allowing the accompaniment to be composed freely around it. In this respect 'Bravura' conforms to the Baroque passacaglia prototype. The original line is also altered by one note (B-A in bar 4 becoming B-B) possibly in order to retain a sense of continuity with the previous bar, where two Cs have been repeated. The second half of 'A Watery Death' is also an example of the original ground being adapted to suit Nyman's creative intentions. Here each three-beat segment is augmented to six, creating a structure that is twice as long as the original.

Nyman's fondness for generating larger structures out of smaller units is seen in 'Queen of the Night', where he takes an entire structure along with its harmonic and melodic details and gradually builds it up. In this case, the entire fifty-two bar structure of Purcell's song 'So when the glitt'ring Queen of the Night' – heard diegetically in its original version at the beginning of the film – is taken and transformed. Certain comparisons may again be drawn with Rzewski's 'accumulative' technique, but in this example musical choice and intuition take precedence over system. The ground bass is isolated and repeated four times during the first two bars before adding the original's melodic line at bar 3 in order to emphasize Purcell's canonic design. The repeating interlocking parts suggest Reich or Andriessen rather than Purcell, while the hard-edged sound seemingly on the verge of spiralling out-of-control resembles the approach of punk rock bands such as The Flying Lizards. Nyman gradually extends the pattern from one bar (bb. 2–3 and 4–5) to six (bb. 6–12), then to nine (bb. 13–22) and finally to include all twenty-nine bars (bb. 23–52). In gradually working their way through the original's formal structure, Nyman's melodic lines move away from, and sometimes converge with, the original material. Towards the end of the sequence a new harmonic reinterpretation of the bass line is interpolated, consisting of a descent from F$^\sharp$ to D via E, suggesting the transposition and augmentation of the bass line's D-C$^\sharp$-B movement.

Grounds based in major keys are represented by 'Chasing Sheep is Best Left to Shepherds' and 'The Disposition of the Linen', although the former was not originally a ground at all but is only re-presented as such by Nyman. Of all the pieces in the soundtrack 'Chasing Sheep' comes closest in resembling the layering method of *In Re Don Giovanni*. Its entire framework is constructed from the opening eight bars of *King Arthur*'s Prelude to Act III, scene 2, and builds, substitutes or re-presents a series of musical layers out of the given material. The initial 15-bar sequence is heard four times (Nyman re-bars the original in such a way that one bar has become two, which also makes it the same length as *In Re*), the second repetition extended to 19 bars through the addition of a 4-bar pattern between bars 10–11. The analogy with *In Re* is most noticeable in Nyman's application of 'terraced textures'. During the first cycle a melody is stated against bustling straight quavers in the accompaniment while strings emphasize beats 1 and 4 of each bar. During the second repetition the bass continues with its straight quaver pattern, strings increase their accents to include all four crotchet beats and the piano emphasizes the fourth beat of each bar. The third repetition reverts to the first, with strings articulating 1 and 4, but this time a new saxophone countermelody is added, played between the notes of the original tune. The final repetition is a combination of the second cycle (featuring strings) and the third (featuring saxophone) by providing the fullest and most complete texture. Nyman may again have adopted this eight-bar fragment because of its generic doo-wop qualities; the sequence is yet another variation on the I-VI-IV-V chord pattern (in this case ii$^6$ substitutes IV).

If 'Chasing Sheep' extends the block layering of *In Re* and 'Queen of the Night' with the additive principle of the 'Blue Danube Waltz', 'The Disposition of the Linen' revisits techniques first explored in the simple 'harmony plus melody' structures of the early waltzes in D and F. A 2-bar, 12-beat ground is established from which other layers are successively and simultaneously derived. This lamina approach emphasizes simultaneous variation rather than successive development. It is difficult to imagine exactly how Nyman could have replicated a 'genuine' waltz under such circumstances, given that he was reworking Purcell material, and this dance form was not established until the following century. 'The Disposition of the Linen' is therefore a waltz in terms of its application of similar methods used in previous waltz compositions by Nyman, though not so much in idiom or style. Based on one of Purcell's 'song[s] upon a ground bass', harmonic and melodic content has been generated from Purcell's material. Two-bar sections from Purcell's melodic lines are gradually repeated and overlaid until the resulting textures suggest a rich simultaneity of Baroque figures and figuration, as opposed to the contiguous presentation of ideas belonging to Purcell's original composition. Apart from the melodic compression, Nyman's deviations from the original appear in the areas of rhythm and timbre. His rhythmicization of the ground bass creates a varied pattern of emphasis that follows a numerical scheme of 1, 5, 4, 2, 3, 1, 2, 6 (the value of each quaver repetition being calculated in terms of the number of repetitions, therefore low C = 1, c = 5, b = 4, and so on; see Ex. 5.2).

**Example 5.2**  *'The Disposition of the Linen' from* The Draughtsman's Contract

All six rhythmic durations are therefore employed over strong and weak beats (1+5 and 2+4 respectively) creating a dynamic and subtly shifting ostinato bass. This

swaying, rocking figure is reinforced in the piano's percussive, metallic timbre, and staccato articulation on bass guitar and cello to yield a powerful fusion of rock and Baroque. Sweeping and sustained upper lines are supported with a solidly efficient bass line, and Nyman's application of sustained four-bar melodic phrases taken from Purcell's vocal line creates the effect of cumulative melodic saturation. These tunes almost burst at the structural seams of the piece, and are perhaps Nyman's most explicit reference to the image of Baroque opulence and decoration.

Nyman's music for *The Draughtsman's Contract* becomes Baroque-but-not-quite as a result of the collapsing and hybridization of past historical models. He avoids attempts at pastiche, emphasizing that the score should be 'on the one hand "Purcell" and on the other "Nyman" and simultaneously both' (Nyman 1989b). Neither does he set out to write a medley, or *pasticcio*, of pre-existing pieces. If parody-as-homage, in its non-satirical sense, might best describe Nyman's approach to pre-existing material here, what is meant by 'parody' in this context?

## Copying texts: parody

Parody often overlaps with intertextuality and is sometimes subsumed within it. If the latter's concepts developed from literary theory then the former has been more commonly associated with art criticism. Hutcheon has claimed that they are synonymous, stating, 'Parody [is] often called ironic quotation, pastiche, appropriation, or simply intertextuality' (Hutcheon 1991, p. 225). On a basic level both parody and intertextuality engage with pre-existing objects and artefacts, whether they are sounds, images or texts. Parody's traditional function may have been to develop a satirical voice or to ridicule conventions, but in recent times it has eschewed certain figurative and stylistic tropes for a broader expressive canvas. Described by Hutcheon as 'repetition with critical difference' (Hutcheon 1985, p. 20), parody's attitude towards the past is dynamic rather than restorative: it seeks to reanimate old forms through new means. Arguing that traditional definitions of parody have been too narrow, Hutcheon states, 'we must broaden the concept of parody to fit the needs of the art of our century – an art that implies another and somewhat different concept of textual appropriation' (ibid., p. 11). In this way, the past is not recaptured in order to preserve its authenticity but so that it can be reapplied and reinterpreted. Parody thus provides new relevance and meaning to existing forms. It distances itself from the past through the use of self-reflexive mechanisms. It draws attention to the illusion of representation and reproduction by simultaneously emphasizing repetition and difference. Irony is used as a kind of 'inversional' device to underscore the fact that 'we are inevitably separated from the past today – by time and by the subsequent history of those representations' (Hutcheon 1991, p. 226).

Built into the internal structures of parodic forms are methods of commentary on the work that establish a series of self-reflexive layers. Such mechanisms allow the object to provide simultaneously its own narrative and metanarrative: the 'how' of communication in addition to the 'why'. Works thus possess a 'structural identity' while also setting up the terms of their own 'hermeneutic function' (Hutcheon 1985, p. 19). Hutcheon has summarized this approach by stating, '[art] forms ... have sought to incorporate critical commentary within their own structures in a kind of self-legitimizing short-circuit of the normal critical dialogue' (Hutcheon 1985, p. 1).

This less prescriptive and more neutral definition of parody is applicable to Nyman's approach to quotation and comes closer to the idea of the 'simulacrum'. This term was adopted in Michel Foucault, Jean Baudrillard and others to describe an image whose original was either lost or impossible to trace, although Ludwig Feuerbach anticipated these changes in the mid-nineteenth century when he described society as preferring 'the sign to the thing signified, the copy to the original, fancy to reality, the appearance to the essence' (Feuerbach 1957, p. xxxix).

The authenticity of the image has been called into question most effectively in the paintings of modern or postmodern artists. René Magritte viewed it as deception or treachery, while later pop artists such as Andy Warhol and Roy Lichtenstein incorporated the notion of commodification as a central theme in their work. De Gaetano has described Nyman's music as 'a kind of "simulacrum" of classical music', suggesting that Nyman's 'copies' make obvious their inherently 'representational' form (De Gaetano 1994, p. 22). Indeed, modern media such as film and video are entirely predicated upon the representation of copies rather than originals. Hutcheon's description of Greenaway's approach to the film genre in *The Draughtsman's Contract* as 'ironic playing with multiple conventions [and] extended repetition with critical difference' could also be applied to the film's soundtrack (Hutcheon 1985, p. 7). Nyman also plays with the multiple conventions of Baroque music, critically commenting upon it by deconstructing its stylistic language and formal structures.

Denham also argues, using Hutcheon, that in Greenaway's work (as in Nyman's case), 'parodic use of irony ... makes intertextual reference into more than playful academia' (Denham 1993, p. 43). Technological media have enabled parody and intertextuality to become more easily absorbed into cultural production. Film promotes the transferring of multiple images, narratives and texts, and music often adds to this sense of polymodality. Intertextuality has also thrived in other technological practices, such as plunderphonics, as will be seen later in this chapter. Nyman's parodic approach thus demonstrates complete respect for the original but also reflects how pre-existing forms and structures may be applied to both late-twentieth-century art and popular styles.

### A Zed and Two Noughts

Unlike that for the *The Draughtsman's Contract*, the musical score for *A Zed and Two Noughts* (or *Zoo*) is diverse and multifaceted, drawing upon an earlier Nyman composition, *Childs Play*. The film score's main theme, 'Time Lapse', also draws on a pre-existing source: the 'Dies Irae' section from Heinrich Biber's *Requiem ex F con terza minore*. James Clements has noted how in the original, after a homophonic opening, a ground bass is introduced to the text 'Quantus tremor est', which consists of the same chord sequence as the one used by Nyman in 'Time Lapse'.[11] As suggested earlier, this sequence replicates in minor mode a version of *1–100* with its Fm-B♭m-E♭-A♭-D♭ movement. The harmonic movement suggests a descending circle of fifths formula typical of much Baroque music. Biber however provides an interesting variation on this generic pattern by substituting both the second and fourth chords with a first inversion triad, resulting in a stepwise pattern that descends gradually in thirds until it arrives at B♭ then ascends by chromatic step via B♮ to C (see Ex. 5.3a).

This sequence is sometimes confused with Purcell's Prelude 'While the cold genius arises' in Act III of *King Arthur* – originally used by Nyman in his homage to the victims of the Heysel football stadium disaster in 1985 – called *Memorial*, and later reused by Greenaway in *The Cook, The Thief, His Wife and Her Lover*. Similarities certainly exist between them, such as a descending, partly chromatic bass line (Beirens 2005, p. 416). Nevertheless, while it is likely that the quotation from Purcell would be recognized as an explicit reference, the Biber extract functions more as a 'stylistic reference to a baroque harmonic stereotype' (ibid., p. 416). In fact, if the first chord is omitted from the Purcell sequence an almost identical pattern emerges to that of Biber's harmony: Fm-B♭m-E♭ (see example 5.3b).

**Example 5.3a**    *Chord sequence from Biber's 'Dies Irae'*

**Example 5.3b**    *Chord sequence from Purcell's* King Arthur

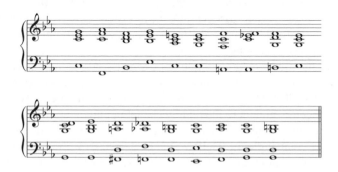

11   Personal correspondence, 1 December 2003.

The half cadence at chords 9–10 of Purcell's sequence, like Biber, approaches the dominant by way of the first inversion secondary dominant's 'chromatic' inflection, but avoids modulating to Biber's tonic key of F minor by resolving onto a minor chord. This in turn generates a second sequence consisting of chromatic movement across first inversion chords (again echoing Biber) before finally resolving onto a chord on the dominant.

The *Memorial* sequence is thus twice as long as 'Time Lapse', sixteen chords instead of the other's eight. The Purcell sequence may therefore appear as a kind of second-generation generic offspring of Biber's 'precursor' piece, which itself had evolved from *1–100*. By reproducing the length of the original versions, Nyman appears to move away from the compressed patterns used in the early works towards broader and more extended harmonic prototypes that possess a greater amount of harmonic complexity and interest (though arguably 'The Queen of the Night' had already done this by using a generative process). The music for *Zoo* also differs from *The Draughtsman's Contract* in that the detached, repeated chords of 'Time Lapse' are used by Greenaway to heighten and strengthen the visual effect and impact of certain scenes, such as the one depicted among the relics of animal experiments inside Oswald's laboratory. Greenaway understood that Nyman's innately musical sense of tempo and timing could be harnessed to cinematographic ends and used the music to dictate the pacing, cutting and editing of scenes and camera shots.

In his analysis of 'Time Lapse', Heldt begins to establish a typology of music and cinematographic features in Nyman's soundtrack by identifying a sense of claustrophobia, absence, hopelessness and resignation represented in the rhythmic, metric and harmonic repetition of Biber's sequence. He argues that its effect is created through the static, enclosed nature of the sequence, and compares it to a similar passage in Bernard Herrmann's score from *The Twilight Zone* series, where a sequence of suspensions accompany a flashback to a character's childhood in order to evoke sadness and nostalgia (Heldt 1989, p. 184). Although Heldt incorrectly hypothesises that Nyman does not quote from any pre-existing source here but rather replaces it with a powerful archetype, his observations demonstrate that one can appreciate the expressive and connotative qualities of Nyman's scores without identifying their intertextual associations. In the Biber case, it is enough to know that here is – in Baroque terms – a composition originally designed to move one's affections and stir the passions.

The rest of the music for *Zoo*, while not explicitly intertextual, makes some use of generic references and self-quotation. Greenaway used a pre-existing Nyman piece called 'Angelfish Decay' (originally composed for the Lucinda Childs dance company) as accompaniment to the rapidly changing photographic images of rotting food and decaying corpses. Nyman also writes another waltz but approaches the form from a different angle. In 'Delft Waltz' he dispenses with the laminate method of the earlier waltzes, opting instead to build a sequence from an essentially non-functional, or at least diatonically unrelated, chord sequence formed out of dominant sevenths (and therefore has parallels with the earlier *Bird List*). A falling melodic pattern introduced in groups of two plays against an oblique motion in the bass in three to form a hemiola effect. These two-bar units are then expanded to three-bar segments, possibly in order to reflect the kind of evolutionary process in eight stages from smallest microcosm to human being that had originally been the starting point for the musical score. Nyman's music explores the internal rhythmic nature of each phrase rather than building up melodic variations. The effect of these contiguous harmonic blocks is more clinical, detached and, as befits the subject matter of the film, more scientific.

### Drowning by Numbers

Though organically developing musical material first used in *The Masterwork* (to accompany 'The Woman Who Had Three of Everything'), and then in *The Falls* (where it shares common ground with Mozart's K. 364 and the character Cissie Colpitts), in many other respects the music for *Drowning by Numbers* presents a radical departure from Nyman's earlier film scores. Many have regarded it as his most personal work of the time, anticipating the more openly expressive style of soundtracks written for *Carrington* and *The End of the Affair*. The film's musical genesis is also different from previous Greenaway films. With the exception of *Vertical Features Remake*, *Drowning by Numbers* was untypical in that Nyman arrived at the work after the filming process had been completed, while the film was being edited. Due to the fact that the film's three (or possibly four) deaths are not meant to be in any sense heroic or dramatic (indeed they are almost trivialized in Greenaway's film), Nyman set out to compose a soundtrack that was 'reflective [and] more elegiac than tragic' (Meyer 1989, p. 44). In many ways the structural subtlety of the film also surpasses previous works. Ritzel has drawn attention to the fact that Nyman's music is first heard in the film when the Skipping Girl reaches the fifty-eighth star in her counting game, which is also the same bar number for Mozart's four-bar sequence from the second movement of the Sinfonia Concertante K. 364, upon which the entire score has been based (Ritzel 1993). The degree of expansion and compositional development of Mozart's material is in marked contrast to the layering processes of *The Draughtsman's Contract*. While the same Mozart sequence is isolated and magnified in *The Falls*, segmented, quoted and superimposed with other Mozart quotes in his setting of a Laurence Sterne text in *I'll Stake my Cremona to a Jew's Trump* (1983), its full implications are only fully realized in *Drowning by Numbers*.

The score therefore demonstrates a high degree of intertextual integration and control. Nyman's approach – of taking a single musical composition and magnifying and developing in different ways its technical and expressive elements – suggests a metatextual approach (see Chapter 4). Given that all the musical cues for the film are taken from this single source, Nyman's recompositions form a series of different commentaries on the work, teasing out aspects that are merely marginalized or suggested in the original.

Nyman's method is to isolate an aspect of the musical material (such as a melody or bass line), take it out of its syntactical context, replicate it, then combine the replicated fragments in various musical sequences to create new continuities (Heldt 1989, p. 181; Meyer 1989, p. 45). While the entire second movement of Mozart's Sinfonia forms the basis for the film score, Heldt has remarked how bars 58–61 possess a particularly important function in both the original and its recomposition. Not only do they mark the end of the exposition section and its thematic material in the original score but they also condense the movement to its rhythmic essence: a group of three quavers functioning as an upbeat to a downbeat crotchet. While the movement's home key is C minor, the eight-bar sequence used entirely throughout *The Falls* – due to its appearance at the end of the exposition – emphasizes the relative major key of $E^b$. Heldt suggests that these bars form the movement's 'syntactic pivot' ('syntaktische Angelpunkt des Satzes') but that part of the cadence's effect is achieved in a certain neutrality, gained in the shift from the expressive minor to the more detached major (Heldt 1989, p. 180).

In very straightforward terms, the major–minor dichotomy between two similarly constructed but emotionally distinct statements provide the film with a basic opposition resembling darkness and light, though such crude oppositions are never brought to the surface in either cinematography or soundtrack. Ritzel even sees Nyman's coupling together of Mozart's implied 'antecedent' (light) and 'consequent' (dark) phrases in compositions such as 'Great Death Game' as a general symbol of 'collusion' in the film (Ritzel 1993). This is supported by the fact that the music accompanying the counter conspirators is also based on the same harmonic sequence. Nyman's soundtrack also often parallels the film's number symbolism, the most obvious being structural repetition and an emphasis on triple-beat time signatures alluding to the female trinity of protagonists.

Ritzel further points out that Nyman's recompositions of Mozart's music most closely resemble the original during points where death is either imminent, enacted or disclosed. Mozart's music is heard over the three drowning scenes, and if Nyman's music is meant to supply a commentary on Mozart's original 'text' it most closely resembles the source music when it frames the drownings or is heard punctuating the 'bargaining' scenes between the coroner Madgett and the three Cissies. The proximity of the text to its intertext is therefore reflected in the increasing gravity of dramaturgical development taking place in the film.

If the second half of the film turns on its dark side, then the first (after the opening scene) emphasizes the sometimes trivial and diversionary nature of games and game playing. The breezy, waltz-like 'Sheep 'n' Tides' accompanies these playful scenes, where a boy called Smut explains the rules for 'Flights of Fancy', 'Dawn Card Castles', 'Sheep 'n' Tides' and 'Bees in Trees' (the last accompanied by a musical variation on 'Sheep 'n' Tides'). One scene depicts Smut being woken up by the voice of Madgett while he retells (in voiceover) a game described as 'Dawn Card Game', one of many games invented by his fecund mind. The waltz is associated here on the one hand with youth, playing and playful qualities, and on the other with an emphasis on correct rules of procedure and attention to detail. Later the music accompanies another game involving Smut jumping out of a barn's hayloft with a mechanism that photographs him doing this (throughout the film he is depicted as a keen photographer and collector of images, in itself self-reflexive given that any film does precisely the same). Scattered across the natural landscape are sheep, birds and other animals. Not only is youthfulness conjured up by the waltz but also a folk-like naturalism suggested by circular shapes and forms, and – through the use of straightforward triadic progressions – a state of musical innocence.

'Sheep 'n' Tides' takes the framework of the original bass line used by Mozart's closing theme as its starting point (a technique later developed in the fusion of both $E^b$ major and C minor versions of this bass line in 'Wedding Tango'). Nyman's harmonic reduction turns the sequence into an even more obvious doo-wop reference. Rigid processes, rather like the rigid rules imposed in Smut's games, operate under the waltz's insouciant veneer. For example, a second variation of the bass line heard in bars 26–41 methodically retrogrades dyads from the original sequence, so that $E^b$ – C becomes C – $E^b$, $A^b$ – $B^b$ becomes $B^b$ – $A^b$, and so on.[12] Similar processes are applied to other pieces during the first half of the film, such as 'Bees in Trees' and 'Wheelbarrow Walk'. As the intentions of the three Cissies become increasingly more conspiratorial, the general mood of the film and of the music darkens.

Of the darker group of compositions 'Trysting Fields' is one of the most arresting. Its focus on creating a musical list parallels other visual and verbal lists supplied throughout the film. As stated earlier, it first accompanies a number narrative set up at the beginning where a young girl skips on the street outside her house at night while looking up and counting the stars. She counts exactly 100, giving each one a name. This in turn triggers off another number sequence from 1–100, which spans the film's entire structure. Sometimes appearing on screen by being physically attached to objects, or at other times heard in the film's dialogue, the number sequence draws the viewer's attention to the fact that any film is artificially constructed, that it lasts a certain length of time, and that its length may be counted out in numbers.

This overarching number sequence represents a teleological ordering principle – a kind of structural paradigm – out of which other number narratives emerge. Nyman also replicates this idea in musical terms by reordering Mozart's material into a series of tables, charts and inventories. In the same way that postmodern criticism treats texts 'not just as object for analysis, but as a means to investigate the terms of that analysis itself, and analysis in general' (Wills and McHoul 1988, p. 8), Nyman's composition becomes a kind of analytical enquiry into aspects of eighteenth-century compositional practice: a piece made out of pieces. He does this by applying a variety of musical processes, including selection according to musical type in 'Trysting Fields', harmonic function and chord position, as in the case of 'Great Death Game' and 'Dead Man's Catch'.

---

12  Beirens describes it as a 'quasi-retrograde of the chord progression' (Beirens 2005, p. 419).

'Trysting Fields' sets out to unfix the 'connective tissue' binding together classical music's phraseological forms and periodicities while simultaneously preserving a memory of the original. This idea has its origins in the experimental music aesthetic where sounds were isolated from their function or purpose so that they could be heard for what they were rather than as vehicles for man-made expression. In Feldman's words, 'only by unfixing the elements traditionally used to construct a piece of music could ... sounds exist in themselves [and] not as symbols ... or memories which were the memories of other music to begin with' (Feldman, in Nyman 1993a, p. 210). The affective poignancy of 'Trysting Fields' is largely attributed to Nyman's choice of the accented appoggiatura as the 'subject' for his recomposition, an unprepared accented dissonance marked by an 'arresting sound that creates an intense expressive nuance, and a grateful release as it resolves by step into the chord' (Ratner 1980, p. 62). As a common feature in music of the late eighteenth century, the appoggiatura is of particular importance in Mozart's music because it constitutes, according to Ratner, 'one of the chief ingredients of his musical speech' (ibid., p. 62).

Nyman has described the process applied in 'Trysting Fields' as an

[act] of musical trawling in which all examples of a particular category of musical material are taken out of their original context and placed side by side in a montage that preserves their original chronological ordering, removes the connective tissue and puts under a microscope ... Mozart's 'affective' deployment of the accented appogiatura [*sic*] ... (Nyman 1989a)

Although 'Trysting Fields' does not adopt the formal plan of the second movement of the *Sinfonia Concertante*, it is in effect bound to it and indirectly governed by it. Charles Rosen has described the second movement of K. 364 as following an 'archaic sonata form, where the second part repeats the material of the first closely, modulating now from the dominant (here the relative major) to the tonic ...' (Rosen 1976, p. 215). An alternative description would be one of abridged sonata form – that is, one without a development section – where bars 1–61 comprises an exposition modulating from tonic minor to relative major, and 62–148 recapitulates the material, initially in a variety of keys, before the tonic is re-established at bar 81. A sense of the original structure is therefore inevitably communicated through Nyman's re-categorization of the appoggiatura figure. Table 5.2 provides a complete list of their location in both Nyman and Mozart's score, while Example 5.4 (p. 108) highlights the first three appoggiaturas from bars 10–14 of the original (see the boxed units).

Nyman also repeats most musical units three times, partly in order to represent the three colluding Cissies in the film. A high proportion of these figures are taken from the first half of the movement, and are concentrated around a cluster of dissonances appearing in the transition from tonic minor to relative major. This chain of dissonances results in an intensification of the figure's effect from bars 16–25, which is also replicated in the last three figures at 81–9. A similar sequence between 34–48 creates the opposite effect due to the fact that – with the new key already

### Table 5.2    Appoggiatura sources in Nyman's 'Trysting Fields'

| Nyman (bar numbers) | Mozart (bar numbers) | Nyman (bar numbers) | Mozart (bar numbers) |
|---|---|---|---|
| 1–3 | 10 | 52–54 | 57 |
| 4–6 | 12 | 55–56 | 65 |
| 7–9 | 14 | 57–58 | 69 |
| 10–12 | 18 | 59–60 | 71 |
| 13–15 | 20 | 61–62 | 73 |
| 16–18 | 21 | 63–65 | 74 |
| 19–21 | 22 | 66–67 | 78 |
| 22–24 | 23 | 68–69 | 81 |
| 25–27 | 24 | 70–71 | 26 |
| 28–30 | 26 | 72–73 | 28 |
| 31–33 | 28 | 74–75 | 81 |
| 34–36 | 29 | 76–77 | 83 |
| 37–39 | 30 | 78–80 | 84 |
| 40–42 | 31 | 81–83 | 87 |
| 43–45 | 32 | 84–86 | 88 |
| 46–48 | 33 | 87–89 | 89 |
| 49–51 | 34 | | |

established – Mozart's interest turns towards developing a more 'conversational' imitative texture between solo violin and viola. Mozart's periodicities are therefore marked out in Nyman's score, and sometimes rise to the surface, such as when the leaping figure at 49–51 signals the end of a concertino section in the original score.

Mozart's musical presence is therefore felt as much by its absence in 'Trysting Fields'. What is not heard – the 'connective tissue' of tonality, its periodicities and divisions – is still implied in the space between the notes. For example, the section half of Mozart's exposition, bars 34–56, provides a lighter and more dextrous contrast to the first half with the opening section's intensity disappearing along with the appoggiaturas. They return during the opening section of the second exposition at bar 65, which functions as a kind of recapitulation in the 'wrong' key. This is reflected in a series of transitions through a succession of tonalities in Nyman, from bars 56–65. The abruptness of the falling figure heard at bars 66–7 is partly attributable to the fact that it lies at an almost equidistant point between the two 'unrelated' appoggiaturas at bars 74 and 81 of the original.

**Example 5.4**   *Excerpt from Mozart's* Sinfonia Concertante *K. 364 (Second Movement, bb. 9–14)*

Nyman then relaxes control over the categorization principle in order to reintroduce two figures previously heard at bars 28–33. They are represented by a characteristic dotted figure underpinned by a chromatic lower neighbour note, which leaps down an octave. Nyman's fondness for this figure may have persuaded him to extend it to a ten-bar phrase consisting of four figures, with one (81) repeated twice. An almost indeterminate logic also asserts itself in places through this 'arbitrary' selection process. In Nyman's score bars 1–15 consist entirely of falling figures, while bars 15–25 reply with a group of rising patterns, establishing a pattern for the rest of the movement.

**Example 5.4**   *concluded*

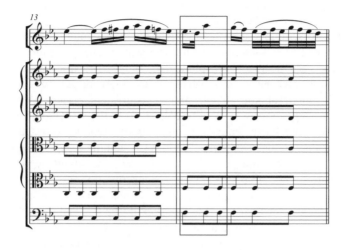

### 'Trysting Fields' and plunderphony

Nyman has compared the process used in 'Trysting Fields' (and also in 'Knowing the Ropes' from the same soundtrack) to the idea of the palimpsest, of 'painting over an [existing] picture … one draws in a manner that enables one to see the original as if one had placed something transparent over it. One can see what [is] painted, but also, what the original looks like' (Meyer 1989, p. 48). There is also a wider context within which 'Trysting Fields' functions. Nyman's methods bear a striking resemblance here to the technique of sampling sounds, although it is unlikely that he would have been aware of this at the time. Developments in sampling technology emerged during the mid-1980s with electronics companies such as Ensoniq and Akai designing samplers that were aimed at the composer and musician rather than studio engineer. This enabled all music in principle, but predominantly pop music, to borrow sounds from previous recordings. Nyman may well have unconsciously transferred its techniques to acoustic music by 'sampling' the text 'as score' rather than 'as sound', although the idea of drawing up musical lists is more likely to have come from serial composition.

Sampling is in many senses the intertextual musical mode *par excellence*. From the 1980s onwards composers and pop musicians harnessed its potential in this way. Indeed Chris Cutler used the term plunderphonics to describe it by (ironically) 'borrowing' the term from Canadian composer John Oswald, whose CD of the same name had been released in the late 1980s. Cutler defines it as 'a compositional practice in which previously recorded compositions – usually drawn from popular sources – are electronically manipulated and used as raw sonic material for an entirely new composition' (Cutler 1996, p. 354). Plunderphonics differs from other forms of borrowing in that it simultaneously preserves and alters the very imprint of the original work through mechanical reproduction. In this sense it paradoxically represents a 'purer' and more radical form of musical intertextuality, where the copy replaces the original by subsuming it.

The ability to sample sounds has brought about a revolution in the way music can be captured, stored, manipulated and transmitted. The consequences according to Cutler have been far-reaching: 'plundered sound carries, above all, the unique ability not just to refer but to be; it offers not just a new means but a new meaning' (ibid., p. 364). Plunderphonics, like its high-art equivalent, parody, borrows methods of 'montage, collage, borrowing and bricolage' from the visual arts (ibid., p. 361). In mapping out four basic types and functions of plunderphony Cutler provides another set of intertextual typologies. The first is complete appropriation, or 'total importation', where 'existing recordings ... become the simultaneous subject and object of a creative work' (ibid., p. 372). The second, described as 'partial importation', grafts pre-existing sounds onto an otherwise 'original' work. A third category, called 'sources irrelevant', consists of the 'recognition of [the fact that the plundered] parts ... [are] not necessary or important' to the music in question. Cutler's final category is 'sources untraceable', where the quoted material has been deliberately obscured by means of manipulation, stretching or other 'radical treatment' (ibid., p. 373). Applied to Nyman's music, Cutler's partial or total importations are certainly present in his work. Inevitably there also exist some irrelevant or untraceable varieties, suggesting that at times identifying the intertextual basis of a work does not always cast light on its function, although it may help explain some of its mechanisms.

Mozart's music when restructured in this way communicates an almost disembodied sense of tension and resolution, of arsis and thesis, which is further emphasized in its superposition with Greenaway's images. Nyman was never required to write music to accompany specific images in the conventional sense, to heighten characters' emotions or even to deliberately create a particular atmosphere. Rather, the music co-existed with the images on screen while at the same time possessing its own logic and structure. It therefore exists at a certain remove or distance from the screen. Its neutrality enables it to be employed in a variety of contexts, and this has been the case with another cue from *Drowning by Numbers*, 'Fish Beach'.

If Nyman's use of the appoggiatura in 'Trysting Fields' results in a complex two-way discourse between text and intertext, subject and object, 'Fish Beach' was incorporated to great effect by Greenaway in his follow-up to *Drowning by Numbers*, *The Cook, The Thief, His Wife and Her Lover*. It provides a straightforward but highly effective intertextual technique based on the simultaneous statement and variation of a pre-existing theme where harmony becomes melody while at the same time being 'heard against itself in augmentation'. Nyman takes the bass line from the endlessly generative doo-wop sequence of Mozart's movement, transfers it to the top line and repeats it twice underneath a single repetition of the same phrase in double values (see Ex. 5.5).

The bass therefore redefines the original bass line here, oscillating between tonic $E^b$ and the relative minor on C (or *vice versa*). The evocative yet enigmatic effect of

**Example 5.5**   *'Fish Beach' from* Drowning by Numbers *(piano reduction)*

this passage is tailor-made for film, suggesting that film music can often say a lot with an economy of means, as demonstrated, for example, by Bernard Herrmann in his famous evocation of extreme fear through the use of a single string glissando in *Psycho* (1960). In *The Cook* 'Fish Beach' is used during the quiet, reflective scenes between Georgina and her lover Michael while in *Drowning by Numbers* it is used to symbolize the solidarity of the Three Cissies. Ritzel suggests that the music may therefore represent a musical type based on unity or solidarity, a unity that is reinforced in the treble line's replication of the bass (Ritzel 1993).

### *Prospero's Books* and beyond

As arguably Nyman's greatest achievement in film music up to this point, *Prospero's Books* remained largely unfulfilled in its filmic form by Greenaway, and precipitated the break-up of their collaboration. Described by Nyman as 'the richest, the best performed [and] the most expensively recorded' soundtrack provided for any Greenaway film (Nyman 2000), Nyman took exception not so much to Greenaway's sparse use of the film score, but rather to the manner in which the film director decided to overlay sound effects (particularly water-based sounds) on top, thereby obscuring the music's primary function and purpose. A work based upon works, *Prospero* signalled a new stage in Nyman's development, where intertextuality is replaced with inter-referentiality; external borrowing with internal self-quotation. The metatext for *Prospero's Books* is *La Traversée de Paris*, a kind of mother-text from which around half the material is derived. The nature of these connections has been outlined in Table 5.3.

*La Traversée de Paris* – a multi-movement work written in commemoration of the bicentenary of the French revolution – forms a rich repository for past and future texts, and seems a particularly appropriate source for a film dealing with the power of texts and their ability to influence thoughts and actions. Previous compositions find their way into *La Traversée de Paris*, such as *And Do They Do* ('Le Jardin'), and

**Table 5.3    Inter-referential connections between *La Traversée de Paris*
and *Prospero's Books***

| *La Traversée de Paris* | *Prospero's Books* |
| --- | --- |
| 'L'entrée' | 'Prospero's magic' |
| 'Débarcadère' | 'Reconciliation' |
| 'Le labyrinthe' | 'Come unto these yellow sands' |
| 'Le theatre d'ombres chinoises' | 'Miranda' |
| 'Du faubourg à l'assemblée' | 'Prospero's curse' |
| 'Passage de l'égalité' | 'Cornfield' |
| 'Cinéma d'actualités' | 'History of Sycorax' |

very many works other than *Prospero* find their way out of it too, including *Out of the Ruins*, String Quartet No. 3 ('L'Arche de La Défense'), *Six Celan Songs* ('Chanson einer Dame im Schatten' is based on 'Les Manifestations') and *The Fall of Icarus* ('Disaster' is based on the piano theme in 'Du faubourg à l'Assemblée').

*Prospero's Books* also departs from the effervescent and often visceral early sound of Nyman's scores. A similar approach is adopted in other soundtracks from around this time, such as Patrice Laconte's *Le mari de la coiffeuse* (1990) or slightly later in Christopher Hampton's *Carrington*. In such contexts the music is often gentler and more understated than in earlier soundtracks, often underscoring the film's tensions by appearing to rise beyond them. Similar forms of expressive detachment are also found in Andrew Niccol's Orwellian *Gattaca* (1997) and in particular Michael Winterbottom's *Wonderland* (1999). Much of the latter's music is written for piano, but unlike the score provided for Jane Campion's earlier *The Piano*, it does not make use of sweeping romantic textures or virtuosic pianistic figurations. Instead, Nyman's style is reduced here to almost Satie-esque simplicity. *Wonderland* is set in London's inner-city urban sprawl, but manages amidst all the noise, grime, frustration and depression of city life somehow to convey a depth, conviction and honesty in the characters' often mundane and monotonous lives. Nyman's music contributes to this sense of overcoming, raising above the troubles and anxieties of the film's characters. It seeks to provide a view from above – or beyond – the film itself.

The intertextual dimensions apparent in the earlier Greenaway soundtracks almost completely disappear in Nyman's later film scores. In *Prospero's Books* a trace of it remains in a quote from the closing bars of a Dowland song, 'Can She Excuse My Wrongs', appearing in the opening bars of Nyman's 'While you here do snoring lie'.[13] In truth, the manner in which this quotation is presented is very different to earlier examples of borrowing from Purcell and Biber, which foreground the act of

---

13  Interestingly, Dowland also quotes an Elizabethan song, here, called 'Shall I go walk the woods so wild?'

quotation and make the original version if not 'known', then at least explicit. The process is taken further in *Drowning by Numbers* where the degree of re-composition renders some passages less familiar – more Nyman than Mozart. In its seamless integration into what is already a fully conceived composition, the Dowland quote advances this idea further still. Here, intertextual devices are only used to support what is already there rather than supplying a framework to an otherwise fairly radical compositional overhaul and rearrangement.

The Nyman–Greenaway soundtracks thus present a variety of intertextual approaches, from the hypotextual relationship between *The Falls* and a Mozart fragment from the *Sinfonia Concertante* to its extension to metatextual proportions in *Drowning by Numbers*. In between these two soundtracks, the polytextual adaptation of various Purcell ground basses in *The Draughtsman's Contract* nevertheless provides unification through generic association. A shift occurs in Nyman's intertextual perspective during the late 1980s. Instead of allowing the precursor piece to dictate the terms on which the Nyman 'hypertext' is based, the latter dictates the position and location of the former. Thus the Dowland song in *Prospero's Books* conforms to Nyman's pre-determined scheme rather than directly shaping and influencing it. This new approach can be traced back to the function and relationship of Nyman's music to Schumann material in his chamber opera *The Man who Mistook his Wife for a Hat*. Here, Schumann's songs are moulded around Nyman's harmonic language and structural framework rather than constructed from the raw materials of the songs themselves (although this also happens in the opera). The music first heard in the opera is Nyman's own set of harmonic variations, and Schumann has to find his own way into the musical and dramatic narrative. That Schumann's music does so with increasing purpose as the work unfolds – culminating in a complete Schumann quotation – demonstrates how intertextual associations could also generate dramatic juxtapositions and conflicts, in addition to stylistic ones, as I hope to demonstrate in the following chapter.

# Chapter 6

# Quotation in Nyman's Neurological Opera

The previous chapter set out to demonstrate that a strong intertextual current runs through Nyman's music as a whole. One could extend this principle further, however, by arguing, as some have done, that intertextuality is an inherent characteristic of all cultural production, be it of a literary, artistic, cinematic, musical or other nature. Language can be understood to be inherently 'heteroglossic', or 'other-tongued', containing within it 'many voices, one's own *and* other voices' (Allen 2000, p. 29). Other terms also point to this relational nature in language. 'Hybridity', used by Bakhtin and others to describe specific contexts in which one voice is infiltrated or contaminated by another, may either take the form of juxtaposition – where all voices retain their own textual autonomy – or liquidation, where voices are absorbed into one hybridized language. If this opens the text up to its location within a series of related texts, it also paradoxically provides a seal upon which the intertext as a whole can close itself off from the outside world. Texts only retain a level of self-sufficiency as a result of the intertext's own autonomy, echoing Jacques Derrida's famous claim that '[there] is nothing outside of the text [there is no outside-text; "il n'y a pas de hors-texte"]' (Derrida 1976, p. 158).

The degree in which hybrid forms manifest themselves in any linguistic context is to a certain extent dependent on whether the reader, viewer or listener is aware of the plurality of voices woven into the text itself. While pastiche or parody draws meanings in relation to a wider constellation of intertexts, quotation goes even further. A phrase or statement carrying quotation marks is conventionally the author's way of acknowledging that the words in question have been spoken or written by someone else. At the same time the very act of quoting allows and indeed encourages words to float free from their original contexts and associations and become part of a potentially limitless series of other contexts, situations and uses. The whole issue of 'what belongs to whom' is more complex than simply ascribing a verbal or musical phrase to its rightful owner. In reality, lines are subconsciously borrowed, previously spoken ideas adapted, narratives retold, and phrases uttered that echo others. By stating 'what has already been said' in a new context, potentially endless continuities are constantly generated.

Quotation may at times even invert the notion of authority bestowed upon the text by its author. Cage, recalling a comment made to him by the poet Robert Duncan, once said, '[Duncan's] poetry was picked up from other people ... [the] only time he felt ... like using quotation marks was when the words he wrote were his' (Cage 1973, p. 13). Duncan's poetic paradox tacitly acknowledges the fact that words possess collective ownership. Everything, and therefore nothing is – or can become – 'quotation'.

Quotation's primary function is to draw to the surface the very act of referring, to re-contextualize a given phrase, and to encourage further dissemination. As a literary or musical device, it is used to support a kind of self-reflexive intertextuality in which dialogues formed between texts form the subject of the work. Sometimes the choice of subject matter draws such creative and interpretative issues to the very surface of a work, as demonstrated in Nyman's chamber opera *The Man who Mistook his Wife for a Hat* (hereafter *The Hat*).

## Quotation

Receiving its first performance at the ICA, London, in October 1986, *The Hat* represented Nyman's first major success away from the film screen and signalled an ambition to work with more traditional forms, such as opera, string quartet and concerto. Despite moving towards established genres, Nyman brought his own experiences to them, gained from outside the classical music world through his work with pop musicians and in the film industry. *The Hat* does not therefore conform to prescribed or conventional operatic descriptions. Its subject matter – a neurologist's account of his investigation into the unusual mental condition of a retired professional singer – is hardly typical of an operatic plot. Indeed, that there exists a 'plot' at all in the opera, at least in the traditional sense, has been the subject of some speculation.

As explained in more detail below, the opera's story unfolds as a series of case studies. First of all a neurologist, Dr S, undertakes a routine physical examination of one of his patients, Dr P, in order to establish why he seems to have difficulty in recognizing familiar faces and objects, despite having good eyesight. The tests elicit no unusual response until the moment when Dr P – preparing to leave the surgery – has difficulty in distinguishing between his shoe and his foot. Dr S concludes from this incident that Dr P looked at him 'with his ears'; his eyes 'scanned' him and, like a radar, 'sought the detail / as if not seeing [the] whole face / but only separate components' (Rawlence, in Nyman 1988b, p. 66). Supported and assisted by his fiercely protective wife (Mrs P) Dr P is then asked by Dr S to identify familiar landmarks from a copy of the *National Geographic* magazine (such as the Manhattan skyline and Empire State Building). Through such empirical analysis Dr S gradually develops a profile of Dr P's condition. What interests him in particular is the fact that, despite mistaking his wife's head for a hat, Dr P continues to live a comparatively 'normal' life, one that is furthermore enriched by his love of music. Dr S decides to explore further the nature of Dr P's musical and artistic perception and prepares to administer a second series of tests in Dr and Mrs P's New York apartment.

At this point in the opera a complete and essentially unaltered quotation of Schumann's 'Ich grolle nicht' is heard from the composer's song-cycle *Dichterliebe*.[1]

---

1  Nyman takes advantage of Schumann's ossia line towards the end of the song to form a duet

It is a key moment in Nyman's opera for many reasons. Appearing slightly before the midway point of the opera, at the beginning of Act Two, its purpose within the opera's unfolding narrative is to represent singer and main character Dr P's profound confession of faith in, and devotion to, music. Heine's suitably ambiguous text for 'Ich grolle nicht' allows the song to be transferred from its original position into a completely different context. Steen K. Nielsen has observed, 'the lied fits well into the work and even adds something to [Dr P's] characterization if one imagines it sung, not about unreciprocated love, but about the advancing disease that Dr P has understood and accepted, bearing no grudge' (Nielsen 1992, p. 84). By hearing the song as Dr P would have understood it, the listener for the first time momentarily enters into his own tragically isolated perception of the world, one where music supplies the only co-ordinates in an otherwise deserted mental and visual landscape.

The inclusion of 'Ich grolle nicht' also makes sense in musical terms. Unlike the opening sequence of songs in *Dichterliebe*, whose keys are connected together to create a seamless musical chain, 'Ich grolle nicht' is complete and self-contained. This may explain why it has been described by Rufus Hallmark as 'the single most popular song in *Dichterliebe*' (Hallmark 1979, p. 62). The song also appears by coincidence slightly before the midway point of Schumann's cycle and marks itself off from the logical sequence of keys that have preceded it. In Nymanesque terms, the piano accompaniment's repeated chords suggests a rhythmically slowed down version of *In Re Don Giovanni*, in addition to offering a wide range of transformational possibilities in the area of harmony and melody. Nyman's choice of song is thus ideally suited to the function of quotation within the context of his opera.

It may therefore appear surprising that the inclusion of Schumann's song has drawn a somewhat mixed response. Anthony Marks saw the quote as merely magnifying the awkwardness of Schumann's romantic lied style when it is mixed in with Nyman's postmodern reworking of it, claiming the effect to be, 'clinical and … clumsy; rather than being integrated with the whole (as it was in Dr P's life) it [seems] grafted on' (Marks 1987, p. 35). On the other hand, Nielsen concludes that the level of engagement between text and intertext is far greater and more highly developed than in previous examples, where Nyman is seen to resort to 'simple structural paraphrasing' (Nielsen 1992, p. 74). Dr P's understanding of the world is filtered through sound rather than sight due to his inability to identify the forms of distinct shapes. This neurological condition, known as visual agnosia, deprives him of the ability to perceive and recognize entities. He cannot add up the parts that constitute an object's *gestalt*, or whole. According to neurologist and author of the opera's case study, Oliver Sacks, he 'construed the world as a computer construes it, by means of key features and schematic relationships' (Sacks 1985, p. 14). The world – reduced to mere schemes – has forced Dr P to substitute what he can hear for what he cannot see. He imagines the world in terms of a completely integrated musical whole.

---

between Dr P and the neurologist, Dr S.

## Science as narrative

It is difficult, almost impossible, for any 'normal' person to imagine how or what the song might mean from Dr P's own distorted perspective. His condition, according to Sacks, may be better described through a narrative process however. Sacks presents Dr P's case history as literally 'his-story', constructed piece by piece, frame by frame. The nature and extent of Dr P's condition thus gradually emerges in front of the viewer's eyes. Sacks consciously eschews the 'abstract and computational' nature of scientific method, calling instead for a '"personalistic", or a "romantic" science', grounded in the case histories and experiential biographies of individuals (Sacks 1985, pp. 3–19). Only from the perspective of understanding a patient's history as narrative can one begin to understand the complex world of neurological dysfunction. Psychology, in this context, represents a kind of halfway house between art and science.

Rather like psychology, music has also historically inhabited a halfway house between art and science. According to Molino, Descartes summarized the art–science dichotomy when he said that music was either 'mathematical proportion or ratio on the one hand [or] on the other hand the "relationship of our judgment to the object …"' (Molino 1990, p. 117). During the Middle Ages music shifted from the scientific discipline of the Quadrivium (arithmetic, geometry and astronomy) to an art-based practice associated with the Trivium (grammar, rhetoric and logic). In its ability to provide a physical image for numbers and calculations, it was considered to bring both mind and body together. While music continues to preside as a predominantly artistic form, the development during the twentieth century of more mathematical compositional procedures (such as serialism) allied with more scientifically-informed analytical techniques suggest that deterministic values are often brought to bear on music's function and meaning. In the sphere of textual criticism, some have sought to question and reject these essentialist approaches. Alan Street, for example, in the late 1980s adopted the deconstructive approach of Paul de Man in order to advocate a new musicological approach based on allegorical interpretation, where 'meaning automatically depends on some form of continuous narrative or temporal unfolding' (Street 1989, p. 102). Sacks has also advanced a form of new neurology that functions along similar lines to the new relativistic musicology proposed by Street. Adopting a narrative process allows Sacks to draw conclusions that would not otherwise be possible through scientific method. Sacks is more interested in what a narrative process might reveal along the way rather than the aims, outcomes and results that drive forward scientific enquiry towards some ultimate goal.

In Sacks's case science aspires to the condition of art rather than the other way round. Neurology as a scientific discipline has been replaced with a narrative process. Diegesis replaces diagnosis and discourse displaces determination. Neurology, like musicology, becomes another area where the old meta-narratives have been challenged and contested. The 'personalistic' manner with which Sacks characterizes the relocation of scientific method inscribes a place for narrative forms. Narrative becomes a vehicle for expressing and articulating what cannot be said through science. In J. Hillis Miller's words, 'what cannot be expressed logically, one is tempted to say, we then tell stories about' (quoted in Lentricchia and McLaughlin 1990, p. 74). The character Ludmilla in one of Italo Calvino's novels expresses similar sentiments when she states that the novel 'should have as its driving force only the desire to narrate, to pile stories upon stories, without trying to impose a philosophy of life on you, simply allowing you to observe its own growth, like a tree, an entangling, as if of branches and leaves ...' (Calvino 1981, p. 76). The kind of synthesis and integration formed in Dr P's uniquely musical conception of the world only serves to expose precisely the sense of 'fragmentation' and 'disintegration' that we observe in his movements and actions. One is inevitably led to the neurological aporia of Dr P's condition through the very process of Sacks's narrative account.

In addition to presenting the 'narrative as process' (Nyman 1988b, p. 9), *The Hat* is also an example of 'narrative as drama'. Nielsen compares the opera's narrative unfolding to a 'whodunit' scenario in which Dr S's aim must be to solve the riddle of Dr P's problem (Nielsen 1992, p. 68). Nyman's intention is not to build into the musical narrative a series of dramatic conflicts and resolutions here, of setting up implications and providing realizations. His music remains somewhat detached from the action, becoming almost 'scientific' in its logical construction. The use of quotations adds to this sense of reflection and distance. In the case of *The Hat*, however, the Schumann material in fact generates its own impetus. While the narrative structure of the opera is not goal-oriented, the narrative dialogue between the two authorial voices provides its own dynamic force. In this sense it conforms to Nyman's opinion that '[music] is not narrative but it becomes narrative on its own terms' (Rivière and Caux 1987, p. 83).

If narrativity may be applied to both disciplines of neurology and musicology, does it also belong to musical composition? If music possesses the ability to narrate, how is it used by Nyman to complement the narrative 'science' of Sacks? According to Jean-Jacques Nattiez, the role of narrative should be distinguished from that of discourse. The former is 'embedded in the syntax of [a] sentence', while the latter inhabits the perception or 'experience' of a listener: 'a narrative emerges, strictly speaking only when a temporal series of objects and events is taken over by a metalinguistic *discourse*' (Nattiez 1990, p. 243). In other words, narratives can be created *about* music, but that may not answer the question as to whether music itself is a narrative form. Narratives retell stories whereas discourses involve dialogue and the exchange of ideas.

Any analytical discourse then aims to plot a narrative pathway through the multiplicity of meanings created by composer, listener and performer. At certain times, however, these pathways cross and collide. Such momentary conflicts occur when the unfolding events themselves become caught in a stasis of sudden self-realization. Carolyn Abbate has observed that music *per se*, 'is not narrative, but it possesses moments of narration, moments that can be identified by their bizarre and disruptive effect' (Abbate 1991, p. 29). The inclusion of 'Ich grolle nicht' is one such example of 'disruption'. What this moment signifies within the opera's overall context will now be addressed.

## Intertexts and contexts

One is left in little doubt that 'Ich grolle nicht' is indeed a musical quotation; for a start it is introduced by the characters and then sung in a different language to the rest of the opera.[2] Its repositioning suggests that while it is clearly the same song as the one heard in *Dichterliebe*, its context has changed. According to Wendy Steiner, context immediately establishes a new set of intertextual variables. Her research into this area has shown how, for example, art exhibitions can provide 'a kind of random intertextuality which radically affects their reception' (quoted in Allen 2000, p. 177). Similar results can also be drawn from the positioning of a musical track on a CD or a piece of music within a recital programme. The fact that, as Komar states, 'a totality is implied by the way the songs [in *Dichterliebe*] are usually performed: the individual songs are rarely heard outside the cycle' (Komar 1971, p. 63), renders its appearance in *The Hat* of even greater intertextual importance. Furthermore, Robert Samuels has pointed out that interpretations of musical works are in themselves intertextual, with each interpretation forming a response to a musical object along a syntagmatic chain of 'unclosed [interpretative] semiosis' (Samuels 1995, p. 4). If the song's immanent structures are unaffected by its appropriation into a changed context by Nyman, one's 'strategies of reception' (to use Molino's term in relation to communication theory) are nevertheless affected in some way by the song's unexpected relocation to a new musical home (Molino 1990, p. 131).

Here, a kind of first-order narrative of perception leads to a series of binary oppositions arising from the song's re-contextualization. Such primary elements set the text's original function with that of the intertext's appropriation of it, as seen in Table 6.1. Lied is turned into aria, song-cycle becomes opera, and even the venue of the concert hall (or nineteenth-century drawing room) has been replaced by the opera house or theatre. Heine's original text suddenly finds itself inhabiting part of Chris Rawlence's libretto, which, in itself, re-contextualizes Sacks's own narrative account.

While these differences only appear to affect surface meaning, one only has to consider how the lyrical quality of the lied tradition assumes a very different character within Nyman's opera to realize that context changes everything. Carl Dahlhaus has described dramatic signification as essentially dialogic, while the lyric element, which strongly characterizes the lieder tradition, 'is an utterance that is not directed ostentatiously at an audience but, in a manner of speaking, is overheard by the audience' (Dahlhaus 1989, p. 105). Nyman's contextual revision of Schumann's song therefore underscores Dahlhaus's notion of the dramatic, not least because it sets

---

2 Beirens has questioned whether 'Ich grolle nicht' is, indeed, a quotation, given that it appears entirely unaltered.

## Table 6.1   The function of 'Ich grolle nicht'

| Schumann | Nyman |
|---|---|
| Lied | Aria |
| Song-cycle (concert hall) | Chamber opera (theatre) |
| Poem (Heine) | Libretto (Rawlence), story (Sacks) |
| Lyric signification (monologic) | Dramatic effect (dialogic) |

up a musical 'conversation' between the two singers and three on-stage characters. This aspect is missing from the original version (although a conversation is also implied in the song-cycle between the singer and his 'absent' lover). The increased dramatic quality of the opera heightens the differences between the quoted and unquoted versions; 'Ich grolle nicht' is therefore made to sound even more unusual.

*The Hat* is not unique in this respect. Abbate has commented at length on other examples from the opera repertory in which characters become aware of their 'voices' and of their ineluctable singing conditions. Abbate describes it as 'the moment at which a character ... appears to pass across the boundary between the phenomenal and the noumenal, and to hear beyond realistic song to that other music surrounding him' (Abbate 1991, p. 119). Such moments arise out of a basic diegetic need to break away from the structure of the plot itself in order to explore the power of music. A duality is therefore set up in the musical narrative between the phenomenal (music consciously sung and heard by the characters) and the noumenal (music sung while being blissfully unaware of the fact). Abbate argues that at 'such moments ... the leap from the normal operatic world is huge, and this very leap – the degree to which the song is set apart as performance – is a means of artistic complexity and tension' (Abbate 1991, p. 121). In Nyman's opera, 'complexity and tension' is further increased through the inclusion of two authorial voices. The voices of Schumann and Nyman undergo processes of construction and deconstruction during the opera, creating a series of narrative cracks and fissures across its surface. Music's meaning is located in the space between these voices, a kind of 'deficit' that is also neurology's 'favourite term' according to Sacks (Sacks 1985, p. 1). In contrast to Abbate's examples of operatic diegesis cited from *Carmen*, *Tannhäuser* and *Die Meistersinger*, Nyman's use of Schumann's work sets up a diachronic narrative: a historical and stylistic gap between Schumann's 'year of song' (1840) and Nyman's own reworking of the material almost one hundred and fifty years later.

To understand the function of 'Ich grolle nicht' it is first necessary to examine the immediate context surrounding it. Table 6.2 provides a chronological succession of events leading up to, and away from this point: the concluding section of Act 1, leading into Act 2, and including 'Ich grolle nicht'. The Schumann quotation is not plucked out of thin air but is precipitated by a number of musical and verbal references. At the very beginning of the opera, inspired by the ambient sounds entering Dr S's surgery

### Table 6.2    The context of 'Ich grolle nicht'

| Bar number | Libretto | Nyman | Schumann |
|---|---|---|---|
| (Part 1) 429 | [Part 1: closing scene]<br>Dr S: He's mistaken his wife for a hat! I was baffled, astonished, aghast. Yet he thought he'd done rather well. Took his leave with a hint of a smile. Did he know? Were they playing an elaborate joke? Who was examining who? I could make no sense of what I'd seen in terms of conventional neurology. How could a professional musician, a practising teacher, mistake his | Melodic variations first heard in Prologue | |
| 448 | wife for a hat? How does he learn his operatic roles? Does he still read music? What sense does he make of the chains of black blobs strung up on five lines? Is he suffering from musical alexia? | | 'Rätsel' from Myrthen (op. 25/xvi) |
| 473 | He did not make sense. On the one hand, perfectly preserved, on the other hand incomprehensibly | Melodic variations | |
| 481 | shattered. There were no textbook answers. I had to see him again on his own ground. Not as a patient in a clinic. | | 'Hochländisches Wiegenlied' from Myrthen (op. 25/xiv) |
| 492 | I needed to watch him cope with the everyday workings of life. Observe the man in his natural | | 'Der Nussbaum' from Myrthen (op. 25/iii) |
| 496 | habitat. | | 'Rätsel' |

**Table 6.2**   *concluded*

| Bar number | Libretto | Nyman | Schumann |
|---|---|---|---|
| (Part 2) 1 | [Part 2: opening scene]<br>Dr S: Bösendorfer!<br>Dr P: I know that voice.<br>Dr S: Magnificent instrument.<br>Dr P: The one thing we saved from Vienna.<br>Mrs P: Dichterliebe!<br>Dr S: How I'd love … would you mind? Will you play and sing?<br>Mrs P: My husband will sing.<br>Dr P: If you'd play.<br>Dr S: I'm a bit rusty.<br>Mrs P: It's his rheumatic hands.<br>Dr P: I no longer play.<br>Dr S: My sight-reading's poor …<br>Mrs P: The damp – it stiffens his fingers.<br>Dr P: I no longer read.<br>Dr S: … not in your league.<br>Mrs P: a little short-sighted …<br>Dr P: Will not … cannot read.<br>Mrs P: … so I'll play the piano for my husband.<br>Dr P: No longer reads music. | Harmonic variations first heard in Part 1, Scene 1 | |
| 49 | [Dr P sings 'Ich grolle nicht'] | | 'Ich grolle nicht' from Dichterliebe (op. 48/vii) |
| 84 | Dr S & Mrs P: He still has a perfect ear! His memory's unimpaired, perfect tonal and rhythmic discrimination and expression – a wonderful musical cortex, temporal lobes intact. | Harmonic variations | |
| 98 | Dr S: But what of the parietal regions? … | Variations on 'Ich grolle nicht' | |

from the busy street outside, Dr P quotes two lines from *Dichterliebe*'s ninth song: 'Da tanzt wohl im Hochzeitreigen / Die Herzallerliebeste mein [amongst the wedding party / my dearest love dances]'. The words do not carry any symbolic meaning here, but rather provide an initial indication that Dr P constantly carries music around in his head as a kind of cognitive *aide memoire*. Only after further examination by Dr S, when Dr P's agnosia is progressively revealed, does Dr P increasingly revert to Schumann songs. These references are gradually brought to the surface of the opera, initially punctuating the dialogue between Dr P and Dr S during 'The Shoe' and 'The National Geographic' scenes in Act One.

When Dr P accidentally mistakes his wife for a hat there follows a series of rapid musical exchanges between Schumann and Nyman. In Schumann's case these include extracts from songs such as 'Rätsel', 'Hochländisches Wiegenlied' and 'Der Nussbaum', while the Nyman material consists of a chromatically-inflected melodic variation first heard in the prologue of the opera and a series of harmonic variations based on nine major chords, which also undergo a process of 'de-familiarization' during the course of the work. 'Ich grolle nicht' thus emerges out of these disguised textual layers as a form of temporary resolution to the authorial exchanges. It signals its own autonomy from the musical world it suddenly inhabits, just as Dr P affirms his own belief in the musically-regulated, self-contained world of his mind.

Nielsen has viewed Nyman's own musical material as representing the world as seen through the viewer's eyes, while the Schumann songs function as substitutes for Dr P's visual 'deficit' (Nielsen 1992, p. 74). As in other quoted material, 'Ich grolle nicht' is later subjected to a series of deconstructive transformations. This suggests a kind of inversion of reality, where Nyman's constructed compositional world provides an appearance of normality, while Schumann's tonal world represents Dr P's abnormality. Nyman expressed this in an interview with Meyer, when he said, 'I determined that the strangeness of the world of this person had to be expressed through something that is familiar to all of us, through Schumann's music' (Meyer 1989).

A similar reversal has been noted by Yayoi Everett in her article on musical parody, where she observes that the use of borrowed tunes and tonal settings within the predominantly discordant world of Peter Maxwell Davies's *Eight Songs for a Mad King* (1969), 'signify the King's entry into illusion and madness, while destructive passages in atonality signify moments of lucidity and awareness' (Everett 2004). Unlike Davies, however, Nyman is not attempting a parody of Schumann here. It is worth noting that in both Nyman's opera and Davies's song-cycle, quotations from pre-existing tonal material represent forms of mental impairment (albeit of very different natures – neurologically-induced in Nyman, insanity in the Davies example).[3] If the narrative in Nyman's opera revolves around the nature and character of Dr P's visual 'loss' or deficit, what about the nature of the musical deficits in the work? How can we begin to explore the relationship between Nyman's text and Schumann's intertexts? What analytical model could be adopted for this purpose?

---

3 Davies's quotation is from Handel's *Messiah*.

## Generative theory and classical tonality

In much the same way that the opera's main theme deals with the way in which music can provide its own sign language and body image in order to overcome the limits of perception, so the application to Nyman and Schumann's music of an analytical framework adopted from the field of cognitive psychology reflects the intertextual tensions operating within the work. Lerdahl and Jackendoff's study of musical cognition in classical and romantic music aims to provide 'an empirical hypothesis about the nature of human perception' (Lerdahl and Jackendoff 1983, p. 42). Here the shift has moved from absolute textual meaning towards the listener's aural conceptualization and reconstruction of a musical work. Sounds are filtered through auditory receptors into groups and shapes, forms and structures. The listener as producer and 'composer' of musical meaning is central to any cognitive theory. As Monelle points out, any generative theory 'is based on the intuitions of a listener and thus describes the process of perception rather than composition' (Monelle 1992, p. 136).

Example 6.1 applies a model of generative analysis to the opening line of Schumann's song.

**Example 6.1**   *Schumann's 'Ich grolle nicht' (opening line)*

The phrase's metrical structure is first of all indicated by a series of vertical and horizontal dots set out underneath the melody. These dots are designed to reflect real-time pulsations and phenomenological accents in the music. Brackets supporting the dots indicate a series of parallel grouping structures, suggesting that the music is perceived in terms of events unfolding in time rather than as a series of isolated and disconnected moments.[4] Musical meaning is generated by the listener through a process of identifying patterns and grouping them into larger shapes. Grouping organizes melodic phenomena while metre organizes the pulsations of a piece into hierarchical patterns. Grouping structures and metrical hierarchies are determined by Lerdahl and Jackendoff's theory through the application of 'well-formed' and 'preference' rules. Well-formed rules are in effect a set of musical universals for tonal functionality. Preference rules have been devised in such a way that they can be

---

4   The brackets used here (and in the following examples) to indicate grouping structure should not be confused with the same symbol employed later on in Lerdahl and Jackendoff's theory to indicate time-spans.

adjusted to specific contexts and depend to a greater extent on listener competence or 'intuitive judgements' (Lerdahl and Jackendoff 1983, p. 53). Indeed the very basis of their theory is constructed around 'the notion of "the musical intuitions of the experienced listener"' (ibid., p. 3).

One feature neglected in Lerdahl and Jackendoff's theoretical model in determining melodic and rhythmic emphases and divisions is the function of extramusical elements, in particular words and word-setting. In such cases certain grouping preference rules require adjustment according to the location of, and emphasis on, words, and the general nature of their musical setting. In Example 6.1 a quaver rest's appearance in bar 2 functions beyond merely that of a breath mark. It serves to divide the phrase into two asymmetrical groups: statement – 'Ich grolle nicht' – and elaboration – 'und wenn das Herz auch bricht'. Further observations may be drawn from this division. The initial group in bars 1–2 is comprised of three short notes and one long. This is mirrored by a similar pattern of three shorts and one long (followed by one short and one long) in bars 2–3. Were the phrase to be segmented differently, according to the preference rule determining that a change or shift in vocal register necessitated a new group, for example, certain notes (such as the first F of bar 2) would be left isolated, contravening the whole notion of a 'group' structure.

While metrical emphasis is normally reinforced by grouping structure, in the case of Example 6.1 I have shown both elements to be 'out of phase' with each other, supporting Lerdahl and Jackendoff's observation that 'groups do not receive metrical accent, and beats do not possess inherent grouping' (Lerdahl and Jackendoff 1983, p. 26). Metrical accents therefore occasionally appear embedded within a grouping structure. In this case it is established by means of harmonic accents supplied in the piano accompaniment. In Example 6.1 the melodic phrase to some extent fights against the underlying metrical structure. While the accompaniment reiterates the tonic chord at the very beginning, the vocal line moves away from it, shifting the focus towards subdominant major and minor. The voice thus appears to trail behind the piano before being forced to realign its course. Read against the singing subject's outward proclamation of self-defiance ('I bear no grudge') Schumann's subtle manipulation of metric and melodic elements in the music suggests that all is not what it appears on the surface.

Example 6.2 extends the principles of well-formed and preference rules to the first 12 bars of Schumann's song. With the accompaniment now included, the aforementioned ambiguity between grouping and metre becomes a mere feature of the opening phrase. Metrical emphasis and grouping structure realign themselves at bar 5 and remain locked together thereafter. Even the opening phrase length's irregularity is resolved on a grouping level organized according to two four-bar patterns. Any ambiguity between metre and grouping is resolved by bar 11 – a significant moment – where the descending bass line finally settles on a dominant pedal, serving as cadential notice for the second statement of 'Ich grolle nicht'. The repetition of this statement provides further emphasis at the end of the first section (bb. 8–12) by creating a four-bar extension. Edward T. Cone sees the 'Ich grolle

**Example 6.2**   *Analysis of grouping and metre in Schumann's 'Ich grolle nicht'*
*(bb. 1–12)*

*continued*

nicht' refrain as, 'an ostinato motif, heard by implication underneath everything that follows … Schumann has made this ostinato explicit, and has chosen logical places to do so' (Cone, in Komar 1971, p. 118).

Thus the two-part division of the opening phrase is reflected in the two-part division of the first section (bb. 5–12, although an additional third phrase follows in bb. 12–18), and even in the song's overall bi-partite structure (bb. 1–18 and 19–36). In this instance the application of principles underlying a generative tonal theory serve to uphold what is, to a certain extent, already known to the familiar listener about its systems and mechanisms: that tonal music is often hierarchical and makes extensive use of order, balance, parallelism and symmetry. Such characteristics are

**Example 6.2**   *concluded*

made even more obvious in the case of the harmonic reduction of bb. 1–12, seen in Example 6.3, which provides an elaboration of the familiar cadential formula I-vi-ii⁷-V⁷-I. While an impression of Schumann's song gained through a generative analysis is one of tonal coherence and balance, what then if Lerdahl and Jackendoff's theory was applied to sections of Nyman's recomposition of Schumann? To what extent does Nyman's music comply with, or work against, the principles of tonal logic?

**Generative theory and the new tonality**

Example 6.4 provides a vocal score reduction of bars 447–87 (also seen in Table 6.2). Here the music oscillates between Nyman and reworked Schumann extracts from 'Rätsel' and 'Hochländisches Wiegenlied' (written in their original versions in Examples 6.5a and 6.5b).

Both again fit into conventions established by the kind of tonal grammar set out in Lerdahl and Jackendoff's theory. 'Rätsel' follows standard tonal conventions of symmetrical phrasing, tonal functionality and standard modulation, although Schumann does avoid becoming too clichéd by including a disconnected unison on the tonic note at the very beginning of the song (see Example 6.5a). This 'rogue' element is balanced out at the end of the consequent phrase by two statements in the relative minor triad. Likewise 'Hochländisches Wiegenlied' also plays around with tonal implications and expectations (see Example 6.5b). A dominant pedal, established halfway through the first bar, steadfastly refuses to resolve onto the tonic, creating an intentionally rustic, barrel-organ effect.

Example 6.6 attempts to apply principles of harmonic functionality and connectedness through generative techniques of tree-formations to bars 442–66 of Nyman's music, where reworkings of Schumann's songs are heard. In a typical tonal example (such as Example 6.3), chords are branched upwards together across local and global levels to indicate structural relationships between contiguous patterns, chord sequences, musical periods, entire sections and even complete movements. According to such rules, the two chords at bars 447–8 are not clearly connected. When Nyman quotes Schumann's 'Rätsel' in the following section, a plausible grouping structure can at least be applied on a local level but its tonal trajectory extends upwards without resolution; the curved branch has no stem to root it to a tonal centre. Rules regulating harmonic logic have thus given way to a kind of combinatorial tonality here, of quoted fragments stacked up in sequential order. Musical events are isolated, segmented and redistributed; harmonic development has given way to juxtaposition. In such contexts a tonal centre can only be heard as a trace or 'resonance' rather than as an omnipresent force. Integrated structures and balanced phrases are eschewed for proportionally related temporal events.

The application of a basic theory of tonal perception found in Lerdahl and Jackendoff fails to add up or make sense in Nyman's music, then. Indeed it was never designed to do so. But the disjunction between conventional tonal practice and

**Example 6.3** *Time-span reduction of Schumann's 'Ich grolle nicht' (bb. 1–12)*

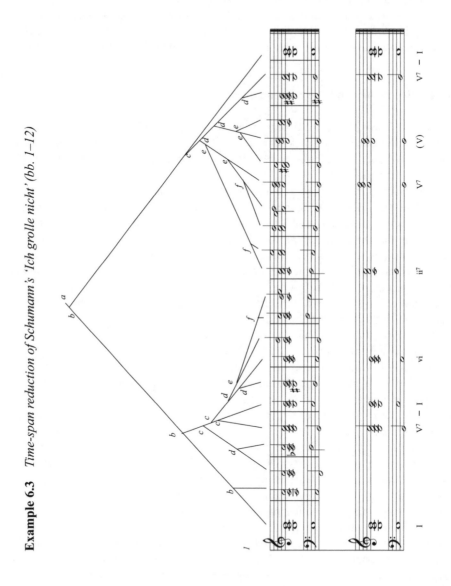

**Example 6.4**   The Hat: *vocal score reduction of bb. 447–87*

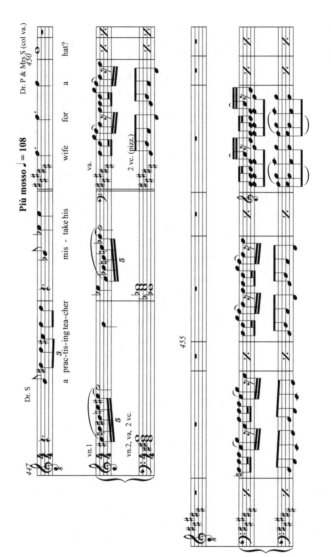

continued

**Example 6.4**   *continued*

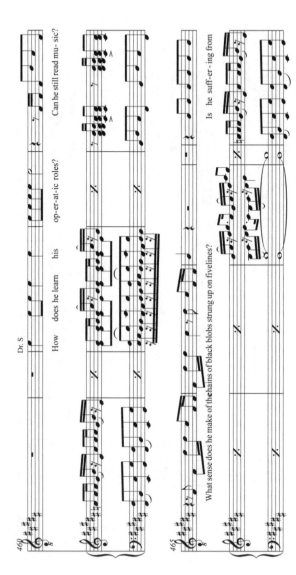

**Example 6.4** *continued*

*continued*

**Example 6.4** *concluded*

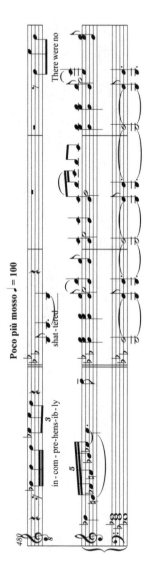

**Example 6.5a**   *Schumann's 'Rätsel' (bb. 1–5)*

**Example 6.5b**   *Schumann's 'Hochländisches Wiegenlied' (bb. 1–4)*

its use in Nyman's opera nevertheless provides a clue to the work's meaning. The tension between tonality and its deconstruction is intended to represent in musical terms Dr P's visual agnosia. Nyman's schematic use of tonality becomes a powerful trope for Dr P's condition.

In her study of repetition in twentieth-century music Rebecca Leydon has observed how a sense of 'cognitive impairment, madness, or logical absurdity'

**Example 6.6**   The Hat: *time-span reduction (bb. 442–66)*

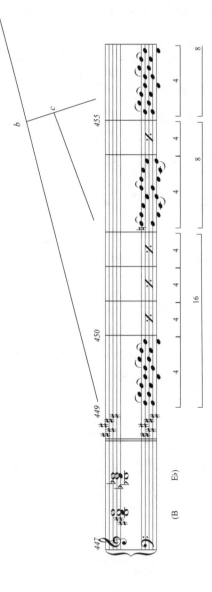

**Example 6.6** *concluded*

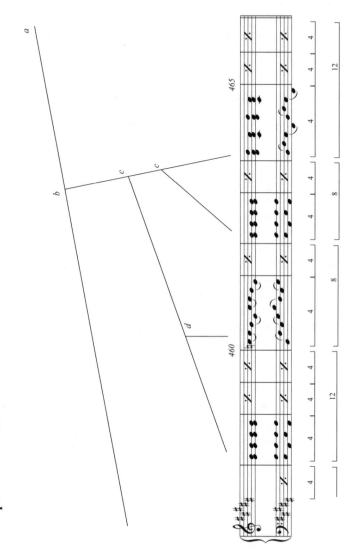

is engendered through the use of such techniques (Leydon 2002). Examining the 'differentiated affects' of repetition in minimalist music in general and Nyman's opera in particular, Leydon concludes that the repetitive trope used in this case is an 'aphasic' one (although a more accurate description would be agnosia) where 'musematic repetition suggests a cognitively impaired subject'. Leydon argues that in certain contexts repetition 'represents the condition of aphasia [*sic*]', but it is often the presence or absence of a tonal grammar that provides the means by which this trope is actualized:

> Throughout the piece, a process in which discursive patterns deteriorate into musemes is applied again and again, not only to [intertextual] sources but to newly composed music as well … [as] the opera progresses, motivic elements become unglued from their discursive context and take on a life of their own as repeated musemes. (Leydon 2002)

Nyman's music goes beyond any straightforward opposition between whole and part, coherence and incoherence, perception and fragmentation, to one where the play of reference and difference generates meaning.

Dr P's world appears to the viewer as a series of broken images, for which the pieces cannot be reassembled to make sense. Yet, as shown, Dr P fashions his own logic – a musical world – that provides a mirror upon his own activities. In the same way, Nyman's music turns its own inverted 'tonal' mirror onto Dr P's life. Chords are connected not so much through progression and function but either by means of common pitch sources or through the numerical logic of a sequential modular process. As detailed below, the former provides Nyman's music with a metonymic function, while the latter is a metaphor for Dr P's agnosia.

## Deconstructing tonality

The idea of combining chords together by means of a common pitch element is evident in one of Nyman's earliest compositions, *Bird List*, where a common note – in this case indicated by the coloured note 'A' in Example 6.7a – provides a link between four dominant seventh chords $A^7$, $F^7$, $B^7$ and $D^7$.

**Example 6.7a**   *Nyman's* Bird List *(chord sequence)*

A7          F7          B7          D7

**Example 6.7b**    The Hat: *harmonic analysis of bb. 473–5*

Apart from this pitch, which functions as a kind of upper 'pedal' note, and the F#
heard in both $B^7$ and $D^7$ chords, none of the other neighbouring chords possess
any common pitches. A degree of chromaticism thus characterizes the sequence's
harmonic content, making any straightforward tonal analysis difficult. The only
obvious 'tonal' function occurs between the 'joins' of the cycle, with $D^7$-$A^7$ suggesting
a plagal progression (IV-I). But even this standard pattern is undermined by the
dominant seventh's inherent instability and need for resolution, which never arrives.
The tritone relationship established between the two 'internal' chords F and B, while
undermining the notion of any straightforward harmonic progression, also obscures
the internal symmetry of each half of the sequence (two sets of chords linked by an
interval of a third).[5] Such chord structures do not conform to the usual grammar of
harmonic or tonal logic enumerated by Lerdahl and Jackendoff.

The coloured notes in Example 6.7b above, taken from bars 473–8, are based on
a melodic variation idea heard at the very beginning of the opera. They also illustrate
non-functional harmonic contiguity based on pitch association rather than chord
progression. As with *Bird List* the emphasis here is on thirds: minor thirds between
F-A♭ or A♭-B, and a major third between A-D♭, again exposing a tritone interval
between F-B. These note-to-note, chord-to-chord associations could be said to
treat tonality syntagmatically rather than paradigmatically – as different but related
phenomena rather than substitutions of one another. As noted above, Nyman's chords
thus function in this context metonymically rather than metaphorically, where one part
constitutes an aspect of the whole rather than representing it (on metonym, see Ayrey
1994, p. 136). This is reflected to a certain degree by the tree diagrams illustrated in
the previous analysis. Whereas Schumann's harmonic language creates in musical
terms a metaphor of 'unity' through his use of hierarchically-related chords and
patterns, Nyman's non-functional but nevertheless related chord patterns do not 'add
up' to anything more than localized references: chords follow one another without
being subordinated to an all-encompassing model or scheme.

Metonym and metaphor are generally viewed as mutually exclusive literary
tropes, but in Nyman's opera these metonymically-constructed chord sequences are
replaced elsewhere by a paradigmatic scheme suggesting metaphoric construction.
Chord sequences follow a process or procedure where units are stacked or grouped
together, suggesting that they do 'mean something' according to their position

---

5   Similar characteristics belong to the chord sequence upon which most of Nyman's original material
is based. The pattern of nine major chords consisting of C-D♭-F-B-E♭-A-D♭-G-B, first heard after the
prologue to Act 1, possesses three contiguous tritone leaps.

within a larger (that is, metaphoric) scheme. Soon after 'Ich grolle nicht', when Dr S sets out to explore the 'parietal regions, fibres, nerves, neurons and synapses of occipital zones' of Dr P's cortex in a series of eye-tests, Nyman makes use of a modular procedure where isolated tonal sequences are taken from Schumann's song, reordered and their identity gradually obliterated through subtraction and addition. Nyman's musical narrative thus parallels Sachs's narrative account but in reverse. Whereas the listener is gradually supplied with more information relating to Dr P's illness in the story, the music's identity and individuality is gradually eroded as the opera unfolds. This is no more evident than in the eye-test scene.

Example 6.8 groups these patterns into four categories, labelled A, B, C and D. All four sequences are taken from the first ten bars of Schumann's song. In addition, each chord is allocated a number so that any renumbering or reordering of chords within a given sequence can be identified with relative ease ($A^1$ thus becomes the first chord of the first sequence, for example). Table 6.3 sets out this sequential distribution in this section.

**Example 6.8**    The Hat: *chord progressions in 'But what of the parietal regions?'*

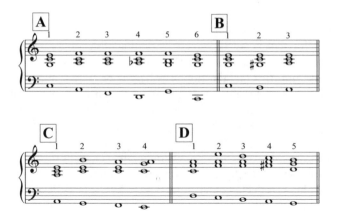

Table 6.3 illustrates first that Nyman eschews any chronological adherence to the original Schumann pattern by starting the section with sequence B. He does, however, adhere to the original order of chords in any particular sequence; $B^2$ always follows $B^1$, for example. Sequence B, consisting of three closely related chords, immediately obscures the possibility of any clear reference to Schumann's song. Sequence A, which follows, is more obviously 'tonal'. Being twice as long as B, it always accompanies Dr P's actions and responses to Dr S's questions. The goal-directed motion of sequence A's cadential figure reinforces Dr P's sense of confidence in being able to identify abstract shapes and complete Dr S's preliminary tests. It is preserved during the opening section of the scene, thus giving each phrase a distinctive shape, but as the tests prove more problematic for Dr P, his uncertainty is reflected in the

**Table 6.3    Distribution of harmonic patterns in the 'Eye-test' scene
(Act 2: bb. 98–221)**

| Bars | A (1–6, bb. 1–4), B (1–3, bb. 4–5), C (1–2, bb. 5–6), D (1–5, bb. 7–10) |
|---|---|
| 98–109 | $B^1+B^2$ / $B^1+B^2+B^3$ / $B^1+B^2+B^3$ / $B^1+B^2$ / $B^1+B^2$ |
| 110–13 | $A^1+A^2+A^3+A^4+A^5+A^6$ / $A^1+A^2+A^3+A^4+A^5+A^6$ |
| 113–18 | $B^1+B^2$ / $B^1+B^2+B^3$ / $B^2$ |
| 118–22 | $A^1+A^2+A^3+A^4+A^5+A^6$ / $A^2+A^3+A^4+A^5+A^6$ |
| 122–7 | $B^1+B^3+B^3+B^2+B^3+B^2$ |
| 127–31 | $B^2+B^1+B^2+C^1+C^2+C^3$ / $B^2+B^1+B^2+C^1+C^2+C^3$ |
| 131–7 | $A^1+A^2+A^3+A^4+A^5+A^6$ / $A^1+A^2+A^3+A^4+A^5+A^6$ / $A^2+A^3+A^4+A^5+A^6$ |
| 137–42 | $B^1+B^2$ / $C^4+D^1+D^2+D^3+D^4+D^5$ / $C^4+D^1+D^2+D^3+D^4+D^5$ |
| 143–52 | $B^1+B^2+B^1+B^2+A^2+A^3+A^6+A^2+A^3+A^6+A^2+A^3+A^4$ |
| 153–62 | $B^1+A^6+A^2+A^3+A^4+A^5+A^2+A^3+A^4+A^5+A^6+B^1$ |
| 163–4 | $C^1+C^2+C^3+C^4+D^1+D^2+D^3+D^4$ |
| 165–68 | $A^2+A^3+A^4+A^5+A^6$ / $A^2+A^3+A^4+A^5+A^6$ $(B^1)$ |
| 169–71 | $B^2+B^1+B^2$ |
| 172–5 | $C^1+C^2+C^3+C^4+D^1+D^2+D^3+D^4$ / $C^1+C^2+C^3+C^4+D^1+D^2+D^3+D^4$ / $C^1+C^2+C^3+C^4$ |
| 175–179 | $B^3+B^2+B^1+B^2+B^3(C^1)+C^2+C^3+A^5(var.)+B^1+B^2+B^3(C^1)+C^2$ |
| 180–82 | $C^1+C^2+C^3+C^4+D^1+D^2+D^3+D^4$ / $C^1+C^2+C^3+C^4+D^1+D^2+D^3+D^4$ |
| 183–9 | $D^1+D^2+D^3+D^4+D^5$ / $A^1+A^2+A^3+A^4+A^5+A^6$ / $A^2+A^3+A^4+A^5+A^6(B^1)+B^2$ |
| 190–99 | $C^1+C^2+C^3+C^4+D^1+D^2+D^3+D^4$ (x 8) |
| 199–205 | $C^1+C^2$ / $C^1+C^2+C^3+C^4+D^1+D^2+D^3+D^4(var.)+D^5+D^5$ |
| 206–15 | $D^1(var.)+D^2+D^3+D^4+D^4$ (x 11) |
| 216–21 | $D^1+D^2+D^3+D^4+C^1+C^2+C^3+C^4$ (x 4) $D^1+D^2+D^3+D^4+C^1+C^2+C^3+C^4+D^2$ / $D^1+D^2+D^3+D^4+C^2+C^3+C^4$ / $D^1+D^2+D^3+C^1+C^2$ |

gradual disintegration of the sequence. Nyman manages to do this because a set of common chords belonging to each sequence serves to blur the differences between them. C major or A minor chords appear in A, B and C, thus a dovetailing effect is often created between the beginning (or end) of sequence A with the beginning of B. Nyman also connects the start and end points of bass lines to join together the end of sequence D with the beginning of C.

While melody, harmony and bass-line move in tandem during the opening fifty or so bars, as the scene unfolds they gradually separate to reflect the sense of musical and visual fragmentation taking place in Dr P's mind. At bar 190, for example, a descending bass line moving through $C^1$ to $C^4$ and $D^1$ to $D^5$ is heard underneath a sixteen-note ostinato derived from sequences C and D (see Example 6.9).

**Example 6.9**    *Descending bass line in* The Hat, *bb. 190–95 (piano part only)*

At bar 206 a further change occurs when the music shifts down a minor third from A to F♯ minor. At this point a melodic line based on D increasingly sheds its harmonic skin while the bass line operates a set of notes taken from C. At bar 216 the opening melodic shape, probably derived from $D^1$ to $D^4$, is then extended when the melodic line for $C^1$ to $C^4$ is transposed up a minor ninth. In truth, by this point any transparent representation of Schumann's chord sequences has become increasingly uncertain and ambiguous.

Nielsen has also observed in his analysis of this section that the music's representation of fragmentation is also reflected in the use of rhythmic diminution. Nyman gradually unhinges the melodic line of sequences C and D from their harmonic bedding and develops a series of rhythmic 'variations' on a theme. For example, at bar 163 the rhythmic value of this melody is stated as a series of dotted minims. At 172 it is reduced to a minim, at 180 to a dotted crotchet, at 190 and 195 to a crotchet, and finally at 216 to a series of quavers. Harmonic rhythm also accelerates in this section. While chords change over twelve crotchet beats at 163, this is reduced to half speed by 216. Indeed the melodic line heard at this point finally represents the last remaining musical trace of Schumann in the entire opera, when it forms the basis for Dr P's vocals as he sounds off at the very end of the work. Nyman's distributional deconstruction of Schumann's harmonic language is thus intended as a metaphor of the visual fragmentation unfolding throughout the work and made manifest in its final notes. The aforementioned musical narrative 'as process' is thus reflected in the increasing atomization of tonal grammar and the gradual disintegration of harmonic archetypes.

If Lerdahl and Jackendoff's theory serves as a blueprint for tonal cognition, it falls short in representing Dr P's obliterated *Weltanschauung*. The aim of their theory is to appeal to universal modes of perception inspired by visual and spatial experiments conducted in the field of Gestalt psychology to determine patterns or modes of perception (Lerdahl and Jackendoff 1983, p. 59). This nevertheless draws to the surface a curious paradox, one that motivated Nyman to set Sacks's story to music in the first instance. What does a generative theory of tonality say about a person who cannot distinguish his wife from a hat, but whose powers of musical cognition remain completely intact? Does music function cognitively in a similar way to other forms of perception?

## Contextualizing quotation

If the opera questions the fundamental supposition that any straightforward parallelism exists between musical perception and patterns of mental recognition, the other question posed by the opera is: what are we to make of quotation in this context? In her study of the subject, Mary Orr develops a more postmodern theory of quotation's function and meaning. Arguing that intertextuality has perpetuated its own set of monological meanings, Orr introduces a series of 'shadowland' concepts, which she describes as 'related and rival terms to describe the processes of cultural rejuvenation' (Orr 2003, p. 15). In discussing concepts such as imitation and – in particular – quotation, Orr brings the subject closer to the aesthetic and creative concerns of late-postmodern culture in general and Nyman's music in particular.

Unlike other related literary devices such as allusion, reminiscence, indirect quotation, paraphrase, pastiche or adaptation, quotation 'marks' the (inter)text off from its 'other'. Orr points out that 'quotation marks placed around any utterance highlight, separate and distinguish it from surrounding phrases' (ibid., p. 130). In occupying a 'neither-here-nor-there' space simultaneously within and outside its immediate context, quotation's importance has been disregarded in aesthetic and literary criticism. On one level unsettling and disrupting the unity of the work, its function is often viewed as a mere supplement to the text, requiring little further explanation. But according to Orr, not only do quotes possess the virtues of 'brevity', aptness and an 'expression that is to the point', they also signal 'the most condensed form of paradigm shift, transmuting the context, form and meaning of the items both inside and outside the quotation marks' (ibid., pp. 132–3). Quotation immediately shifts the textual focus from content to context, from inside to outside, setting it apart from other figures of writing. A quotation will open the text up to its position within a network of other texts and encourage other phrases to act accordingly: '[as] multiple expressions in singular form, therefore, quotations invite onward transmission, whereas the new context, although often particular to accommodate it will rarely make "quotable quote" status itself' (ibid., p. 133).

Although traditional methods of citing may have become *dépassé*, 'surpassed by electronic citation as the cut–copy–paste facility or postmodernism's protean and mixed-media styles ...' (ibid., p. 131), quotation has successfully adapted to the needs of late-twentieth-century consumerist society. Indeed contemporary culture has become almost a 'culture of quotation', being emphasized in the brevity of a caption or slogan, the impact of an advertising board, news headline or media sound bite. Its appropriateness to a culture which fetishizes the image cannot be overemphasized, as 'quotation's powers of concentration or crystallization [create their own] concise "word pictures" or verbal images' (ibid., p. 135).

Nyman may have been drawn to quotation because of its ability to simultaneously project or embody a compelling musical image while referring beyond itself. Although remaining statically within the text, quotations are also inherently dynamic, constantly shifting between text, context and intertext. Quotation becomes in Nyman a trope for repetition itself, an application of the principle that any part of any text may be repeated within the context of another. Repetition in Nyman's music therefore goes beyond localized or structural functions to include the repetition of ideas within and between compositions. In Kristevan terms, quotation is therefore intrinsically genotextual. Associated with the musical elements of language (such as rhythm, intonation, melody and repetition) Kristeva identifies the genotext as 'that part of the text which stems from the "drive energy" emanating from the unconscious' (Kristeva, in Allen 2000, pp. 50–51). The dual presence/absence signification of each quotation provides it with a kind of 'pulsation', a textual depth and reverberation. If the phenotext is connected with unity, the genotext is associated with dispersion: quotations are spread across vast textual areas, becoming reanimated and rejuvenated in the process. Orr's observation that quotation prefers dialogic discourse to that of monologic meaning – 'always [an] enrichment by inclusion, integration and proclamation of otherness, a dialogue not a monologue' (Orr 2003, p. 133) – echoes Nyman's observation that 'one of the problems with recycling other composers' music is that it has to be an enrichment not a diminishing' (Nyman 2000).

When 'Ich grolle nicht' is heard in its new context it is no longer associated with the words of Schumann's song 'Ich grolle nicht und wenn das Herz aus bricht' ('I won't complain even though my heart may break'), with the poet Heinrich Heine's theme of a failing *affaires des coeurs*, or even the double-edged quality of his lyric technique, the 'mocking Weltschmerz' of his poetic style (Hallmark 1979, p. 6). The song, stripped bare of its cyclic clothing, takes on a new complexion. It appears to the listener as it does to Dr P. He is no longer held within the unstable phenomenal world of disintegrated objects, but is released by music into the noumenal sphere of pure sound. In Dr P's mind music paradoxically assumes the outward manifestation of reality. Temporal and spatial relationships between musical events function as extended tropes for the measurement of objects and distances in Dr P's routine activities of washing, dressing and eating.

Yet his performance of 'Ich grolle nicht' extends beyond the pragmatism of these 'orientation songs'. Little or no correlation exists between sound–word and body–movement in these songs. The dressing song 'Der Nussbaum', for example, speculates over meanings embodied within the swaying movements of a walnut tree. Secondly, these songs appear as textless, songless interpolations during the opera; they are kinds of musical ephemera or snatchings of tunes that restore a regulative pattern to Dr P's life. 'Ich grolle nicht' on the other hand becomes a statement of self-affirmation, while simultaneously confirming in Dr S's mind that Dr P 'still has a perfect ear ... [his] memory's unimpaired, perfect tonal and rhythmic discrimination and expression – a wonderful musical cortex, temporal lobes intact' (Rawlence, in Nyman 1988b, p. 83).

Through music Dr P retains a measure of proportion and stability in his life, and ultimately a sense of freedom and reconciliation within a deeply unbalanced world. In Dr S's final words: 'I think that music, for him, took the place of the image. He had no body image; he had body music. And to this inner soundtrack, he moved and he acted, fluently, cogently. But ... when the music stopped, so did he ...' (Rawlence, in Nyman 1988b, p. 143). This dichotomy between body music and body image was subsequently explored in Nyman's next stage work *Vital Statistics*, which in turn spawned a work of substantial architectural intertextual proportions, *Facing Goya*, which will be analysed in Chapter 9.

Alongside the exploration of intertextual devices in his film soundtracks and stage works, Nyman also developed a variety of referential and self-referential functions in the string quartet genre. Whereas quotation simultaneously served as a symbol of identification and fragmentation in *The Hat*, its appearance in Nyman's String Quartet No. 1 was, by contrast, a means of allowing the composer to identify with (or distance himself from) the genre's venerable traditions. The first quartet becomes the focal point of the following analysis because its approach to pre-existing material is at times systematic or free, controlled or improvised, and such contrasts have characterized the variation principle that has underpinned Nyman's reworking of Purcell in *The Draughtsman's Contract*, Schumann in *The Hat* and both Bull and Schoenberg in the first quartet. In addition, the first quartet's multi-referential character is unique in Nyman and draws him closer to the collage technique of modern composers such as Kagel or Schnittke. All four quartets address aspects of intertextuality through their use of quotation, appropriation, self-reference and recomposition, and as such provide a series of insights into Nyman's processes and procedures.

Chapter 7

# Unchained Melodies: Intertextuality and Inter-referentiality in the String Quartets

Spanning a period of ten years from the completion of his first string quartet in 1985, Nyman's compositions in this medium form a comprehensive inventory of intertextual techniques that include quotation, appropriation, revision and re-composition. Taken together, they provide a snapshot of the diversity and variety adopted by Nyman towards pre-existing musical materials. Bridging a gap between the structural processes of his earlier works and the large-scale inter-referential designs of later works, such as *Facing Goya*, the string quartet facilitated Nyman's return to more conventional musical forms in the 1990s, in particular the concerto, while still remaining true to the aesthetic principles underlying his compositions predominantly for the Michael Nyman Band during the 1980s (as seen in the Nyman–Greenaway soundtracks studied in Chapter 5).

Figure 7.1 maps out the intertextual topography of the four quartets. The first quartet (7.1a) sets up conflicts between three somewhat unlikely sources. The second (7.2b) composed three years later is based on a series of rhythmic templates taken from the South Indian Bharata Natyam dance tradition. The third quartet (1990) is modelled on another Nyman composition, *Out of the Ruins* (1989), while also referring to Romanian vocal and instrumental music (7.2c). The fourth, completed in 1995, is a large-scale example of wholesale musical interpolation, where parts for second violin, viola and cello are added to an independent pre-existing composition by Nyman for solo violin, *Yamamoto Perpetuo* (1993).

In addition, multiple layers of intertextual association and discourse are formed around the third and fourth quartets, as shown in Figure 7.1c. Originally based on *Out of the Ruins*, the third quartet in turn provided themes for the soundtrack to *Carrington*. One theme used in this film, 'Ham Spray House', is derived from 'La nef de Paris' from the earlier *La Traversée de Paris*. Another movement from the latter work, 'L'arche de la défense', also forms the basis for *Out of the Ruins*. The fourth quartet is therefore indirectly influenced by *La Traversée* while at the same time related to the third through the *Carrington* connection. The third quartet was specifically requested by director Christopher Hampton for use as a 'temp track' to the film, suggesting that on occasions certain types of intertextual associations are

**Figure 7.1 References in Nyman's String Quartets 1–4**

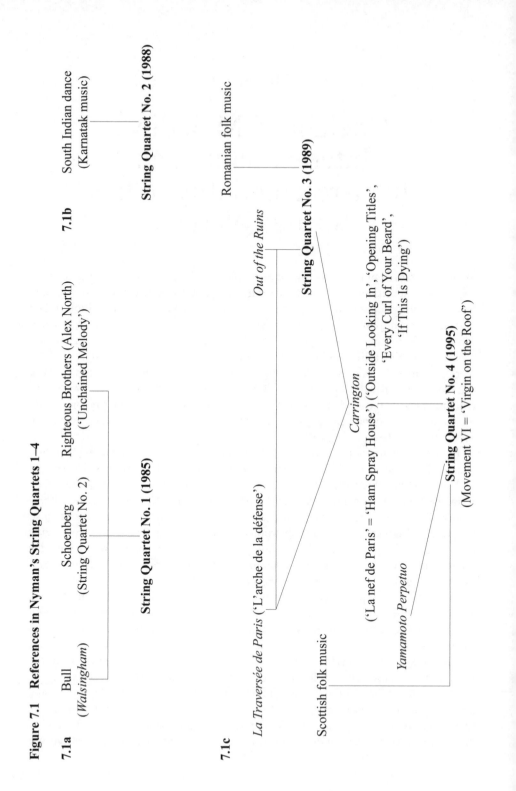

**7.1a**

| Bull | Schoenberg | Righteous Brothers (Alex North) | | South Indian dance |
|---|---|---|---|---|
| (*Walsingham*) | (String Quartet No. 2) | ('Unchained Melody') | **7.1b** | (Karnatak music) |

**String Quartet** No. 1 (1985)

**String Quartet** No. 2 (1988)

**7.1c**

*La Traversée de Paris* ('L'arche de la défense')

*Out of the Ruins*

Romanian folk music

*Carrington*
('La nef de Paris' = 'Ham Spray House')

('Outside Looking In', 'Opening Titles',
'Every Curl of Your Beard',
'If This Is Dying')

**String Quartet** No. 3 (1989)

*Yamamoto Perpetuo*

Scottish folk music

**String Quartet** No. 4 (1995)
(Movement VI = 'Virgin on the Roof')

the result of external requests or decisions, as suggested by the fourth intertextual 'type' outlined by Nyman in his inventory (see Table 4.1).

One cue in *Carrington*, called 'Virgin on the Roof', also forms the opening theme to the fourth quartet's sixth movement. All four works are therefore directly or indirectly connected and linked, either partly through isolated themes, chord structures and sectional divisions, or wholly through the complete integration of another composition. In fact, in certain other respects the third quartet follows on from the previous two quartets in that all three are composed in single, uninterrupted movements. Nyman's intertextual procedures therefore operate in relation to both detail and overall design, to the whole or to its parts.[1] If the first and second quartets appear to be intertextually 'self-contained', then the third and fourth form an indirect but related pair. Being indirect, this relationship is not necessarily noticeable in the music *per se*, but nevertheless demonstrates the complex and often multilayered nature of Nyman's compositional approach. The idea of the palimpsest – developed by Genette in his intertextual study of literature – is adopted by Nyman here: he writes on to, and over, previous compositions in the same way that a parchment obscures the traces of earlier texts.

The previous chapter examined the function of quotation and its elaboration in the context of a single work. While the introduction of an external source set up an opposition of sorts – of conflict between style, expression and musical language – in order to provide the opera with a dramatic scenario, consistency was nevertheless maintained by the use of one composer (in this case Schumann) as the focus for intertextual extrapolation. A similar set of circumstances dictates the intertextual basis of the Nyman–Greenaway soundtracks, as seen in Chapter 5. The string quartets pose a different set of problems, however. Intertextual unity is replaced here by diversity, and reflected, for example, in the multi-authored origins of the first quartet, the generic North Indian rhythmic structures of the second, and the inter-referential (that is, self-quoting) elements surrounding the third and fourth. Applying a generic analytical methodology – as in the case of *The Hat* – would therefore serve only limited purposefulness. Instead, a comparative approach has been adopted which, while less rigorous in its objectives, nevertheless allows the original source and its manifestation in the new quartet context to be scrutinized in more detail.

## String Quartet No. 1

Three layers are formed around the intertextual structure of Nyman's String Quartet No. 1, and may be described in turn as primary, explicit and implicit. The primary source comprises a set of thirty keyboard variations on the popular song *Walsingham* by seventeenth-century English composer John Bull. Partly intended as a personal homage to Thurston Dart, who had presented Nyman with his *Musica Britannica*

---

1 The Fourth Quartet has in addition generated material for *Strong on Oaks, Strong on the Causes of Oaks* (1997).

edition of Bull's keyboard music while a student at King's College, London, its function directly influences and transforms the quartet's musical content and material (Dart 1963). The second, implicit, source is Schoenberg's Second String Quartet, a landmark composition in the quartet repertory not only because it broke free of the genre's medium by including a female voice in two of its movements, but also was one of the first works to compose music freely outside traditional tonal conventions. Viewed in the context of the implicit quote, it may seem surprising that the third, explicit type is a quotation of the Righteous Brothers 1965 pop hit 'Unchained Melody' (composed by Alex North), heard in the middle section of the work.

What are the reasons for tying together such disparate strands, separated by three centuries and belonging to different musical traditions, practices and contexts? In alluding to Schoenberg's work Nyman inevitably positions himself in relation to the medium's stylistic past and subsequent development. Certain factors may have contributed to this decision. First, Nyman's compositions had up to this point been written for non-standard combinations of instruments rather than established formats such as trio, quartet or quintet. Apart from a few choral commissions, Nyman had composed primarily for his own group, whose sound had become distinctive through its fusion of classical, jazz and rock instrumental timbres and mixed elements from a variety of performing practices. Although the Michael Nyman Band's instrumentation became more settled during the 1990s, and in fact included a standard string quartet (in essence the Balanescu Quartet), Nyman's band constantly underwent various transitions, revisions, transformations and alterations during the 1980s, as demand dictated.

When Nyman occasionally strayed away from the safe haven of his own sound and its own inbuilt set of conventions – such as when he wrote *A Handsom, Smooth, Sweet, Smart, Clear Stroke: or Else Play Not at All* (1983) for the Austrian Radio Orchestra – performances were on the whole less convincing. Nyman soon discovered that in order to replicate the loud, amplified sound of a small ensemble within the context of an un-amplified but large symphonic context, orchestral players had to be versed in a different kind of awareness, concentration and response mechanism if they were to acclimatize themselves to the demands of his music. The Michael Nyman Band's gradual expansion during the 1980s resulted in compositions that were effectively for extended ensembles, such as the *Six Celan Songs* (1990) and *Prospero's Books*, and these works subsequently paved the way for the series of concertos composed during the 1990s. The turning point came in 1992 when Nyman consciously moved away from his ensemble's instrumental combinations and wrote for a variety of line-ups, as heard on the CD *Time Will Pronounce*.[2]

Secondly, although clearly capable of replicating orchestral sonorities, the string quartet's four-part textural division could also adopt at the opposite end of the spectrum the form and function of a standard four-piece rock band, where the roles of lead guitar (first violin), rhythm guitar (second violin and viola), bass guitar

---

2 *Time Will Pronounce* featured performances by James Bowman and Fretwork, Trio of London, Virginia Black and London Brass (Argo 440 282-2).

(cello) and drums (all four) could be utilized. The application of rhythmic and textural elements derived from rock to that of a quartet format had the desired effect of bringing the medium closer to the performance practice of the Nyman band. While the notion of the string quartet as a kind of rock band may appear at first outlandish, it is worth noting that composers such as Reich, Riley and Volans around this time also set about to unlock the medium's rhythmic drive and energy, simulating a style closer to the spirit of rock. Nyman similarly sought new ways of harnessing the visceral qualities of his own ensemble to that of an established genre weighed down by the burden and expectation of musical tradition.

Nyman's musical borrowings when played by his band often drew attention to an inherent paradox between the material and its form: the musical material would suggest 'the past', but its form – how it sounded – belonged to 'the present'. One challenge facing Nyman, then, was what to do in the case of a medium where the form was already well established? His solution was to invert this dichotomy – to treat the material itself as a new resource – and draw upon established references in order to imbue them with altogether different meanings.

He does this by ensuring first of all that the Schoenberg references are obscured in the work while the *Walsingham* material is always audible and often clearly discernible. His preference for the past (Bull) over a more recent reference (Schoenberg) suggests that Nyman wishes to comment on the quartet tradition from an unconventional perspective and from a certain distance. If read accordingly, one might suppose that Nyman is providing a critique of the genre's venerable history by first presenting a historical precursor composed on a very different type of string instrument (the harpsichord) some 150 years before the quartet came into existence. A canonical modernist work is then grafted onto the work's structure, but its function is limited to short sectional bursts, its potential for development controlled and suppressed, and its influence ultimately negated. Nyman's aim may partly have been to provide the medium with an alternative aesthetic. The quartet's single-movement grid-like design of opposing blocks of ideas rather than the developmental structures of classical art music appears to support this idea. However, traces of a modernist aesthetic are still to be found in the function of metre and form in the quartet, where they establish a series of conflicts and tensions before finally resolving.

*Metric modulation and form*

Nyman's first quartet was a commission from Irvine Arditti, for whose quartet a regular performer of Nyman's music, Alexander Balanescu, played second violin. The Arditti's were revered for their authoritative and commanding interpretations of complex modern music. Particularly highly prized performances and recordings by the Arditti quartet included Elliott Carter's quartets. Carter was noted for developing a rhythmic and metric language where parts of a movement could be connected through proportionally-related tempos and various subdivisions of a pulse. This structural use of rhythm and the relationship between tempi in certain respects drew him closer to Cowell and Cage's methods, but Carter's notational refinements were essentially his own, and the technique became known as 'metric modulation'. Strangely enough, analogous processes of structuring time would also have been familiar to Nyman from his work with motion pictures. Mathematical calculations in the margins of Nyman's film scores bear witness to the fact that he was sometimes called upon to calculate exact numbers of beats and rhythms required to fit specific lengths of time (although this was essentially contrary to his basic working method with Greenaway). Nyman's application of the principle of metric modulation in the first quartet suggests that the formal design of the work operates on one level according to classical formal archetypes of conflict and resolution.

He appropriates Carter's methods in the quartet by setting up four proportionally-related tempos. Their function is summarized in Table 7.1. Commonalities between them are explored during the first section where a demisemiquaver at crotchet equals sixty is played at the same speed as a semiquaver at a tempo twice the speed, a sextuplet semiquaver at crotchet equals eighty, and a quintuplet semiquaver at crotchet equals ninety-six. Nyman rewrites all rhythmic parts in such a way that a constant pulse remains throughout. In doing so he subtly undermines the principles upon which Carter's technique was formulated. This ironic comment is further emphasized by the minimalist gestures of rapidly repeated notes of the second violin, although it is likely that Nyman was using Balanescu here as 'conductor', time-keeper and instructor in a style unfamiliar to the rest of the quartet.

Nyman may be subtly parodying the concept of metric modulation in the opening section of the quartet by drawing attention to the sometimes unnecessarily complicated lengths modern composers go in order to provide their music with a semblance of difficulty, inaccessibility and exclusivity. The question as to whether he is parodying a technique here is left ambiguous, and one suspects that its purpose is not so much to question the validity and efficacy of Carter's invention but rather to draw attention to the concept of notational practice as an end in itself in certain forms of contemporary music. On a more pragmatic level, Nyman also presents the temporal scheme in order to establish in the players' minds a proportional and relational scheme according to a common beat and constant pulse. Metre may therefore remain static, but the patterns derived from Bull's *Walsingham* provide a sufficient amount of melodic differentiation.

Subtle gradations between slow and fast, single-speed and double-speed tempos are first made clear in the metrical scheme in Section 2 (letter D). An eight-chord sequence is transposed four times, with all four tempi accompanying one statement of each transposition. Unlike the first section, where metrical differentiation is nullified, here it changes in relation to melodic and harmonic stasis. At letters E and F the tempo remains within crotchet equals ninety-six and sixty respectively, providing at least brief respite from the preceding instability. Letter G juxtaposes the two fastest tempos – 96 and 120 – with the former eventually prevailing over the latter. Letter I heralds the return of a tempo not heard since letter D, crotchet equals eighty. J recapitulates for a second time the same juxtaposition of tempos heard at G, but this time the outcome is different to their previous 'encounter', with the fastest tempo prevailing. Also at J the eight-chord sequence first heard at letter D returns, this time without metrical variation, signalling that the conflict between all four tempos is drawing to a close. When the work enters its final section at K, the very first tempo – crotchet equals sixty – is firmly re-established, and resolution is achieved.

**Table 7.1   The function of metric modulation in Nyman's String Quartet No. 1**

| Rehearsal letter | Tempo types (crotchet equals 60, 80, 96 or 120) | Description | Function |
|---|---|---|---|
| A–C | All | Metrical stasis *vs* Melodic differentiation | Conflict between notation and intention |
| D | All | Metrical differentiation *vs* Melodic stasis | Conflict |
| E | 96 | Moderately fast tempo established | Temporary resolution |
| F | 60 | Moderately slow tempo established | Temporary resolution |
| G–H | 96 & 120 | Conflict and juxtaposition with the slower tempo winning out | Conflict and temporary resolution |
| I | 80 | Moderately slow tempo established | Temporary resolution |
| J | 80, 96 & 120 | Conflict and juxtaposition with the faster tempo winning out; letter D material returns but this time in one tempo | Conflict and temporary resolution |
| K | 60 | Slow tempo established | Final resolution |

If Nyman had indeed conceived of the quartet according to principles of conflict and resolution, then the quotes from Bull and Schoenberg simultaneously support and weaken it. The use of two contrasting ideas provides the work with two thematic 'subjects' not dissimilar to the kind of scheme adopted in conventional quartet structures. However, the fact that these 'subjects' do not belong to Nyman undermines the sense of formal and creative autonomy presupposed in such classical structures.

The juxtaposition of two very different sources in one work is relatively uncommon in Nyman. Normally one composer (and often only one work) is sufficient because Nyman's interest is primarily in the transformation of material rather than in collage or superimposition. Inter-referentiality, or self-quotation, occupies a different role in this respect. Ideas are often combined from a diverse range of works and from a variety of sources safe in the knowledge that they will all bear individual traces of Nyman's own 'signature'. The first quartet is therefore different to any other consciously intertextual work by Nyman. Indeed, when an explicit reference to 'Unchained Melody' is also thrown in, the kind of poly-stylistic approach reminiscent of Schnittke or John Zorn is implied, rather than the formal design and stylistic coherence of a classical quartet.

*Baroque source: Bull's Walsingham*

Bull's tour-de-force in seventeenth-century keyboard variation – itself an example of musical intertextuality – supplies Nyman with a significant portion of the quartet's material. The reference to a pre-classical work demonstrates, as in the case of Purcell, Nyman's fondness for employing fixed variation schemes rather than the technique of developing variation later advocated by Schoenberg and other modernists from the notion of the *grundgestalt*, or 'basic shape'.[3] Nyman has preferred the term 'developmental variation' to explain this technique, with the emphasis lying more with 'variation' than 'development'. Bull's use of a rigid eight-bar template for all thirty variations allows Nyman to identify, isolate and endlessly reshape and repeat pre-existing material.

Nyman identified as a characteristic feature of Bull's chord sequence an 'internal repetitiveness' (see Ex. 7.1). Melodic parallels can be found for example in the odd numbered bars (1, 3, 5 and 7). Bars 1, 3 and 5 employ a rising and falling C-D-E-D figure, while a 'B' added at the beginning of bar 5 is reflected in bar 7's B-C♯-D melodic shape. The even-numbered bars (2, 4, 6 and 8) are also related, this time harmonically, each one providing alternative versions of an A minor triad, or in the case of bar 8, its major equivalent. Bull's variation principle enables statement and elaboration to become indivisible. Variations are thus written within an established variational scheme. Nyman adopts its guiding principles and structured framework in his quartet. Any musical unit or segment located at any point during Bull's variation may in principle be matched up and recombined with an equivalent unit. *Walsingham* thus provides the quartet's compositional design with an 'active' ingredient: a way of moving through the intertext and reordering its properties.

A general progression from a fixed approach to a freer one is also evident in Nyman's approach. Certain parallels lie with Bull's method of providing increasingly florid elaborations and decorations to his melodic and harmonic frame. Table 7.2 sets out the process as applied to the *Walsingham* material in the first main section of the

---

3   For a detailed exegesis on the *grundgestalt* see Epstein's *Beyond Orpheus* (1979).

**Example 7.1**   *John Bull's* Walsingham *(first variation)*

work, from rehearsal letters A to C (B consists of the Schoenberg material, which will be discussed later). This analysis follows on from earlier studies by Nimczik (2000) and Beirens (2005, pp. 428–32).

Nyman applies a fairly methodical structural process in this section by gradually uncovering aspects of the original source, adopting a similar 'reconstructive' technique to the one used for the cadential chord sequence in Mozart's *Sinfonia Concertante* K. 364 in *The Falls* and *Drowning by Numbers*. The process is different to that of *In Re Don Giovanni* and *The Draughtsman's Contract*, where fully

**Table 7.2** **Arrangement of the *Walsingham* material**

| Quartet (bar nos) | Bull, *Walsingham* (variation no. and bar number in the original) |
| --- | --- |
| 1–2 | Var. 1, b. 8 (8) |
| 3–4 | Var. 2, b. 8 (16) |
| 5–6 | Var. 3, b. 8 (24) |
| 7–8 | Var. 4, b. 8 (32) |
| 9–10 | Var. 5, b. 8 (40) |
| 11–13 | Var. 6, bb. 1 + 8 (41+48) |
| 14–16 | Var. 7, bb. 1 + 8 (49+56) |
| 17–19 | Var. 8, bb. 1 + 8 (57+64) |
| 20–23 | Var. 9, bb. 1 + 8 (65+72) |
| 24–6 | Var. 11, bb.1 + 3 + 8 (81+83+88) |
| 27–9 | Var. 12, bb.1 + 3 + 8 (89+91+96) |
| 30–33 | Var. 13, bb.1 + 3 + 8 (97+99+104) |
| 34–8 | Var. 16, bb. 1 + 3 + 4 + 8 (121–8) |
| 39–45 | Var. 17, bb. 1 + 3 + 4 + 8 (129–36) |
| [46–57 | Schoenberg, String Quartet No. 2] |
| 58–62 | Var. 1, b. 7 + Var. 2, bb. 7–8 (7, 15–16) |
| 63–7 | Var. 3, b. 7 + Var. 5, bb. 7–8 (24, 39–40) |
| 68–72 | Var. 6, b. 7 (x 2) + Var. 8, b. 7 (x 3) (47, 63) |
| 73–4 | Var. 8, b. 8 (cello) + Var. 11, b. 8 (vln 1) (64, 88) |
| 75–7 | Var. 15, b. 7 + Var. 16, bb. 7–8 (119, 127–8) |
| 78–82 | Var. 17, b. 7 + Var. 18, bb. 7–8 (135, 143–4) |
| 83–6 | Var. 20, bb. 1–2 + 7 (153–4, 159) |
| 87–90 | Var. 22, bb. 1–2 + 7–8 (169–70, 175–6) |
| 91–7 | Var. 24, bb. 1–2 + 5–6 + 7–8 (185–6, 189–90, 191–2) |
| 98 | Var. 3, b. 1 (17) |
| 99 | Var. 6, b. 2 (42) |
| 100 | Var. 7, b. 3 (51) |
| 101 | Var. 9, b. 4 (68) |
| 102 | Var. 17, b. 5 (102) |
| 103 | Var. 20, b. 6 (158) |
| 104 | Var. 29, b. 7 (231) |
| 105–6 | Var. 1, b. 8 (8) |

formed chord sequences act as a framework for increasingly elaborate melodic and rhythmic variations.

Nyman first sets out the *Walsingham* material as a musical list by extracting the final bar from each one of variations 1–5, which results in a series of alternative readings of an A major chord. He then continues to move chronologically through Bull's sequence by bolting onto the first bar of every succeeding variation the final bar of the previous one. This additive technique in effect combines the ends and beginnings of variation sets, while also producing alternating tonic major and minor versions of an A chord. At bar 24 Nyman deviates from this scheme by omitting variation 10, probably because the dotted rhythmic pattern introduced by Bull at this point would have cut across the sense of momentum generated by the accumulation of increasingly elaborate figurations. He does something similar later to variations 14 and 15.

Nyman gradually fleshes out the *Walsingham* segments so that in bar 24, beginning, middle and end segments are placed together, creating a series of minor–major–minor sounding sequences. This additive process is continued until bar 26, with bar 4 tagged on to 3, mirroring the earlier combination of 8 and 1. Half the accumulated contents of variations 16 and 17 are heard towards the end of this section – albeit in the edited form of middles, ends and beginnings. As the music increasingly assumes the modal language of early-seventeenth-century English keyboard music, the Bull source gives way to a quotation from Schoenberg's second string quartet, discussed later.

The quartet re-engages with the Bull material at bar 58. Pairs of single bar and two-bar segments derived from the ends of variations are now selected, paralleling the procedure adopted in the opening section. Although Nyman is seen to move chronologically, that is, from beginning to end through the *Walsingham* sequence, he does not always use successive variations. Thus variations 4, 7, 9 and 10 are omitted as the rigorous method of selecting patterns is gradually relaxed. Indeed his intertextual methods become increasingly innovative and almost virtuosic from herein on. At bar 73 two variations (eight and eleven) are heard simultaneously for the first time. Between bars 83–97 a cumulative process is adopted, resulting in the most complete statement of any single variation (six out of the possible eight bars of variation twenty-four are heard here) and this almost complete reconstruction announces an end to the intertextual process. Nyman concludes the section by creating a completely new 8-bar sequence by selecting in correct order relevant segments belonging to different variation sets. Thus bar 1 of variation 3 is followed by bar 2 of 6, 3 of 7, 4 of 9, 5 of 17, 6 of 20, 7 of 29 then reaching full circle by ending on bar 8 of variation 1 (see Examples 7.2a and 7.2b).

In employing Bull's material in this way, Nyman's quartet evokes in essence various elements of Elizabethan music: its harmonic language, melodic shapes and contrapuntal motion. At the same time, the isolated musical units only serve to obscure and even obliterate any sense of narrative logic belonging to Bull's variation technique, replaced instead with Nyman's own non-narrative variation technique. Anticipating techniques adopted in *Drowning by Numbers*, he selects and combines

**Example 7.2a**   *String Quartet No. 1: bb. 98–106*

elements according to type and character rather than function. In providing a series of variations upon a work originally based on the principle of variation, Nyman is seen by Beirens to adopt the concept of a 'meta-variation' by addressing 'the subject of the variation principle itself' (Beirens 2005, p. 411).

By contrast, the very last section of the quartet faithfully resembles Bull's variation principle but does not evoke so much its soundworld. Initially heard in solitary isolation at bar 193, the theme that draws the quartet to a close appears to have been derived from a conflation of vertical and horizontal elements from bar 3–4[1] (see Ex. 7.1). The notes contained within the boxed section in Example 7.1 are also found in Nyman's melody, apart from the F♮ which has been altered to an F♯ (a

**Example 7.2a** *continued*

*continued*

similar concatenation of notes, this time with an F♯ included, may also be derived from the end of bar 4). Nyman ties in Bull's variation technique with the principle of metric modulation in the final section. A series of twelve four-bar variations are heard in all, flanked by two augmented eight-bar versions of the theme. Nyman applies a series of rhythmic diminutions and melodic elaborations to the theme, reflecting the seventeenth-century practice of the 'division', its minim values halved into crotchets,

**Example 7.2a**   *concluded*

halved again to quavers, by a third to triplets and then by a quaver to semiquavers. Meanwhile, a countermelody in the second violin moves by turns from quintuplets to sextuplets to demisemiquavers. The accumulative effect of melodic and rhythmic diminution is only disrupted by the quartet's final cadence, which returns to explicit quotation by reproducing the harmonic and linear motion of *Walsingham*'s own final cadence. Nyman once stated that this section did not belong to either source, but the melody seems to have sprung – whether intentional or not – from the *Walsingham* source (Nyman 1993b). One could describe this, as in other examples, as a kind of indeterminate or non-intentional intertextuality.

   Between the beginning and end sections, Bull's variations are subjected to a series of elaborate melodic transformations, the ninth variation providing the basis for compositional 'development' during the middle of the work.[4] At letter E Nyman takes the bass line from bars 1–2 of this variation, moving through each four-note

----

   4  Nyman also comes closest to developing the pre-existing material in what would traditionally be regarded as the development section.

**Example 7.2b**    Walsingham: *variations 3, 6, 7, 9, 17, 20, 29 and 1*

unit and extending it to five by repeating the penultimate note in each pattern (see Ex. 7.3).

**Example 7.3**   Walsingham *(variation 9) and the String Quartet No. 1 (bb. 123–6)*

An irregular seven-beat rhythmic pattern is also applied to the note sequence, heard against an eleven-beat ostinato. Nyman is prepared to deviate from the original, however, when he considers it necessary to do so. More evidence of this is seen in the fourth cycle of the sequence. Following Bull's bass line slavishly would have yielded an A and G dyad at the end, rather than the B and C used by Nyman. At bar 148 – the point at which bar 2 of Bull's ninth variation commences – Nyman swaps around the last two notes, but when this sequence returns (at 181) he adheres to Bull's original sequence. It is likely that Nyman deliberately 'misreads' the original in this instance. Such instances of misreading have been identified in some literary critics' theories as forming the basis upon which intertextual relationships are seen to emerge. This concept has been discussed at length by Bloom in relation to poetry and literature and is touched upon in Korsyn's analysis of nineteenth-century music by Chopin and Brahms (see Chapter 4).[5]

Furthermore, at bar 159, the point at which the music arrives at the fifth and final four-note unit in Bull's two-bar sequence, Nyman appears to transpose the pattern up a perfect fifth while at the same time altering its final note. The resulting pattern, C#-A-B-D (not G#-E-A-G#) demonstrates how in straightforward terms the application of a transformational procedure onto a second- or third-generation variation may distinctly alter its relationship to the original source. Carried to greater extremes, commonalities between the two shapes would eventually disappear, although they would still share the same length and duration. A correlation can be made in this respect between levels of similarity and variation characterizing Nyman's compositions as a whole. An economy of means allows Nyman to use the variation principle to generate larger structures from smaller units. In the section from bars 163–92, the entire first half of the variation nine sequence is heard against a more dense polyrhythmic texture, enabling Nyman to carve out a whole section lasting

---

[5] See Bloom's *A Map of Misreading* (1975). Elsewhere Nyman 'misreads' the original source in his paraphrase of the 'Bonnie Jean' folk melody in 'Big My Secret' (bar 15 'should' read E-F#-A-B not E-F#-G-A).

almost seventy bars from an isolated two-bar unit. Later, at letter J, the cello adopts a similar procedure by taking the same two-bar fragment and generating nine two-bar blocks out of its ten four-note groups.

Two intertextual techniques emerge, then, from Nyman's use of the Bull variations. The first involves quoting, listing and juxtaposing musical features while the second recomposes the original material into larger structures through variation processes. Letter G combines these selection and variation processes by adopting and adapting specific features from the *Walsingham* source (see Ex. 7.4).

**Example 7.4**  *String Quartet No. 1: bb. 220–23*

Bar 220 reorders the theme's opening C-D-E figure to C-E-D, then does the same with the theme's seventh bar. The pattern heard at bar 222 is likely to have been derived from the descending line that adjoins bars 5–6. Even the seemingly unrelated G-F♯-D pattern appears in the bass line at bar 8. Nyman isolates distinctive landmarks scattered across Bull's musical landscape, reconfigures and repeats them, then combines them to create larger blocks. Exploring connections between primary and secondary texts can lead to some fascinating comparisons, but of equal importance is the manner with which Nyman constructs a 'grid-like' structure out of Bull's three-note cells. An example of this may be found in the four modules and their derivations. Identified in Table 7.3 as A, B, C and D (see also Ex. 7.4), their progress is charted as follows:

**Table 7.3    Modular process in the String Quartet No. 1, letter G (bb. 220–37)**

| Bar | 220 | 221 | 222–3 | 224 | 225 | 226–7 | 228 | 229 | 230–31 | 232 |
|---|---|---|---|---|---|---|---|---|---|---|
| Module | A | $B^1$ | $C^1$ | A | $D^1$ | $C^2$ | $B^1$ | $D^2$ | $C^1$ | $B^1$ |

| Bar | 233 | 234 | 235 | 236 | 237 |
|---|---|---|---|---|---|
| Module | $B^2$ | $B^1$ | $B^2$ | A | $B^3$ |

As with other aspects of his music, Nyman's modular structures are also inherently variational. The first half is comprised of three statements of three three-unit groups: A+B+C, A+D+C and B+D+C. Each group forms a variation out of the preceding one, B in the first variation is replaced with D in the second and B replaces A in the third. Variations on B are then explored, before the reintroduction of A with B at the end. It is interesting to note that A and B are only conjoined at the beginning and end of the sequence, but even here B is altered. Nyman thus avoids predictability, imbuing his minimal structures with subtle variety. The process is taken a step further between bars 238–55 where an entire modular block is repeated with changes in rhythm, register and pitch.

*Popular source: 'Unchained Melody'*

Letter H, like E, is a somewhat freer rendering of the variation 9 bass line in the viola and cello parts, a freedom underscored by the use of indeterminate rhythmic notation in the violins. Such free notation is uncommon in Nyman's music, and one – along with the Schoenberg references and use of metric modulation – that may have been intended to provide the work with a modernist (or possibly an anti-modernist) dimension. This section returns in an abridged form at bars 297–313.

In between these two statements is arguably the quartet's most startling and unexpected moment, The Righteous Brothers' 'Unchained Melody'. Its arrival at bar 274, almost exactly midway through the work, is not entirely unheralded. As with the 'Ich grolle nicht' quote in *The Hat*, a number of intertextual indicators prepare and anticipate its introduction. The idea of including a more recent popular tune probably occurred to Nyman while looking at *Walsingham*, which is also based on a popular tune of its time. Indeed Nyman acknowledged that Bull had managed to turn the tune's inherent lack of melodic and harmonic variation to his own advantage. Limited by formal constraints, Bull was forced to develop 'from within' and engage in endless melodic and rhythmic elaborations. By choosing to work with pre-existing material and its 'developmental variation' Nyman imposes a similar set of constraints. That *Walsingham*'s status as popular artefact had all but faded away meant that Nyman needed to engage with a more recent example. He found the perfect match in 'Unchained Melody', the melody of which had also been quoted by folk-pop singer Joni Mitchell a few years earlier in her song 'Chinese Café'.

An uncanny resemblance exists between the *Walsingham* theme and 'Unchained Melody'. The pop tune's opening three-note C-D-E pattern is a variation on the *Walsingham* melody. By quoting and thereby literally 'unchaining' the melody from its source, Nyman continues to adopt the process of melodic reconfiguration used in letter G. Connections run deeper between the two than melodic variation, however. Four bars into Bull's ninth variation, the bass line moves in a progression from C major to A minor to F major (see the variation 9 segment in Ex. 7.2b). Heard in isolation and in the context of pop discourse the pattern again suggests doo-wop. Its extensive application in pop songs had turned this sequence into an intertextual type. Here was a chord sequence that signalled 'pop' even to those who were unfamiliar with its sounds. In prefacing the I-VI-IV pattern with V (G major) Bull's progression also inadvertently contains this standard pop sequence. Nyman's recombination of these chords makes the doo-wop reference explicit.

Both harmonic sequence and 'Unchained Melody' are quoted together in bars 274–96. The doo-wop sequence is subjected to an extended harmonic variation treated in similar fashion to the *Walsingham* segments at the beginning of the quartet. Bull's complete seven-chord sequence, consisting of chords I-VI-IV-I-IV-V-I, is heard at the end of the section, but Nyman introduces it gradually, thus allowing him to bring the doo-wop pattern to the surface (see Table 7.4):

**Table 7.4   Doo-wop pattern and *Walsingham* harmony in
the String Quartet No. 1**

| bb. 274–7 | C | A min | F | – | – | – | G |
|---|---|---|---|---|---|---|---|
| bb. 278–82 | C | A min | F | C | – | – | G |
| bb. 283–8 | C | A min | F | C | F | – | G |
| bb. 289–95 | C | A min | F | C | F | C | G |

*Modern source: Schoenberg's String Quartet No. 2*

At the other end of the quartet's intertextual spectrum lies Nyman's use of a melodic sequence from the last movement of Schoenberg's second quartet. Unlike the *Walsingham* material, these extracts play a more passive role in the work's design. They function in a more introversive way, providing a kind of static counterpoint to the dynamic re-workings of the Bull extracts.

Schoenberg's material is introduced for the first time at letter B (bar 46). While the tonal and improvisational character of Bull's music is slowly unlocked by Nyman's process, the Schoenberg source amounts to a single two-bar fragment in the original heard at the very beginning of the final movement, consisting of a linear eight-note figure transferred from cello to first violin via the two middle voices (see Ex. 7.5).

**Example 7.5**   *Schoenberg's String Quartet No. 2: Fourth Movement (opening)*

In the original, an eight-note figure encompasses a span of almost two octaves, but in Nyman's version it is compressed to less than one octave. As a result, a pattern that in tonal terms is already unfamiliar is further de-familiarized, echoing the Georg text heard later in this movement, that Schoenberg's music '[breathes] the air of another planet'. Unlike the blocks of material spliced together from *Walsingham*, the Schoenberg fragment turns in on itself, restless and lacking any clear direction (see Table 7.5).

The Schoenberg material disappears almost as soon as it has arrived, and when it eventually returns at letter I (b. 314) it has acquired a very different musical character. Descending chromatic tremmolando figures accompanying the initial quote are replaced by Nyman's trademark syncopated rhythmic figures, despite retaining the eight-note character of Schoenberg's theme. Pitches 1–8 are stated between bars 314–19 followed by pitches 9–16 at 320–24. The entire sixteen-note pattern is then repeated between bars 325–32 before introducing the next sequence between bars 333–6, which include pitches 17–24 of the original. Nyman then applies a kind of

**Table 7.5   Schoenberg references in the String Quartet No. 1**

| Quartet (bar nos) | Schoenberg, String Quartet No. 2 / iv, 'Entrueckung' (bar nos) |
|---|---|
| 46–7 | bb. 1–$2^1$ |
| 48–9 | bb. $2^1$–$2^2$ |
| 50 | bb. 1–$2^1$ |
| 51 | bb. $2^1$–$2^2$ |
| 52–3 | bb. $2^2$–$2^3$ |
| 54 | bb. 1–$2^1$ |
| 55 | bb. $2^1$–$2^2$ |
| 56–7 | bb. $2^3$–$2^4$ |

**Example 7.6**   *String Quartet No. 1: the distribution of Schoenberg material, bb. 314–48*

Numbers 1-32 indicate the pitch sequence taken from Schoenberg (see Ex. 7.5)

segmentational process similar to the one applied to Bull's variations, by repeating notes 1–8, skipping 9–16, and proceeding to notes 17–32 (bars 337–48).

Obscuring these regular pitch repetitions is an irregular bar structure of 10, 13 and 12 bars respectively, as shown in Example 7.6. These three basic sections are divided as follows: the first is a six-bar repeated group followed by a pair of two-bar units, the second unit repeated. The second section consists of a nine-bar unit followed again by a pair of two-bar units, both repeated this time. A third section consists of an eight-bar group followed by a three bar unit and rounded off by a single bar. Pitches 1–8 are contained within the opening six-bar unit (although even here internal repetition of pitches 1–4 can be seen) but any continuity between pitches 9–16 has been eradicated by the internal repetition of bars 322–3. The dovetailing of pitch sequence with bar structure means that notes 15–26 become part of a new cycle at bar 324. Likewise, pitch continuity from 17–24 is hidden by internal repetition at bars 333–4. The final pitch sequence, notes 25–32 of the original, is also blocked by repetition, so that notes 31–2 stand alone at the end of this section.

## String Quartet No. 2

The heterogeneous character of the first quartet, both in terms of intertextual appropriation and the variety of methods applied to them, results in a work that lies, according to Ortwin Nimczik, somewhere between Bull and Schoenberg, a work that partakes of both worlds yet exists in neither. The second quartet also lies between two traditions and two cultures, in this case the East and West. It displays the structural organization of South Indian Karnatak music while at the same time the melodic and harmonic features of Western music. Yet in other respects the second quartet is very different to the first. Its references are general rather than specific, conceptual rather than real. There are no direct melodic or harmonic quotations here.

The second quartet was originally written for a solo dance performance called *Miniatures*, choreographed and performed by Shobana Jeyasingh and based on the South Indian Bharata Natyam dance tradition. As in the case of *Carrington* and the third quartet, the rhythmic structure of the second was indicated entirely by Jeyasingh, both in principle and note-to-note detail. Nyman had to follow a set of prescribed rhythmic grids and patterns, but was nevertheless free to interpret the manner in which these rhythmic prescriptions were represented.

Therefore the principles which shape Indian Karnatic music and its systems tacitly form the basis for Nyman's composition, although he does not attempt to emulate or imitate its sound and expression. In its most basic form, Karnatic music is founded on the twin concepts of *raga* (melody) and *tala* (rhythm). The latter manifests itself both rhythmically, in terms of patterns created according to the 'number of individual beats', and also metrically, in terms of beats 'grouped into larger units' or cycles, while *ragas* are constructed from specific modes which form the basis for melodic construction, elaboration and variation (Viswanathan and Allen 2004, p. 35).

Nyman shares with other minimalist composers (La Monte Young, Terry Riley and Philip Glass) a fascination with South Indian classical music. Analogies may be drawn between his own musical language and the rhythmic and metric foundation of the performance and improvisation of Karnatic music. In Nyman's music, repeating patterns are played alongside or against a constant pulse, sometimes reinforcing a sense of regularity or working against it. Parallels also exist between the melodic principles of construction in Indian music. The process of stating, embellishing and constructing extended lines through additive techniques is as much a feature of Nyman's music as it is of the Indian tradition. The adoption of generic forms rather than any stylistic or expressive nuances allowed Nyman to employ a structural framework that belonged to Indian music but did not sound like it. Both rhythmic and melodic aspects manage to reference the Karnatic tradition while still remaining true to Nyman's own compositional aesthetic.

The basic rhythmic structure of the quartet broadly adheres to the five rhythmic classes of Karnatic music. These types, called *jatis*, are based on patterns constructed according to groups of 3, 4, 5, 7 and 9. In the second quartet Nyman adopts a similar pattern of 4, 5, 6 (this being a multiple of 3), 7 and 9. They are employed successively in the opening five movements, while the final movement combines them all. Nyman adopts these numbers as a metrical basis, allowing him to set rhythmic patterns of varying lengths against the pre-defined pulse of the movement. Throughout the work, the Karnatic rhythmic intertext is highly explicit, audible and totally generative, but nevertheless articulated into a different cultural and musical context.

The first movement sets off unequivocally in four beat measures. Rhythmic patterns are clearly subdivided into a regular metrical framework providing an overwhelming sense of four to the bar. This undifferentiated union between rhythm and metre continues until bar 57. At this point a melodic line grouped into three is heard for the first time in the first violin. This subtle deviation from a regular pulse is reinforced at bar 69 by a viola line, which – although still playing in four – subverts the natural emphasis of the downbeat by playing in groups of eight quavers across the bar. This pattern becomes increasingly irregular so that by bar 73, rhythmic blocks consisting of seven and nine patterns are being built around alternating two- and three-quaver units.

The pre-established rhythmic scheme forms in this case the basis for a series of rhythmic variations not dissimilar to the Western classical idea admired by Nyman of building melodic variations upon a chaconne or ground bass. In the first movement rhythmic variations are presented in terms of statement and counterstatement, of regular patterns disrupted by irregular deviations. In the second movement the two are combined from the very outset. The previously established four-beat structure is maintained by a syncopated rhythmic figure heard in the first violin, but it is played against an underlying five-beat pulse resulting in a rhythmic cycle that loops around every twenty beats. The process is developed in the third movement, where three large sixteen-beat segments are heard against eight six-bar groups. Connections between underlying metre and counter-metre are further complicated by the fact that the pattern is at first stated on the second beat of the bar, at $13^2$, and therefore cycles over a forty-eight beat structure, realigning itself at bars $21^2$, $29^2$, 37 (ostensibly extended to seventeen beats here), $45^2$ and $52^2$ respectively.

The fourth movement highlights the ambiguity surrounding rhythmic subdivisions of 7 by presenting it in groups of 3+2+2 or 2+2+3. At bar 22 in the second violin the former division is preferred, while at bar 43 the first violin employs the latter grouping. At bar 43, fifteen quaver-beat patterns are stated against the established seven-beat pulse while the second violin and viola's rhythmic groupings are divided into 4+4+4+2 and 3+2+2 / 3+2+2 respectively, further increasing linear density and activity. Movement five sets up a similar scenario, where a sixteen quaver-beat (or eight crotchet-beat) group is played against a constant nine-beat pulse, resulting in a structure that cycles across sixteen bars, at bars 17, 33, 49 and 65. Similarly, at bar 69 an eight-quaver group plays against a nine-beat bar resulting in cyclic overlapping at bars 77, 85 and 93. This nine-beat structure forms a rhythmic template for subsequent Nyman compositions, including 'Le Labyrinthe' from *La Traversée de Paris* and later, 'Come unto these yellow sands' from *Prospero's Books* (1991).

All five rhythmic structures are integrated in the final movement against a four-beat pulse that is featured at various times throughout the work. After a six-bar introduction, the complete number sequence is stated back-to-front in the cello part, starting with a rhythmic idea heard over nine-quaver beats, then seven (at bar $11^2$), five (at 15), three (at $17^2$), before realigning itself with the established four-beat pattern at bar 19. This twelve-bar rhythmic process is extended to sixteen through the addition of four bars: two to synchronize the pattern and two to provide an upbeat for the beginning of the next cycle, which starts at bar 23 and is repeated at 39 and 55. The first violin also plays across the four-bar regular division at this point with rhythmic groupings consisting of seven (2+2+3) and nine (2+2+2+3) notes. A coda encapsulates these rhythmic differences where groups of 5, 6 and 9 notes are heard (see Ex. 7.7).

While Nyman's melodic ideas are made to work within the rhythmic structures established in each movement, they too follow the principle of statement and elaboration. The theme introduced in the third movement provides an example of this technique. Initially stated in minims and crotchets against an undulating accompaniment in the viola, additional patterns are added to it when transferred to the first violin at bar 37. Nyman's method is consistent with his adopted principles of melodic variation here, occurring within a prescribed rhythmic structure rather than attempting to develop beyond it. A similar method of filling in the temporal spaces between the notes occurs in the following movement, where a seven-beat pattern, or 1+2+2+2, at bar 4 becomes 1+2+1x4 at bar 6, then 1x7 at 16. The principle of statement and elaboration, of variations within a series of pre-established time spans is applied not only to rhythm and metre, then, but also to melody. It is a principle that not only governs single movements of the quartet but is mapped across the entire work. While melodic references remain implicit in the second quartet, its rhythmic design from an Eastern perspective is intertextually explicit. However, it is also worth noting that when overt cultural references of a non-Western kind feature prominently, Nyman either works around the integrity of the original, as in the case of his 'Sangam' collaboration with Indian musicians U. Shrinivas, Rajan and

**Example 7.7**   *String Quartet No. 2: Coda section*

Sajan Misra, or adapts its principles to his own (Western) way of thinking. He strives towards a balance between a local dialect and global concerns in order to reflect a kind of harmonious co-existence of diverse cultural practices.

## String Quartet No. 3

If the second quartet is modelled on the generic structures of Indian classical dance, the third is derived from a very different source, Nyman's choral work *Out of the Ruins*. Unlike its predecessors, the third quotes from a single specific source from Nyman's own catalogue of works while also combining a strong Romanian folk element. In drawing upon ideas already used in previous compositions Nyman imposes an inter-referential element that has become a recurring feature of his compositions from the 1990s onwards.

Nyman has described the transformation of an old work into a new one as a form of 'translation'. This term is defined by the *New Shorter Oxford English Dictionary* as the 'rendering of something in another medium, form or mode of expression', and as such provides an accurate description of the various processes used by Nyman in this work (Brown 1993, p. 3371). He 'renders' a choral piece in a new medium, adopts the original's form and adheres to its melodic lines, harmonic sequences, rhythmic patterns and phrase structures. The third quartet thus evokes the original's very 'mode of expression', yet rather than functioning as a mere reproduction of the original it also deviates from its close relation in a number of important respects. In this sense translation may also suggest more radical emancipation from the original through 'transformation, alteration [and] change' (ibid., p. 3371). Neither a simple case of straightforward repetition nor entirely different, Nyman therefore applies the variation principle to the re-composition of this work. The quartet thus becomes a kind of commentary on the precursor piece, and the extent to which it follows and deviates from the former work will serve as a basis for the following analysis.

*Out of the Ruins*

*Out of the Ruins* was composed for a programme following the lives of those affected by the devastating earthquake which struck Armenia in 1988, killing over twenty-five thousand people, and formed part of the BBC's documentary series '40 Minutes'. For this work Nyman set a text dating from the tenth century by the Armenian poet Grigor Narekatsi, interspersing three sections taken from the poet's *Book of Lamentations* with two sections using vocalised sounds. The wordless sections already supply the choral work with an instrumental quality that would have readily lent itself to string quartet adaptation.

The first section of *Out of the Ruins* is anchored in the aeolian mode and introduces at the outset a restless seven-note 'ostinato' in the bass. This figure, repeated over and over in the manner of a responsory, acquires its most forceful realization in the final section, where it is declaimed loudly in the upper register of the sopranos against dorian-derived harmonies. The opening section also employs a gradually rising and falling four-note figure, first heard in bar 3, and subjected during the work to a series of subtle alterations and transformations. It is moved up a third at bar 5, rhythmically altered to a five-note theme at bar 12 and appears in retrograde and with further rhythmic variation at bar 15 (see Ex. 7.8).

**Example 7.8**   Out of the Ruins*: pitch cells*

The return of the opening material for a second time at bar 55 is heralded with increasing melodic and rhythmic elaboration. For instance, a countermelody is added in the altos and transferred to the sopranos at bar 69. The entire opening section is also extended when it reappears at the end of the work.

The two textless sections are in fact more freely composed, making greater use of contrasts, and are also less constrained by the open section's modal context. At bar 34 Nyman establishes a tritone relationship between A minor and $E^\flat$ major via $A^\flat$, underneath a melody that gradually extends itself from three, to four, to five notes. Tritone-related chord structures established via more conventional tonal cadences are not uncommon in Nyman's music, and are sometimes used by him to express anxiety or restlessness. A similar pattern appears in 'The Mood That Passes Through You' from *The Piano*, where a $B^\flat$ minor chord shifts to E major via B minor, though it is difficult to establish any direct correlation between the two.

How then does Nyman succeed in adapting *Out of the Ruins* to the string quartet medium? In general terms, choral works are relatively compatible with the quartet medium. Both adopt the 'standard' texture of four individual lines or parts, but additionally possess the ability to reduce or increase it. While the number of vocal lines self-evidently depends on the number of singers available, the string quartet, consisting of a finite number of players, may only enhance its linear and harmonic potential by employing double and triple stopping. Both mediums are capable of producing 6, 8 or even 10-note chords. Textural density in *Out of the Ruins* ranges from the monophonic line heard at the very beginning to seven superimposed lines at various points during the final section. The third string quartet, by contrast, creates an almost orchestral sonority during equivalent moments, often playing in six or seven parts, though rarely beyond this. Such dexterity in the quartet allows Nyman, at bar 102 for instance, to conflate all necessary choir lines into three parts, enabling the first violin to overlay the texture with additional material derived from Romanian folk music.

Likewise, a vocal ensemble's range – with the exception of the violin, which can reach well beyond that of a human voice, and also the lowest open string on the cello – is roughly similar to that of a string quartet. In Nyman's quartet the second violin becomes the carrier of the original choral melody, the viola often provides an additional folk-influenced layer, while the first violin adds new melodic material and colour. For example, at bars 107–22 the second violin reproduces the choral theme heard at bar 77, while a more improvised line in harmonics is heard in the first violin.

Differences also clearly exist between both groups. Choral writing is conditioned and determined by such factors as breathing and text, while string instruments can move from one section to the next without pause, as happens when a new section is elided at letter F (bar 122) without the caesura included during the selfsame moment in *Out of the Ruins* (bar 92). String instruments sustain notes for indefinite periods of time and execute rapid passagework with arguably greater ease and agility. As a result, sections starting at letters B or G in the third quartet have been completely re-orchestrated in order to accommodate the variety and flexibility contained within the medium.

*Translation and transformation*

To translate a work is partly to bring to the surface a whole range of similarities and differences that lie between the original and its reproduction. A cursory glance at the last six bars of both works on the final page of each score indicate a strong degree of association between the two works. Sometimes similarities outweigh differences, such as in bars 55–62 of *Out of the Ruins* and bars 84–91 from the quartet. Here the quartet almost quotes verbatim from the choral work, the only difference being that the two uppermost choral lines have been swapped around in the quartet's texture. The quartet also adheres closely to the original during the following section (63–8 in *Out of the Ruins* and 92–7 in the quartet) where even the internal voicing is maintained.

Even on the final page of both scores, however, a solo line has been interpolated in the viola part, and layered over the choral canvas of its precursor piece. While the ascending melodic figure first heard in the violin at the very beginning is derived from *La Traversée de Paris* ('L'arche de la défense'), other examples serve to emphasize the new context established by the quartet's folk material. At bar 63 the cello plays an elaborate quasi-improvised melody against the duplication in the other string parts of the choral section from bar 34. A viola melody at 98–101 also provides an additional folk layer in this section.

While the quartet is constructed from a predetermined grid, there is still room for elaboration and differentiation. The original is sometimes altered, such as at bars 125–6, when the second violin transforms the original melody into figuration. The quartet's increased flexibility allows it occasionally to develop themes to more distant harmonic regions. This occurs at bars 17–24, for which there is no exact equivalent in the choral work. At such times the quartet's narrative develops its own internal logic beyond that of the precursor piece, moving away from it, but Nyman prefers on the whole to remain within the original's template rather than striving beyond it.

How then does Nyman adapt the expressive needs of one work to fit the other, given that they both deal with two different historical events? One interesting area of comparison is the way in which the quartet transforms the material it shares with *Out of the Ruins* to radically different expressive ends. Composed in response to a natural disaster, *Out of the Ruins* is intended as a thoughtful, dignified, reflective and sometimes emotional response to a natural disaster that could not have been averted. A sense of hopelessness and helplessness is communicated, but Nyman's score does not express moral indignation, retribution or outrage.

In contrast, the third quartet 'celebrates' the fall of Romanian dictator Nicolae Ceauşescu, though any sense of joy or jubilation is tempered by anger, fear and outrage at the pain and suffering caused during his twenty-five year despotic reign. Nyman's score expresses the sense of embittered triumph and pyrrhic victory. Contrasts between these two works are thus predicated on context, as in a comparison between bars 23–4 of *Out of the Ruins* and bars 25–6 from the third quartet. The former is quiet and reflective, the latter aggressive and agitated. Another contrast may similarly be seen by comparing bars 32–3 of the choral work and its analogous section, bars 55–62, from the quartet. The arched vocal line at this point in *Out of the Ruins* suggests an intense expressionism – a cry for help – while the accented string writing in the equivalent section is on the contrary forthright and aggressive.

At such moments the expressive language employed in both works has been harnessed to quite radically different ends. Nyman's occasionally extreme recasting of the original material suggests that a form of musical critique or commentary is taking place: he wishes to represent the precursor work in an altogether different light. From this pretext, one may arrive at a reading of the musical form of the third quartet that extends beyond its role as a mere faithful note-for-note translation of the original. In Adornian terms the quartet may be said to contain a 'conceptual breach … a rupture which allows for [a] critique of that system in terms of itself' (Williams 1989, p. 188). Thus the enclosed musical 'system' constructed in *Out of the Ruins* has given way to a musical 'critique of that system' in the third quartet. If the comparison with Adorno seems a little far-fetched, it is worth noting that his philosophical ideas were adapted by Jacques Derrida in the area of language, where he claimed that meaning is seen to '[exist] in a continual state of substitution' (Derrida, in Williams 1989, p. 188). As a basic premise upon which linguistic deconstruction is formed this description seems particularly applicable to Nyman's own deconstructive approach to musical 'texts' (ibid., p. 190). At times Nyman works with the grain of the original, at other times he moves across or against it. This sense of an unresolved dialectic – a lack of resolution between not only the copy and its original but also between the copy and itself – conveys the same sense of empty satisfaction and false joy brought about by Ceauşescu's downfall.

**String Quartet No. 4**

Having written an article extolling the virtues of simplicity as an absolute concept in 1980 (Nyman 1993a), Nyman rarely set out to compose music where technique and virtuosity was championed for their own sake. Certainly, virtuosity has often been group-led rather than individually focused in Nyman's music. Having established a band with relatively unchanged personnel enabled Nyman to write for specific individuals and identify unique features and characteristics of their playing or singing. In the area of vocal music, Nyman often made effective use of 'the grain of the voice', either in terms of the breadth and control achieved in extremely high registers by Sarah Leonard's voice, Hilary Summers's deep and affective contralto, or Ute Lemper's highly individualized interpretations and stylistic versatility. Contrasts are also emphasized in Nyman's characterization of particular sounds. The rasping rhythms of John Harle's alto saxophone are often countered in Nyman's scores by the plangent lyricism of his soprano instrument.

The balance between sound and technique is nowhere more apparent than in Nyman's compositions for the violinist Alexander Balanescu. Having written a set of pieces for string duet in the early 1980s also featuring Elisabeth Perry, where extended ranges and techniques are explored (*2 Violins* and *I'll Stake My Cremona to a Jew's Trump*), Nyman's *Zoo Caprices* (1986) for solo violin takes the notion of virtuosity in his own music to hitherto uncharted territories. *Zoo Caprices* arranges into a suite of movements musical excerpts from the soundtrack to the film *A Zed and Two Noughts* (see Chapter 5). Nyman had to provide musical solutions to the task of applying multi-layered and multi-textured dimensions of the original to a solo instrument nevertheless capable of replicating subtle contrapuntal and harmonic motion. *Zoo Caprices* thus reproduces the film score's harmonic layers while at the same time imparting its own 'grain' on the original, as heard in the combination of raw edge and precision of Balanescu's recording of 'Time Lapse'.[6]

The fourth quartet takes the principles adopted by Nyman in his *Zoo Caprices* a step further, however. It uses as its basis another Balanescu-inspired work for solo violin, *Yamamoto Perpetuo* (1993). The title is an affectionate play on the name of the fashion designer who commissioned the work, Yohji Yamamoto, his name forming one half of 'moto perpetuo' – a musical technique where continuous rhythmic patterns are used to impart a sense of accumulated energy – of which the third movement is one such example. Unlike the material that furnished *Zoo Caprices*, *Yamamoto Perpetuo* was composed specifically for solo violin. Nyman is not working here according to the principle of reduction (ostensibly the case in *Zoo Caprices*) but rather with extension and expansion. The fourth quartet is thus a work beyond a work. By completing something that has in a sense already been completed, Nyman demonstrates that the musical text is never fixed down or inherently controlled.

The fourth deviates from the single movement scheme established in the first three quartets by being constructed according to twelve short movements, paralleling the epigrammatic quality of *Zoo Caprices*. This sectionalized approach is also used within certain movements, such as 2 and 4, where sharp contrasts in tempo and dynamics are employed. In other respects however, the third and fourth quartets have more in common with themselves than their precursors. Both use folk-like elements, which gives them a lyrical quality absent from the first two. The fourth quartet is also connected to the third via Nyman's soundtrack to the film *Carrington*. The main theme for the film was based on the third quartet, demonstrating an interesting example of second-generation borrowing of ideas. A separate theme from *Carrington*, called 'Virgin on the Roof', also finds its way into the fourth, but is not used in the third quartet. The two works are therefore indirectly related.

Pre-existing material may be viewed in this quartet in two ways, according to its 'internal' use of folk-like elements, and externally in terms of its relationship with *Yamamoto Perpetuo*. A legacy of Nyman's integration of folk ideas in his film *The Piano* (which enjoyed enormous popularity and success in Japan), Scottish elements are also brought to bear at various points in the quartet, but their presence is never made explicit. Indeed, Nyman incorporates a subtle allusion to the film's soundtrack in bar 11 of the eleventh movement, which plays on the opening chord

---

6   For a detailed analysis of *Zoo Caprices*, see Beirens 2005, pp. 361–8.

sequence of 'The Heart Asks Pleasure First' from *The Piano*. Other folk references are masked by string figuration, such as the theme first heard in the first violin at bar 24, which subsequently appears during the third and twelfth movements (bars 27 and 98 respectively).

The manner in which the quartet works within and around these self-imposed constraints is one of its most interesting features. Like a copy or reproduction, the quartet is indivisibly attached to *Yamamoto Perpetuo*, but it nevertheless marks out its own distinctive sonic image. This will be analysed by looking at its relationship with the precursor text according to three aspects: integration, opposition and development, all of which Nyman draws upon in his rewriting of the precursor piece.

First, the original source imprints itself upon the secondary source in the level of *integration* between the two. For example, the solo violin line will sometimes generate elements of melody and harmony in the other string parts. A melodic line may be extracted from a pre-existing figure, such as the line in the second violin and viola at bar 25 of the first movement, whose A-G-F-E descent may be heard as an augmented version of a folk fragment simultaneously heard in the first violin. At the beginning of the third and fifth movements the second violin, viola and cello essentially underpin, underline or amplify what is already stated in the solo violin. In the eleventh, additional parts merely sustain notes derived from the arpeggiated sequences of the solo violin. Sometimes integration between the two sources is achieved by means of generic convention, such as the division of melody and accompaniment assigned to the solo violin and three string parts respectively in the fourth movement. In this case, the three instruments add an accompaniment to a solo line that already in effect has one in its own part. A 'harmonic' realization of the tune is heard in the eighth movement, an idea also adopted at bar 19 of the eleventh.

Integration is *developed* further at other moments, often in the form of new material. In the seventh movement a new melody is introduced in the middle parts of the ensemble. At other times, the accompaniment is used to alter the sense of accent and metre of the original by providing its own commentary on the solo violin's part. For example, the delayed single-line effect created by the close imitation of string parts at bar 60 of the fourth movement would be impossible on a solo instrument without the use of a tape delay system. At other times, material stated during the preceding section is developed in the added parts despite the fact that the solo violin may be playing a different idea. For example, at bar 96 of the fourth movement the second violin continues to play a figure previously heard between bars 60–95, despite the fact that the solo violin has ostensibly moved into a different section. This reinforces a sense of continuity from one section to the next that would have been impossible to create in the original work.

At other times the relationship between the two texts is one of opposition. This sometimes results from the use of a kind of bi- or poly-textuality, layer placed upon existing layer. For example, at the very opening of the quartet a sense of opposition is established where violin 2 and viola play in octave unisons following a different rhythm and metre to the solo violin, almost as if two independent pieces have been superimposed, which, in a way, is true about its very 'composition'. The ninth movement reintroduces this texture but with an even greater sense of difference due to the almost improvisational quality of the internal parts (see Examples 7.9a and 7.9b). A similar scheme is established in the seventh movement where the two internal parts 'shadow' the original in such a way as to produce a very different image.

**Example 7.9a**   *String Quartet No. 4: First Movement (opening)*

**Example 7.9b**   *String Quartet No. 4: Ninth Movement (opening)*

Intertextual elements thus appear in a variety of different guises in Nyman's string quartets, from the use of multiple referential quotation, generic and formal appropriation to self-quotation, translation, re-composition and addition. Nyman's growing interest during the 1990s with self-quotation, reflected in the third and fourth quartets, stems from his reworking of past music in his own compositions from the 1980s. But whereas the latter works engage diachronically with issues of style and authenticity, encompassing almost three hundred years in the case of Purcell's music, Nyman's own reworkings do not indicate in quite the same way an involvement or engagement with history. The third quartet's folk origins may suggest 'the past', but the abstract nature of these quotations rarely brings them to the surface of his music. In the case of the fourth quartet, only through knowing *Yamamoto Perpetuo* does any meaningful exchange of signifiers emerge between one work and another.

These inter-referential processes thus serve to consolidate the primary position of the composer rather than to complexify it. By quoting himself, Nyman reinforces a sense of authorship and self-presence. In Bloomian terms (as seen in Korsyn's analysis in Chapter 4) this could be understood as a form of 'anxiety'; having been open about his music's referential nature, Nyman seeks to close himself off from such influences by drawing on his own work, but nevertheless maintains a link with it through the very act of self-reference. Quotations in the works from the 1990s – even when they are derived from an outside source – often create the opposite effect to those composed in the previous decade because they often serve to support what has already been composed by Nyman. A fascinating example of this is to be found in Nyman's soundtrack to Jane Campion's film *The Piano*. If the film's reception has often revolved around the question 'who is composing here?', then critical response has often been to discount the composer and look at the role of music in the film. As I hope to demonstrate in the following chapter, both text and author are two sides of the same coin in this instance, and it is the composer who eventually emerges on top in the soundtrack to *The Piano*.

# Chapter 8

# The Author Returns:
# Music at *The Piano*

A common tendency in previous writings on Nyman's music for Jane Campion's film *The Piano* (1993) has been to move away from the musical 'text' – the notes and sounds themselves – in order to examine the music's function in relation to extra-musical factors such as film narrative, plot and meaning. This approach may appear to be an entirely valid one for a medium where music often plays a subsidiary role, but in the case of *The Piano* the music–image relationship has arguably been completely reversed. Instead of hiding somewhere along the margins of one's semi-conscious comprehension of it, music lies at the very centre of the film's cinematic imagery. It redefines characters' actions and feelings and even appears to be redirecting the course and outcome of the film. It draws the viewer closer, encouraging a direct engagement with its sounds, structures and expression. In contrast to music's perfunctory role as mere accompaniment to images, in *The Piano* it marks out its own discursive territory within the film as a whole.

Part of the film's appeal has been attributed to the fact that meaning is left open and provisional by Campion's story. Margolis has supported this idea by saying, '[the] message of *The Piano* may be that it does not offer a message [but] that it makes available a variety of readings' (Margolis 2000, pp. 28–9). Gelder also points out that the film's metaphors are always 'open and ambiguous', citing Barcan and Fogarty's claim that *The Piano* sets out to validate 'a position of ambivalence' (Gelder 1999, p. 161). In much the same way, Gorbman's analysis of the musical content is conducted in order to underscore the film's overall ambiguity. She concludes by stating that the music is as inscrutable as the film itself; its referents eschew stability and doggedly '[shun] illustration' (Gorbman, in Margolis 2000, p. 53). Music is thus seen to support and strengthen the overall meaning of the film, contributing to an 'impression of depth, openness, and psychological ambiguity' (ibid., p. 53).

The high level of integration between sound and image in *The Piano* is a direct result of the piano-playing role assigned to the film's main character, Ada, although it could even be argued that the film's central character is not so much Ada herself but the piano (indeed all the film's characters are to some extent affected by it). A high proportion of the film's musical cues form part of the action and supply it with a strong diegetic aspect; that is, music played, heard and experienced by the characters themselves. Gorbman has argued that Nyman's music casts Ada's playing onto 'a sea of indeterminacy' (ibid., p. 57), but Ada's character (played by Holly Hunter) is to a large extent defined by her ability to render convincingly this diegetic music animate and authentic. In Hunter's powerful and haunting evocation of Ada's playing, music acquires a profound and almost palpable sense of existence. By placing added significance onto the role of music in the film, however, Gorbman's critique in fact ends up undermining its aesthetic value.

Both Gorbman and Margolis suggest that a clue to the film's meaning lies in its ability to articulate structures of authenticity. These are provided by the presence of the physical body – in this case the female body – and its willingness to engage with performance as a means of empowerment. Margolis's analysis concludes that *The Piano* 'enhances the *authenticity* of [Hunter's] performance as Ada' (ibid., p. 30). Hunter's playing is seen to be emphatically 'embodied', and this articulation of authenticity distinguishes *The Piano* from other film genres (ibid., p. 47). Other writers have also identified the music's 'performance' as a key to unlocking what Purkis describes as the film's 'authentic meaning' (Purkis 1995, p. 39). Purkis sees the film's music as being 'extended in scope precisely because it is the means to enter into a state of "performance"', by arguing that it is precisely through the act of performance that the body asserts itself in the film. The viewer not only witnesses the music's 'coming into being', then, but is also made acutely aware of the physical impulses that drive it forward, as if eavesdropping on the very act of creation (although Ada's apparent disinterest in musical notation may be viewed as a critique of women's creative disempowerment as composers during the nineteenth century). Drawing on the work of Richard Poirer, Purkis argues that the film is '*about* "performance" … in the moments of "performance" life *is* (my emphasis)' (ibid., p. 39). Poirer believed that literary criticism lost sight of the creative drives that bind together artistic endeavour, arguing for a reconsideration of the function of performance by posing the question, 'what must it have felt like to do this – not to mean anything, but to do it [?]' (Poirer 1971, p. 111).

Paradoxically, a focus on the music's actual representation as performance has consigned its existence as 'text' (and that of its composer–author) to the hermeneutical margins of discussion. Dai Griffiths' observation in a conference report on Purkis's paper, that 'Nyman [seems] to be a rather distant figure', before adding, 'perhaps [this] says something about Nyman's music', suggests that the music has only been a means to discuss wider issues relating to gender, sexuality, possession, empowerment, and so on (Griffiths 1995, p. 10). This neglect seems strikingly at odds with the commercial popularity of the film's soundtrack recording, which has sold over three millions copies (Russell and Young 2000, p. 95). But even the music's success has been dismissed by Gorbman as 'more likely … an example of the "halo effect" [in which] filmgoers purchase recordings of the soundtrack driven by their desire to reexperience [sic] the story through listening to the music' (quoted in Margolis 2000, p. 42). On the other hand, the music's ability to free itself from the confines of the film's narrative and context suggests that it possesses the means to exist in and of itself, as *music*. Indeed Campion approached Nyman to write the score precisely because she recognized in him 'the ability to create a self-contained independent world in music' (Russell and Young 2000, p. 100).

### Re: positioning *The Piano*

Any reading of *The Piano* needs to take into account the complex series of multiple author-as-composer positions engendered by the music's function. There are at least three possible composers at work in the film (four if one also considers Campion's editing and reordering of the soundtrack for the final cut). First, there is Ada as fictional composer and performer. Viewed voyeuristically by the other characters in the film, her playing is a means of closing herself off from the surrounding world. In this context, the music is her inner voice, or her 'mind's voice' (Purkis 1995, p. 39). Introspective to the point of solipsism, Ada is essentially '[playing] for herself' (ibid., p. 40).

Secondly, there is Holly Hunter who, as actress composer and performer, not only plays for the cinema audience but also to the camera, something she later recalled as a 'formidable, frightening task' (quoted in Campion 1993, p. 151). Nyman has noted that, in composing the music, he was writing as much for Hunter as for her character: 'I had to find music which she, Holly [Hunter], the pianist ... rather than [Ada], was emotionally attracted to, so that she could really be engaged by it' (Campion 1983, p. 150). Whereas Ada's world has been sealed off by the film's internal reality, the viewer is aware that Hunter is aware of her performances being watched. This intensification of 'being watched' is often emphasized in Campion's films, according to director of photography Stuart Dryburgh. He states that the camera is used deliberately as a means of 'directing the viewer's attention in a very intimate way' (ibid., p. 141). While these moments of illicit, self-conscious observation are constructed in such a way as to impart a sense of intense cinematic frisson, it is equally likely that the viewer, aware of the fact that Hunter's transformation into quasi-recitalist inevitably results in a momentary lapse of her character identity, similarly disengages himself or herself as furtive onlooker. In such double-edged contexts Ada's playing simultaneously proclaims a hermetically sealed interiority while Hunter openly displays a sense of emancipated creative prowess. Her performances appear boundless yet at the same time restrained, effusive yet strangely enigmatic. During such conflicting interpretative moments, *The Piano*'s 'authenticity' may be understood to be a mere foil for the film's openly self-reflexive qualities.

Finally, there is Nyman the composer. He exists in this context almost as a kind of Pythagorean figure, the acousmatic author hiding behind the soundtrack's cinematographic veil. Yet his position provides its own set of variables: Nyman's music is derived from a number of Scottish folk-tunes, quoted, adapted, arranged and recomposed by him, or occasionally from 'sampled ... segments repeated from Chopin's "Mazurkas"' (Russell and Young 2000, p. 100). In addition, the music's own folk genealogy is itself a pluralistic distillation of centuries of voices performing, adapting and transforming the repertory. If Hunter authenticates Ada's character through performance, then Nyman also reinterprets the nineteenth-century Scottish folk-song repertory as his own. Part of the film's complexity lies in separating out who is really playing, writing and composing here.

Purkis comments that any discussion of the film score's signification would in fact 'be limited to current musicological abilities: all that would be "new" would be the object to which the methods of investigation were being applied, i.e. film [in general], and this film in particular' points to a general reluctance to critically engage with the musical substance of the film (Purkis 1995, p. 40). The music's content – as separate from its function – is relegated to mere decoration, suppressing its ability to defer and differ meanings. According to such an approach, *music* is considered to be more important to the film than *the* music. While Nyman's music is often inextricably bound to the processes of its own performance in the film, it nevertheless marks out an autonomous space for itself. Thus it is necessary to return the ignored author–composer back into the film's discursive framework. Absent from the film's critical history so far has been Nyman's own creative input and how this may shed further light on our understanding of music's role in the film. *The Piano*'s deliberate play on such ambiguities can be read in terms of the replacing of modernist notions of Romantic authenticity with postmodern recreations of Neo-Romantic simulacra. Purkis already recognizes postmodern elements manifesting themselves at a general level in the film through 'the way that it plays with the canons of Hollywood popular cinema/costume drama and Modernist/art-films', and also, in particular, through performance's ability to 'actually transgress' (ibid., p. 39). This notion of stylistic transgression, described by Gelder as 'literary cinema', also allows Nyman the freedom to 'transgress' by reclaiming a 'lost' musical language and by freely interpreting the improvisational techniques and aural tradition of the nineteenth century.

**Approaching *The Piano***

As previously discussed in the chapter on the Greenaway soundtracks, prior to *The Piano*'s success, Nyman's music was designed to retain its independence while at the same time coexisting within a pre-determined structural or numerical plan. His scores for Greenaway's films were mostly composed without recourse to the film's images. The music was not designed to provide the mood of a scene, to intensify certain character's feelings towards one another or to accompany the action as it unfolded on screen, but rather as an element in and of itself. In an interview with Rivière, Nyman described the relationship: 'I write specific pieces of music for specific settings, not responses to images [...] the music I've written has never been for images: but in response to an idea, a methodology, a structure' (Rivière and Caux 1987, p. 78). Nyman has viewed film music's proper function as being equal to that of any other genre, including classical 'art' music. He once maintained that film music should retain a degree of autonomy and self-sufficiency and be easily adaptable to other contexts, including concert music: 'My attitude when composing film music is the same as when composing concert music, largely because I don't see any distinction between the two. My film music is played as concert music, and my concert music is equally used as film music' (Simon 1982, p. 232).

While Nyman's approach to film music resembled that of an 'art' music composer, he nevertheless developed in parallel with writing scores for Greenaway's films a more direct and accessible style. His first commercial undertaking, *Keep it up Downstairs* (1976), required that he composed pastiche Edwardian salon music and ragtime. He later worked with rock musician Sting on *Brimstone and Treacle* (1982) before breaking away from the multi-layered structural arrangements of Greenaway's work in the late 1980s in a series of intensely expressive scores for Patrice Laconte's films *Monsieur Hire* (1989) and *Le mari de la coiffeuse*. While the combination of art-house techniques with that of more mainstream cinematic approaches may suggest the kind of plurality associated with postmodernism, at the same time Nyman's belief that film music is central rather than incidental has its aesthetic origins in nineteenth-century formalism. Nyman has always acknowledged his debt to the European Art tradition but at the same time he has willingly appropriated techniques associated with more recent non-European forms, such as minimalism and rock. This, according to Jonathan Kramer, is a feature of certain European composers' interpretation of contemporary culture: 'steeped as they tend to be in dialectical thinking [they] enter into a struggle with postmodern cultural forces' (Kramer 2002, p. 22). Such tensions are actively brought to the surface in the score for *The Piano*, which is culturally, historically and geographically located between the old and new worlds of the West and the East. However, unlike postmodernism's depthless 'plurality of voices', Gergen has suggested that the Romantic self is characterized by a depth of passion, soul and creativity (ibid., p. 21). In *The Piano* Nyman reconfigures both elements: a Romantic sensibility is refracted through a postmodern lens. The old and new coexist.

Before analysing the soundtrack's function and meaning it is first necessary to chart briefly the genesis of the music's formation. Nyman initially spent some time working through the script with Campion, highlighting moments where music would be required (Russell and Young 2000, p. 100). He then arranged to meet Hunter in New York during pre-production in order 'to establish not only a repertoire of music for the film, but a repertoire of piano music that would have been Ada's repertoire as a pianist, almost as if she had been the composer of it' (Campion 1993, p. 150). The solo piano music was therefore composed first, 'in the autumn of 1991' with the aid of Campion's script (Nyman 1994, p. 5). This was then used by Campion as a temp track for editing various scenes (Russell and Young 2000, p. 100). The orchestral music followed during the summer of 1992 when Nyman was probably working from the film's rough cut. While this suggests a procedure where the piano music 'fed into' the orchestral cues, it is more likely that Nyman was constantly drawing from a wider pool of ideas during both stages of writing, partly using the Scottish folk material at his disposal and partly generating music from scratch. A study of the order of pieces in the score manuscript suggests that Nyman either intended the musical cues to be used in a different sequence to those eventually decided upon by Campion, or that he deliberately set out to compose the music in a non-sequential manner. The music accompanying the opening credits, 'To the Edge of the Earth', appears for example

Table 8.1    The music of *The Piano*: order, inventory and reference

| CD track listing | Order in film (scene no.) | Order in full score | Folk and classical references | Function |
|---|---|---|---|---|
| 1. 'To the Edge of the Earth' | 1 | pp. 22–4 (#8) | | Non-diegetic |
| 2. 'Big My Secret' | 2, 54, 55, 91 | | 'Bonnie Jean' | Diegetic |
| 3. 'A Wild and Distant Shore' | | pp. 25–32 (#9) | End quotes 'The Heart Asks Pleasure First' | Non-diegetic |
| 4. 'The Heart Asks Pleasure First' | 12, 29 (suite version with 'coda'), 62, 116 | | 'Gloomy Winter's Noo Awa' | Diegetic |
| 5. 'Here to There' | 16, 84 | pp. 5–8 (#2) | 'Gloomy Winter's Noo Awa' (2nd half) | Non-diegetic |
| 6. 'The Promise' | 17, 24, 30, 151 | pp. 1–4 (#1) | 'Gloomy Winter's Noo Awa' | Quasi-diegetic |
| 7. 'A Bed of Ferns' | 43, 87 | p. 9 (#3a) | | Non-diegetic |
| 8. 'The Fling' | 50, 149 | | 'Flowers o' the Forest' | Diegetic |
| 9. 'The Scent of Love' | | p. 33 (#10, end only) | 'Bonnie Jean' | Quasi-diegetic |
| 10. 'Deep into the Forest' | 97 | pp. 19–22 (second part) | 'Gloomy Winter's Noo Awa' | Quasi-diegetic |

at the midpoint of Nyman's score. Other pieces, such as 'Dreams of a Journey', accompanying the end credits, do appear to have been written in sequential order.

Table 8.1 organizes the music according to the track name and listing on the original CD recording (Virgin CDVE 919). This order is (with one or two exceptions) consistent with each musical cue's first appearance, as can be gleaned from following the numerical sequence of scenes taken from Campion's published script of the film (1, 2, 12, 16, 17 and so on).[1] Two piano pieces, 'The Attraction of the Pedalling

---

1  A later CD release (CDVEX 919) also includes an edit attaching 'The Heart Asks Pleasure First' to 'The Promise' at the end of the recording.

**Table 8.1**  *concluded*

| CD track listing | Order in film (scene no.) | Order in full score | Folk and classical references | Function |
|---|---|---|---|---|
| 11. 'The Mood that Passes Through You' | 75, 105 | | | Diegetic |
| 12. 'Lost and Found' | 137 | pp. 9–10 (#3b) | | Non-diegetic |
| 13. 'The Embrace' | 90 | pp. 34–5 (#11) | 'Bonnie Jean' | Non-diegetic |
| 14. 'Little Impulse' | 110, 112 | pp. 11–14 (#4) | See also 'The Mood That Passes Through You' | Quasi-diegetic |
| 15. 'The Sacrifice' | | | 'Gloomy Winter's Noo Awa' | Diegetic |
| 16. 'I Clipped Your Wing' | 119, 131 | pp. 35–40 (#12) | | Non-diegetic |
| 17. 'The Wounded' | | p. 15 (#5) | | Non-diegetic |
| 18. 'All Imperfect Things' | 146 | pp. 16–17 (#6) | | Non-diegetic |
| 19. 'Dreams of a Journey' | 151 | pp. 40–47 | 'Flowers o' the Forest' | Non-diegetic |
| X. 'The Attraction of the Pedalling Ankle' | 51, 57, 88 | | Chopin *Mazurka* op. 7/i | Diegetic |
| Y. 'Deep Sleep Playing' | 100 | | | Diegetic |

Ankle' and 'Deep Sleep Playing', appear in the soundtrack but are not included on the CD. A list of folk and classical references in the table also indicates that up to half the score's cues refer to, or borrow from, pre-existing sources. The nature of these references and their diegetic or non-diegetic function is of particular significance in any analysis of the music's function in the film.

**Inside** *The Piano*

First, a clear and important distinction should be made between the function of the solo piano pieces and Nyman's orchestral score. The former provides the film with an autonomous 'diegetic' dimension – music that speaks to the characters themselves. The latter occupies a more illustrative role, signifying the weather-beaten landscape and the Maori inhabitants' relationship to their environment and the 'natural order' of things. These non-diegetic cues are orchestrated for a relatively homogeneous combination of string orchestra and saxophones, imparting a softer and less percussive attack than occasionally utilized on the piano. Both elements are not however mutually exclusive. Other cues function in the film in order to bridge the gap between them. These form a kind of halfway house between the two elements, whose function may be described as partly- or quasi-diegetic. They combine both piano and orchestra and reflect the music's dual role at both conscious and subconscious levels. In these cues music 'speaks' and thinks on behalf of the film generally and of Ada in particular. As Nyman has pointed out, 'the piano music is a crucial part not only of the film's soundworld but of the expression of Ada's character' (Russell and Young 2000, p. 100). This three-layered, or tri-diegetic arrangement, allows the piano to shift constantly between the film's foreground (diegetic) or background (non-diegetic) narrative. The disposition of these three musical functions across the film's entire span is illustrated in Table 8.2 and described below.

Diegetic and non-diegetic cues punctuate the opening two scenes, rather like the statement of two thematic subject ideas in a nineteenth-century piano sonata. At scene 17 the piano is heard for the first time in a quasi-diegetic context, accompanied by string orchestra. During the course of the following set of cues, this quasi-diegetic element gradually asserts itself while simultaneously establishing the piano within the general fabric of the soundtrack (the piano having already firmly established itself as an image in the film's cinematography from the very opening scene). Relatively even distributions of diegetic, non-diegetic and quasi-diegetic cues are maintained during this introductory section, until the point at which the piano is delivered to Baines's hut in scene 43. During scenes 50–75, the point at which Baines strikes a bargain with Ada allowing him to 'do things' while she plays in return for her piano, to the moment when they both lie naked together on Baines's bed, the music becomes entirely diegetic. This places the piano's image and sound at the very centre of the film's actions. Non-diegetic music is eventually heard again in scene 84, accompanying Baines's decision to return the piano to Ada when their increasingly sexual relationship threatens to spiral out of control.

From thereon in to the end of the film, the non-diegetic element appears to undermine and challenge the piano's supremacy. It even signals the instrument's ultimate downfall even though it accompanies Ada and Baines's first true 'embrace' (scene 90). This is a significant moment because it indicates that Ada has relinquished her love of the piano for her passion towards Baines. Her relationship with Baines is passive, or in his case voyeuristic, when she plays the piano. At

**Table 8.2  Scene categorization in *The Piano* according to musical function**

Introduction

| 1 | 2 | 12 | 16 | 17 | 24 | 29 | 30 | 43 |
|---|---|----|----|----|----|----|----|----|

Exposition of the diegetic element

| 50 | 51 | 54 | 55 | 58 | 61 | 62 | 75 | 84 | 87 | 88 | 90 | 91 |
|----|----|----|----|----|----|----|----|----|----|----|----|----|

Conflict between diegetic and quasi-diegetic elements

| 97 | 100 | 105 | 110 | 112 | 116 |
|----|-----|-----|-----|-----|-----|

Resolution of the non-diegetic element

| 119 | 131 | 137 | 146 | 149 | 151 |
|-----|-----|-----|-----|-----|-----|

Key:

| Diegetic | |
|----------|--|
| Non-diegetic | |
| Quasi-diegetic | |

scene 91, however, the piano diegetically accompanies their love scene 'off screen', signalling an inherent crisis in their affair (Ada has already been married to Stuart 'by arrangement' at the beginning of the film). The piano is also heard on its own at scene 100, when Stewart incarcerates Ada in their home, in an attempt to prevent her from seeing Baines. At this point the 'conflict' between diegetic and non-diegetic elements is at its greatest. In sonata form terms, this could be seen as the equivalent of a kind of development section. Diegetic and quasi-diegetic elements reassert themselves during scenes 105–16 when Baines plans to leave the area and Ada seeks solace away from Stuart's inept advances by absorbing herself in a series of highly individualized piano extemporizations. Her dark improvisations prompt Aunt Morag to observe that she 'does not play the piano as we do ... she is a strange creature and her playing is strange, like a mood that passes through you. You cannot teach that … one may like to learn, but that could not be taught' (Campion 1993, pp. 91–2).

The emotional intensity of the previous sequence of diegetic cues has now given way to a kind of obsessive brooding culminating in Stewart's callous removal of Ada's finger. In stark contrast to Baines's earlier obsessive behaviour towards her, Ada's love is recognized by the other characters as a form of illness or madness, remedied only through censure and punishment. Stewart already casts doubt over her sanity soon after she arrives, wondering whether 'she's not brain-affected' (ibid., p. 39). Her later bouts of somnambulism confirm his thoughts. In her portrayal of Ada, Campion is rehearsing a standard theme in eighteenth-century women's fiction, expressed by Kaup when she said that 'nineteenth-century romance "ends", for women, in either marriage or death, which would then have to be read as the heroine's success or failure' (Kaup 1993, p. 81).

Whether in fact Ada chooses marriage or death becomes significant in determining the film's ambiguous resolution. Her amputated finger signals both a physical and symbolic loss. Deprived of her only means of self-expression, Ada falls silent. From this point on until the very last set of cues Nyman's music is entirely non-diegetic. Thus we are not granted the proportional and aesthetic reassurance of any sonata form-style recapitulation, but instead the uncertain harmonic meanderings of 'I Clipped Your Wing'. When the piano does eventually return, it revisits not the erotically charged music enveloping Ada and Baines's trysts but rather a mechanically reproduced technical exercise ('The Fling'). If the amputation scene triggers a kind of terrible realization – Ada's peripeteia, if you will – her covered face, dark clothing and detached presence in the concluding 'Nelson' scene suggests that her body does indeed lie, as quoted by Ada's voiceover from Thomas Hood's sonnet 'Silence' at the very end of the film, 'under the deep, deep sea' (Campion 1993, p. 123).

While the music's 'plot' runs parallel with the film's action it is also seen to map out its own autonomous course, one in which musical ideas live out their own narrative desires and drives. To this end Nyman incorporates levels of thematic integration involving Scottish folk material sourced for the score. This may take on an explicit reference, as in 'Silver-fingered Fling's' use of the melody 'The Flowers o' the Forest'. In this example (taken from Nyman's published suite of pieces for the film) the melody is transformed through successive applications of rhythmic augmentation and diminution, creating a grid-like structure based on statement and elaboration. The first section (not used in the film) incorporates an augmented version of the original melody (Ex. 8.1a; the pitch content of the original folk melody has been included above the piano part here, and in Examples 8.1b, 8.2 and 8.3). A second section (simply called 'The Fling' on the CD soundtrack) transforms the melody by means of rhythmic diminution into a series of repeated pentatonic and modal patterns (a similar technique to that used in 'Here to There'). Each one-bar segment of the original melody is systematically 'deconstructed' in order to yield another variation, a technique commonly associated with American minimalist music and previously encountered in *Drowning by Numbers* (1988) (Ex. 8.1b). Unlike the

**Example 8.1a**    The Piano: *'Silver-fingered Fling'*

**Example 8.1b**    The Piano: *'The Fling'*

American minimalists, however, Nyman's permutational processes are firmly rooted in the European folk-art tradition. He appropriates for his own European musical ends an American technique, creating an unorthodox synthesis which parallels the film's paradoxical world.

At the opposite end of the intertextual spectrum, Nyman utilizes a complex paraphrasing technique where a folk melody is subtly embedded within an otherwise lush romantic texture. This occurs in 'Big My Secret', which uses the Scottish tune 'Bonnie Jean'. Unlike 'The Fling', where the melody is clearly stated, 'Bonnie Jean' is initially sandwiched between a freely flowing two-part texture and remains for the most part cleverly disguised (see Ex. 8.2).

From around the midway point the folk melody appears in the top part (as if exchanged between the two embracing bodies) but is still obscured by the continuous use of free, elaborate and decorative foreground material. Nyman also hides the melody through octave displacement, possibly in order to reflect the wide span of

**Example 8.2**    The Piano: 'Bonnie Jean' paraphrase in 'Big My Secret'

the original tune. In keeping with Ada's characterization in the film, the effect is of a performer freely extemporizing over a given melody, 'as if she had been the composer of it' (Nyman, quoted in Campion 1993, p. 150). The desired effect, however, has been carefully controlled, organized and composed out of the music. In much the same way that Campion writes into the film's script a sense of impulsiveness and spontaneity through carefully controlled cinematic techniques, Nyman does the same in his music. In the case of 'Big My Secret' he achieves this by means of various melodic and rhythmic transformations of the original tune, with rhythmic augmentation again the most prevalent technique. Stretching the original material out in this way results in the transformation of the original 16-bar melody into an extended 32-bar piece lasting almost three minutes. There are parallels here with certain fifteenth- and sixteenth-century paraphrasing techniques of using borrowed melodies in sacred polyphonic works (see Sparks 1975). In addition to pitch structure, other features of the original tune have also been retained in 'Big My Secret'. Caesuras and phrase endings, including the two resolute cadences in D major, reflect the melodic structure of the original tune. Elsewhere however, Nyman consciously avoids repeating the same harmonic or rhythmic material. If anything, he varies as much as possible certain non-pitched aspects within the self-imposed limitations of the folk melody in order to create a sense of moment-to-moment composition and studied improvisation. During the melody's second cycle, then, there is an attempt to further intensify the arched melodic line through extended harmonies of added minor ninths and a faster-flowing rhythmic movement creating a sense of suspended animation.

**Example 8.3**    The Piano*: 'Gloomy Winter's Noo Awa' from 'The Heart Asks Pleasure First' (opening)*

'The Heart Asks Pleasure First', described by Gorbman as 'Ada's theme' (in Margolis 2000, p. 51), combines elements of both explicit and implicit paraphrasing techniques.[2] The melody, 'Gloomy Winter's Noo Awa', is stated against a rapidly undulating accompaniment, possibly in order to represent the elemental forces of nature (see Ex. 8.3).

In contrast to 'Big My Secret', the accompaniment here merely draws the melody to the surface rather than obscuring it. A sense of impulsive spontaneity is created in 'The Heart Asks Pleasure First' through Nyman's melodic and periodic reconstruction of the original tune. He extends the sixteen-bar melody by way of an additional beat into a seventeen-beat phrase and also shifts in the last clause of the musical phrase away from a predominantly Aeolian sound to the diatonic minor. In fact the opening eight-beat introduction may have been derived from the final measures of a musical cue never used in the film by Campion called 'A Wild and Distant a Shore', which suggests again that non-diegetic music could also furnish material for diegetic elements, or *vice versa*. Nyman's musical introduction to the folk material was also a way of 'distancing' Ada's theme by constantly interrupting it with additional refrains. Nevertheless, the order of the 'Gloomy Winter's Noo Awa' melody is also adhered to in Nyman's rearrangement of it, though harmonically his shift to the relative major (C major) at bar 11 is arguably more forceful than in the original. Simple song-like structures are thus transformed into sublime, sweeping

---

2   The title of this track is an allusion to an Emily Dickinson poem of the same name.

statements, as if emerging fully formed from the wellspring of a hidden, suppressed and censured nineteenth-century female piano repertory.[3]

## Outside *The Piano*

In mastering the piano, Ada masters one of the most patriarchal of all instruments. A vehicle for profound self-expression and a symbol of grandeur, might, strength and breadth, the piano signifies 'maleness' in every sense. Even Baines treats it as a kind of totemic symbol. The piano became a nineteenth-century contrivance and was also a classic Victorian status symbol. Its solid steel frame and coil strings, encased in wood, allowed it to look natural and organic. According to Carolyn Jones, '[despite] the piano's highly technological manufacture, it presents a body that conceals a metallic, mechanical interior in a sheath of organic wood and ivory (an android rather than a cyborg). Modest Victorians saw the piano's body in such anthropomorphic terms, clothing its naked legs in decent draperies' (Jones 1993, p. 631). Ada herself also arrives in the New World as the intended status symbol of Stewart. The piano's arrival in the New World is in itself a form of colonial intrusion to which Ada tacitly subscribes through playing. Yet its symbolic power is not recognized or grasped by its inheritors, who merely ascribe value to objects according to their worth, and this includes Ada herself. For them it is a question of whether these objects are able to be possessed, exchanged or exploited. Ada's playing does not conform to the crude socio-economic formula inscribed upon everything by the settlers. Assumed to be of no objective worth for having been 'bought' by her husband, Ada creates a space for the renegotiation of her own self – she emancipates herself from Stewart's ownership before succeeding in harnessing Baines's untamed physicality.

Likewise, the piano is deemed to possess little value in the New World's colonial market place. As if it had been washed upon the shore, the piano wavers uncertainly between nature and culture. Ada is also represented as being highly responsive to the forces of nature, a view shared by Aunt Morag when she compares her to 'a pet' because she cannot speak, and later describes her as a 'strange creature' (Campion 1993, p. 92). If Ada is closer to nature, she also appears to belong outside her own place and time. She appears to possess an almost late-twentieth-century sensibility. Likewise the cultural meaning of 'civilization' is also inverted in order to reflect the noble, peaceful and even idyllic existence of the indigenous Maori people, representing, according to Gelder, 'the "unfettered" unconscious of a repressed civilized world' (Gelder 1999, p. 159). Ada's articulation of the old and new, of tradition and innovation through a fusion of a highly subjective folk-vernacular interpretation with the rhapsodic spirit of romanticism, parallels the film's overall concept and design. The Romantic Movement sought to combine a

---

3   Used by the Lloyds/TSB bank in promotional adverts during 2003, 'The Heart Asks Pleasure First' has since been imitated by other jingles, such as the online car insurers morethan.com in 2005.

spirit of unrestrained individualism, balanced and ordered by previously acquired knowledge. It thus allowed full vent to music's power to 'express the inexpressible'. During the mid-nineteenth century, under the impact of Schopenhauer's philosophy, music was accorded an unprecedented high status among the arts. Schopenhauer identified music as being the closest embodiment of his concept of the 'will'. He described the 'will' as the essence that belonged in everything, and considered music to be the ultimate expression of it. Music was therefore considered by Schopenhauer to be 'far more powerful and [to] penetrate far more deeply than that of the other arts; for they communicate only shadows, whereas [music] communicates the essence' (quoted in le Huray and Day 1988, p. 219). In *The Piano* Ada becomes the physical embodiment of Schopenhauer's 'will' that has been combined with a subconscious, pre-Oedipal impulse (Gelder 1999, p. 165). When, according to Stuart, she does 'speak', it is to say 'I am [afraid] of my *will*, of what it might do, it is so strange and strong' (Campion 1993, p. 115). Then later, having risen to the surface of the sea, she declares ambiguously, 'my *will* has chosen life!?' (ibid., p. 121).

Ada carries within her traces of the Old World order, her folk inheritance, but she deliberately misreads (or mishears) the tradition, preferring instead to compose spontaneously. Her performances on the piano are therefore not slavish recreations or resuscitated imitations of 'dead' arrangements but are rather alive and re-lived at every moment of their re-composition. She starts off as the self-consumed, autonomous Romantic artist, but gradually relinquishes her pursuit of pure aesthetic objectives for economic exchange and objective value. As Gelder puts it, Ada has to 'negotiate her pleasure, to see pleasure-as-excess (improvisation, autonomy) always in a dialectical relationship with work-as-restraint' (Gelder 1999, p. 166). Therein lies the ultimate paradox of the film. In presenting Ada and her music as victims of the colonial market place, Campion tacitly inscribes her own, and Nyman's, relationship to the work. *The Piano*'s literary qualities stem from Campion's own self-image as the autonomous auteur. Like Ada, she strives in her work for balance between self-expression and commercialism, playing the cinematic conventions in order to privilege the former. Likewise the music forms its own autonomous, neo-romantic space – the music of the mind – while on the surface implying commercialism and accessibility. The music's neo-romanticism inscribes its own textual and intertextual dimensions. A vitality and strength of purpose witnessed in Ada's acts of performance have already been written into the notes themselves, and its autonomy is reinforced through the 'composing out' of diegetic, non-diegetic and quasi-diegetic functions in the film.

Nyman's music thus operates both within and outside *The Piano*, hence the reason why it has become such a success as 'absolute' music and been adapted to a variety of different instrumental forces and contexts. Despite working intertextually on a variety of levels through its reference to a lost, gender-related music of the past and its reconstruction of a found, folk-related tradition, Nyman's soundtrack stands alone in his oeuvre, almost as if it had suddenly sprung from nowhere. Generic patterns do appear from earlier works, as shown in Chapter 4, but they are absorbed into the work's closed-off soundworld. *The Piano*'s strength no doubt lies in its ability to evoke this sense of musical self-sufficiency. Other works reaffirm their own independence in a more paradoxical fashion, however, by drawing on a multiplicity of inter-referential sources. While such procedures are seen to operate in the third and fourth string quartets, its application on a much larger scale occurs in Nyman's opera *Facing Goya*. Here the function and position of self-quotation will be studied across the architectural sweep of the opera in order to examine its relationship to the opera's dramatic subject matter and overall meaning.

# Chapter 9

# Gene Sequences and Musical Sequences: *Facing Goya*

The multifaceted natures of Nyman's intertextual method has enabled him to travel across chronological time-scales and move between musical genres. A musical phrase or harmonic progression used in a more recent work may well have its origins in another piece written many years earlier. This can cause problems in providing, for example, a conventional account of stylistic development. The interchangeability of ideas suggests that Nyman's musical language was fully formed early on and that his task has been to realize in various ways its harmonic, rhythmic and melodic potentialities. It is nevertheless possible to talk of a shift in emphasis from one period to the next. The early years are characterized by small-scale single-event compositions. Nyman has described them as 'very straightforward, self-explanatory systems pieces ... they only do one thing: you set off an explosion and watch it explode' (Ellis 1997). A broadening of expressive range during the middle period led to a greater emphasis on lyricism. The later period has brought together both elements within the context of much larger musical structures. While acts of self-quotation sometimes seamlessly merge into a new work, obscuring connections with past origins, on other occasions entire blocks are fitted into a pre-determined scheme or the scheme fitted around a pre-existing block. These issues inform the musical and artistic design of one of Nyman's most substantial works to date, his four-act opera *Facing Goya* (2000).

## Pretexts

Described by Worby as 'a classic example of intertextuality' (Worby, in Nyman 2002), *Facing Goya*'s musical, textual and dramaturgical genealogy is multifarious and complex. Premiered in August 2000 in Santiago de Compostela, Spain, the first version was extensively revised for its second 'premiere' in Karlsruhe, Germany, in October 2002. The 'Santiago' version in fact shares more in common with an opera completed soon after *The Man who Mistook his Wife for a Hat*, called *Vital Statistics*, than the 'Karlsruhe' version.[1] *Vital Statistics* was performed in June

---

[1] In Act 1, for example, both the 'Santiago' and 'Karlsruhe' versions have a craniometrist and assistant sing the lines 'Ignore Broca at your peril / And mankind will go to the devil', but in the former version it is preceded and followed by a section dealing with body measurements and proportions taken from *Vital Statistics*.

1987 at the Donmar Warehouse, London. Dean's unflattering description of it as a 'relentlessly loud ... orgy of ostinatos discharged with more aggression than Philip Glass' indicates that *Vital Statistics* was not very favourably received by some, and was soon withdrawn by Nyman (Dean 1987, p. 449). In this sense the genealogy of the opera is very different to *The Man who Mistook his Wife for a Hat*, which is an essentially self-contained work, its only previous precursor reference being Schumann.

The subject matter of *Vital Statistics* – how one's mental ability and character is judged according to physical features and appearances – still fascinated Nyman however. He has referred to this idea as 'body-image', and it plays a central role in *The Man who Mistook his Wife for a Hat* where Dr P substitutes musical images for physical ones in order to map out and structure his everyday movements and activities (eating, washing, dressing, and so on).[2] This concept becomes more apparent in *Facing Goya*, when remarks, such as the following from Leonardo da Vinci, are used: 'the face shows the indications of the nature of men, their vices and temperaments' (da Vinci, in Baxandall 1974, p. 59).

In fact, Nyman first set da Vinci's words in 1985 when he collaborated with painter Paul Richards on a music/art video production called *The Kiss* for Channel 4. Conceived as an 'operatic duet' between a male and female singer, the texts used by Nyman for this work consist mainly of aesthetic observations by fifteenth-century Italian painters taken from Michael Baxandall's *Painting and Experience in Fifteenth Century Italy*. Nyman went through Baxandall's exegesis on the 'social history of pictorial style', selecting appropriate passages of text in order to 'deliberately and ironically ... give the erroneous impression that I believed that the visual images that are frequently combined with my music are stronger than the musical images' (Nyman 1988a). A quote from Michel da Carcano which acts as a kind of refrain in *The Kiss* does not appear in either opera: '[images] were introduced because many people cannot retain in their memories what they hear, but they do remember if they see images.' Other quotes from Baxandall's book, such as Piero della Francesca's '[by] measurement we mean profiles and contours put proportionally in their proper places', appear towards the beginning of Act 1 of the opera but are not included in *The Kiss* (ibid., p. 141).

Having sourced a series of texts from early Renaissance art, Nyman then read Stephen J. Gould's book *The Mismeasure of Man* (1981). Gould examines the way in which medical science from the late eighteenth century manipulated, misrepresented and distorted scientific – specifically numerical – facts in order to reinforce an ideology of class, race, gender, intelligence and even criminality. During the nineteenth century craniometrists such as Paul Broca (1824–80) measured the sizes of skulls in order to 'determine the relative position of races in the human series', selectively editing data in order to secure the place of the white male at the top end of the evolutionary scale (Topinard, in Gould 1981, p. 86). Broca's selectively interpreted data establishing

---

2  See Chapter 7.

the pre-eminent status of the white male at the top end of a hierarchical evolutionary ladder – with Negroes, Hottentots, Eskimos, Australian aborigines and other non-European races laying underneath – led to Francis Galton's research into hereditary intelligence, and his subsequent coining of the term 'eugenics' in 1883. Through his research, Galton advocated the breeding selection of people according to their looks and ancestral background, which subsequently led to the idea being placed into chilling practice by the Nazis during the Second World War in order to construct a pure Aryan race.

Other examples are based on the notion of biological essentialism, such as Cesare Lambroso's concept of innate criminality and the 'natural born killer', painter Peter Camper's measurement of facial angles, and Lavater's claim that '[facial] profiles reveal our innermost nature'. All these find their way into *Vital Statistics*'s subject matter. But therein possibly lies the work's main problem. Some might argue that discussions about cranial measurements do not necessarily provide the most appealing or attractive ingredients for a dramatic scenario.

To be sure, Nyman's operatic 'plots' in general possess a strong cerebral quality that eschews the kind of dramatic conflict and resolution favoured in traditional stage works. He has described *Facing Goya* as 'an opera of ideas', where the drama takes place as much inside the characters' minds as in the physical actions on stage. The main difference between *Facing Goya* and its previous incarnation lies of course in the inclusion of Goya, the Spanish artist (1746–1828). In 1998 Nyman read an article by Robert Graham, who hypothesized over the strange circumstances surrounding the disappearance of Goya's skull after his skeletal remains were exhumed from the cemetery at La Chartreuse, Bordeaux sixty years after his death (Graham 1998). The notion that Goya may have instructed someone to remove and hide his skull so that it could not be measured or used in experiments for the purposes of calculating the level of his intelligence or the source of his artistic genius was not entirely implausible in an age when Broca and other craniometrists were conducting research in this area. From these sources Nyman and librettist Victoria Hardie (who had also provided the libretto for *Vital Statistics*) produced a plot based around a hypothetical journey through two hundred years of history featuring Goya's missing skull.

## Synopsis

Goya the artist does not emerge in any physical sense until the final act of the opera, but his presence is felt throughout its two-hour span. In Act 1 an art banker, who represents a type rather than a character, and moves through each historical period in the opera, is passionate about Goya's work and this takes her on a quest to recover his missing skull. She is led to a nineteenth-century craniometry lab where a heated debate takes place between some craniometrists. They try to decide whether or not the measurement of skulls and weighing of brains can tell them anything about character, personality and feelings. When one craniometrist asks for the measurements of his hat, to prove that 'the length and width of [the] skull decides whether [a person's] good or bad, sane or mad, clever or dull, white or black, master or slave' an assistant counters, quoting da Vinci again, that 'talking about the unmeasurable is what makes a person so great and pleasurable'. Goya assumes a more central position during these exchanges when at one point an apparition of him makes a fleeting appearance. Throughout the course of the opera Goya's paintings are projected onto a screen, including in Act 1 his etching 'Dogs Drowning in Sand', the famous 'Nude Maja', a self-portrait and the symbol of the 'One Eye'. The audience is informed towards the end of Act 1 that Goya's skull is amongst those being measured. His facial profile 'snub nose, sunken eyes and chubby cheeks' will provide sufficient evidence that he is a 'degenerate' human. During the final scene a craniometrist attempts to smash Goya's skull with a hammer, but to her horror it does not crack.

Goya's skull therefore survives into Act 2 and to the next phase in history: 1930s Germany. Here, art in general and Goya's paintings in particular become the subject of arguments between art critics on the nature of 'degenerate art'. In national socialist Germany eugenicist art critics were employed to censor so-called 'subversive' art, and the notion of the ideal body – a combination of Nordic beauty and the Classical Greek figure – was advocated as part of the Aryan ideal. Artists whose work did not conform to this view were labelled 'degenerate' and their paintings were often censored and destroyed. These included Rembrandt, Rodin and Otto Dix, while Rubens, Arno Breker and others were praised for their ability to capture 'ideal types' rather than individuals. Nineteenth-century scientific practice, which had explored the shape and measurement of the human mind and body, was now – in the hands of doctors, painters, architects and art critics such as Max Nordau and Paul Schultze-Naumburg – being used to advocate theories of selection, racism and ultimately the Final Solution. Political, scientific and ideological expediency prevailed over moral issues or artistic judgments. Therefore at the end of Act 2, a bonfire containing examples of degenerate art is set alight and Goya's skull is also thrown into the burning pyre. At this point the art banker reflects ruefully on the fact that, in his art, Goya had anticipated these atrocities by 'seeing' Hitler before Hitler saw Goya.

Acts 3 and 4 are set in the twenty-first century, separated only by a few weeks. The scene is now a laboratory belonging to a commercial Bio-Tech company. The art banker has in the meantime managed to rescue Goya's skull from the flames of the bonfire and finds herself in the company of a microbiologist, the chief executive of the company, a doctor and an academic. She has obtained the rights on Goya's DNA patent, which she has extracted from the remains of his skull. Having been distrustful of the craniometrists' and eugenic art critics' motives in Acts 1 and 2, the art banker now falls prey to the allure of personal profit by selling Goya's patent to the company. The chief executive extols the healthy virtues and advantages of genetic mutation, arguing, 'the patent on Goya's talent gene will be a document for teaching'. The genetic fingerprint of each individual has now replaced profiles and measurements in determining who is 'good or bad, sad or mad, or if they live or die'. We are made to believe that such advances will help to anticipate and identify conditions such as Usher's Syndrome, which may have caused Goya to go deaf. An academic counters by claiming, 'those who control the gene control the next page in history [by creating] a genetic underclass'. The art banker is nevertheless excited by the prospect of meeting Goya face-to-face. Tempted by financial profit, she hands over the epindorph phial containing Goya's DNA to the chief executive. At this point a dark figure looms in the background and Goya finally makes his entrance.

The final act begins with the art banker rueing her decision to sell Goya's gene patent, conceding that she had 'lost Goya to science, because my imagination was deserted by reason'. She is still obsessed with Goya, however, and accedes to his demands to have his DNA patent returned when he appears before her, fully cloned. Goya then confronts the chief executive about his actions. A microbiologist counters by claiming, as the craniometrist had done in Act 1, 'Scientists are the artists now … [transforming] evolution into works of art'. Goya responds by stating, 'a clone is only a shadow of invention'. The art banker finally admits to 'only [understanding] money', although she loves art. Goya tells her that she has sold her own soul (and his, too) for pure profit. In a bid to turn back the clock she asks Goya to smash his own skull, but he cannot bring himself to do it. Ironically, he is only 'human' after all. Goya's skull is taken away from him by the art banker and smashed onto the floor. The opera ends poignantly with Goya alone on his hands and knees, desperately trying to put the pieces of his own skull back together again.

**Primary intertexts**

The opera is divided into four acts, each act sub-divided into a series of arias or numbers, and each number divided into a series of smaller sections. Between six and nine 'numbers' appear within each act and each number consists of around the same number of sections, sometimes even more. Table 9.1 partly reproduces the sectionalized nature of the opera, but it is worth noting that only intertextual and inter-relational features have been identified here, while new material has been omitted. The last number of Act 2 provides an initial indication of the complex nature of each number, for example, where at least eleven sections have been discerned in this scene.

Nyman has said that 'if *Facing Goya* is directly a "grand opera" reincarnation of *Vital Statistics*' then it is 'marginally a "continuation" of *The Kiss*' (Nyman 2002). *Facing Goya* is literally an extension and development of *Vital Statistics*, rather than a straightforward case of 'pillaging' material. In the same way that the intellectual and conceptual idea accumulated from *The Kiss* and *Vital Statistics*, so did the music. Most of the opera's inter-referential material has been derived from these two primary sources, although additional musical or extra-musical references do appear. Some themes are transplanted from *The Kiss* to *Facing Goya* via *Vital Statistics* while others are taken directly from *Vital Statistics*.

**Table 9.1   The disposition of intertextual material in *Facing Goya***

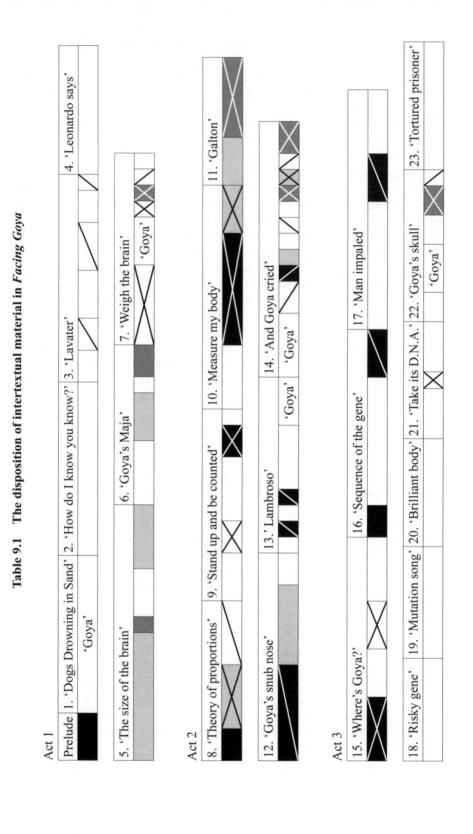

Act 4

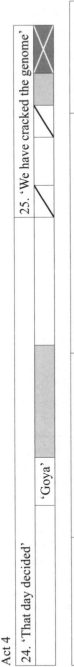

24. 'That day decided'

'Goya'

25. 'We have cracked the genome'

26. 'I wanted rid of it'  27. 'And cloning is here to stay'  28. 'How can you be so stupid?'  29. 'Forgive me'

'Goya'

Key

= 'Gattaca' themes (and variations)

= Minor seventh chords / hemiola figure (*The Kiss*)

= Cadential figure (*The Kiss*)

= Theme based on parallel fourths (*Vital Statistics*)

= Rhythmic figure using 'additive' process (*VS*)

= Syncopated rhythmic figure (*VS*)

= Rhythmic figure in quavers and semi-quavers (*VS*)

= Theme first accompanying words 'Remarkable Artists' (*VS*)

= A minor theme (and miscellaneous others) (*VS*)

= 'Its as simple' / 'The nose never lies' themes (*VS*)

= Octatonic scale

Two main musical ideas common to both works find their way into *Facing Goya*. The first is a harmonic sequence based on a succession of minor seventh chords underpinning a three-note semiquaver figure which spans an octave with a fifth added (see Ex. 9.1 and Table 9.1 white boxes with a black diagonal line from bottom left to top right).

**Example 9.1**   Facing Goya*: chord sequence taken from* The Kiss

The three-note figure stated in this idea is played in groups of four, resulting in a hemiola effect. Heard at the beginning of *The Kiss* and *Vital Statistics*, this figure (which I call the 'Kiss' theme) does not appear in *Goya* until the third number of Act 1. As in the case of *The Kiss* it is also accompanied by a quote from Baxandall's book.

This thematic figure increasingly assumes a life of its own during the course of *Facing Goya*. Even when it is first stated, its original harmonic and melodic identity has been combined with a rhythmic figure not heard in *The Kiss*, but derived in fact from another passage in *Vital Statistics*, to the words 'Weigh the brain'. Two other variations of this theme appear later on in the third number of Act 1; the first is heard in relation to a dissonant melodic line of abrupt minor ninth leaps, semitones, tritones and minor sevenths, the second supplies a diminution of the harmonic rhythm. It appears again towards the end of the first number in Act 2 where an ascending vocal line created out of alternating tones and semitones is gradually added to it (see Act 2/viii, bb. 59–96 and xiv, bb. 105–13).[3] This scale-like figure, based on the octatonic scale, is also taken from *Vital Statistics* and makes an important individual appearance towards the end of Act 2 (indicated by the black box with a diagonal

---

3   All score references and bar numbers are to the 'Karlsruhe' version published by Chester Music & Novello & Co.

white line from top left to bottom right in Table 9.1). Indeed soon after this section the 'Kiss' theme returns again, this time as an accompaniment to a non-octatonic melody in the bass voice.

Rather like Goya's own character, the 'Kiss' theme also disappears at various points, such as during the third act, but returns in the fourth by first accompanying a horn-call figure (Act 4/xxv, b. 1ff). It is then very subtly disguised by the absence of the hemiola figure later on in the scene but can still be identified by its harmonic motion (Act 4/xxv, bb. 110–20). Finally at number twenty-seven in the opera it is turned into a three-chord sequence where the first two chords are repeated seven times. Rhythmic, melodic and counter-melodic layers are therefore added to this basic harmonic framework resulting in the kind of multi-layering effects typical of Nyman's style. These pre-fabricated musical blocks can be adjusted to any length, shape or form, allowing – in comparison with earlier methods – a greater degree of flexibility. The theme's virtue lies in its ability to adapt to a variety of musical and dramatic levels, and its detached, neutral quality allows it to accompany almost all characters and situations at some point or other.

The function of the other primary quotation from *The Kiss* (and one that again finds its way into *Vital Statistics*) is more clearly fixed and defined. Consisting of four chords heard over a repeating two-bar sequence, it first appears in the fade out to *The Kiss* recording. The predominantly major-triad sequence of A$^\flat$-B$^\flat$-E$^\flat$-D$^{7\flat9}$ has the final chord resolving onto a straight D$^7$ chord (see Ex. 9.2, taken from the version that opens *Vital Statistics*; in Table 9.1 it appears as a white box with a black diagonal line extending from top left to bottom right).

**Example 9.2**     Facing Goya: *cadential figure from* The Kiss

As with other harmonic progressions belonging to Nyman, this sequence establishes a sense of tonality while simultaneously disrupting it. The first three chords suggest a perfect IV-V-I cadence in E$^\flat$ major, but the chromatic shift downwards to D and then back to A$^\flat$ creates a tritone relationship, which cuts across any tonal stability. If the sequence's circularity suggests an open-ended quality while its internal cadence remains momentarily closed, the overall effect of the 'Kiss' cadence is one of 'reiterating a statement through repetition'. Indeed it is often used in this way in the opera to support the repetition of a verbal slogan or truism.

Its structural function also appears to be more unequivocal than the use of the 'Kiss' theme. Positioned towards the end of Acts 1, 2 and 3 respectively, its role – as one might literally expect from a quasi-cadential figure – is to close off the previous action. However it does not so much provide a summary as assume the character of summarization. First it accompanies the cold rationalism of the craniometrist (Act 1/vii, bb. 107–14). In Act 2 it is heard twice in relation to observations about Goya, or ones made by him. On the first occasion the words '[the] dream of reason produces monsters' are heard, then it accompanies the art banker's statement that 'Goya saw Hitler before Hitler saw Goya' (Act 2/xiv, bb. 26–33 and 161–8 respectively). In Act 3 it provides support to the humane sentiments of the doctor and academic, then later the avarice and exploitative designs of the microbiologist and chief executive (Act 3/xxii, bb. 87–98). Significantly this figure does not reappear in the final act. If it is in fact meant to symbolize 'considered opinion' and 'rational judgment', its absence in the final act suggests that, according to the opera's underlying narrative, 'rational judgments' have finally been replaced by impulsive, irrational thoughts and actions.

## Secondary intertexts

While delineating the 'Kiss' elements in *Facing Goya* is relatively straightforward, tracing the plethora of patterns generated from *Vital Statistics* alone has proved to be more difficult, given the level of interconnection between them. In addition to the ascending octatonic line mentioned earlier, at least seven other 'figures' are identified in *Facing Goya* from the precursor work. In reality there are probably many more than the seven 'figures' outlined in this analysis. Some have been transformed to such an extent that they have lost any relationship with the original source. When one considers that together they only form an aspect of the complete work (the rest being themes constructed specifically around the work itself) one begins to get a sense of the manifold archaeological layers of music that make up *Facing Goya*.

Patterns and figures from *Vital Statistics* act as secondary intertexts in the opera. The first appears in the fifth number of Act 1 (shaded light grey in Table 9.1) and consists of a driving quaver figure circling initially around a minor third interval and often harmonized in parallel fourths (in this sense it has an almost 'heavy rock' guitar-riff quality about it). Together with another pattern that gradually extends outwards in a rhythmic sequence based on numbers 3-5-7-9-11 (shaded dark grey), both of them are laid almost end-to-end during the middle section of Act 1, closely resembling their original context. The intertextual pathways of the opera are often labyrinthine, and short-term associations between two or more ideas are established at times to serve as musical signposts, drawing two or more sequences together. The parallel fourths theme recurs at fairly regular intervals and often generates rhythmic tension and momentum. In Act 2 it appears in contrast to two gentler and more lyrical themes, while in Act 4 it accompanies Goya's anger and unease over his cloned self, then soon after loses its 'parallel fourths' identity.

A series of similar though essentially unrelated rhythmic patterns weave in and out of the opera's sections, including a syncopated figure (white box with a black cross) and a figure consisting of quavers and semi-quavers (light grey box with a black cross in Table 9.1). The former first appears at the beginning of Act 1's seventh number, making another brief appearance before the end of the act, while the latter's presence is heard in Act 2, where it plays an important role in the opening number and towards the end of the third.

A figure analogous in function if not in sound to the 'Kiss' cadence is a four-chord pattern first accompanying the lines 'It's as simple as it's clear' at the end of Act 1 immediately prior to the former pattern's first appearance in the opera (dark grey box with a white cross). This melodic line consists initially of an arpeggiated figure over a harmonic pattern more modal than tonal, making use of the flattened submediant chord, and bears a certain resemblance to 'Prospero's Magic' from *Prospero's Books*. By the time the number titled 'Galton' is reached in the middle of Act 2, the original chord sequence is essentially unaltered but a completely new melodic line has been placed over it (to the words 'the nose never lies'). While both themes appear different on the surface they are essentially variations upon a similar harmonic ground. They punctuate important points during the opera, such as at the end of Act 2 where the 'original' triadic pattern returns, or at the end of the twenty-fifth number in Act 4, where the aforementioned second melodic variation is included. Another theme is characterized by a five-note descending figure in straight crotchets sometimes grouped into 10, 11, 12 or 14 notes and accented irregularly (white cross against black background). The number sequence underpinning this and other patterns provides an effective musical equivalent to the opera's central theme of DNA replication. It first accompanies the words 'Remarkable Artists, Superior Races' in Act 2, number nine, starts off Act 3, and makes an ironic appearance towards the end of the opera when the chief executive extols the virtues of genetic engineering.

A more lyrical theme centred round the key of A minor first appears at the beginning of number twelve (white line from bottom left to top right against black background). This has been combined on Table 9.1 with a series of other less noticeable figures from *Vital Statistics*, but it is worth pointing out that one of these, which appears between two versions of the A minor theme in Act 2, in fact marks the very end of *Facing Goya*. What appears initially unassuming (Act 2/xii, bb. 13–25) therefore acquires greater significance in its final moments (Act 4/xxix, bb. 69–82). The opera does not, however, begin with a quote from *The Kiss* or *Vital Statistics* but arguably from another source.

## Extraneous intertexts

The Prelude to *Facing Goya* draws thematic inspiration from the soundtrack theme to Andrew Niccol's futuristic film *Gattaca* (1997). *Gattaca*'s maxim, 'there is no gene for the human spirit', resonates with the opera's overall message. Robert Worby has pointed out that *Gattaca*'s main theme, 'The Morrow', is heard in the second number from Act 3 of *Goya*, called the 'Sequence of the Gene' (shaded in black in Table 9.1) (Worby, in Nyman 2002). In fact this theme is also suggested in the very opening melodic line. An initial four-note pattern based on a minor triad with an added sixth is stated three times at the beginning of the opera. This figure is nested within the *Gattaca* theme, although it is slightly altered rhythmically (see Ex. 9.3).

**Example 9.3**    Facing Goya *(opening) and 'The Morrow' theme from* Gattaca

In *Facing Goya* the four-note theme is extended to five- then seven-note groups, representing in musical terms the helical spiral that forms around the two DNA strands, and is even reflected visually in the film by the spiral staircase in Jerome's apartment. Subsequent variations of the opening idea, such as at the beginning of Act 2, may therefore be connected by implication to this theme. While the reference to *Gattaca* may have been unintentional in the opening theme from *Facing Goya*, its function in the film soundtrack is similar to that of a thematic 'citation', where a type of 'genetics music' is established and referred to during subsequent scenes without further explanation.

A less direct allusion may also be traced to the music Nyman wrote to *The Ogre* (1996), Volker Schlöndorff's cinematic adaptation of Michael Tournier's novel *The Erl-King*. This film traces the life of a reclusive and enigmatic character called Abel who, due to the cruelty and hypocrisy of those around him, lives very much inside his own imaginary, internalized and occasionally delusional world. Set around the time of the Second World War, Abel becomes an innocent accomplice in the Nazi regime's implementation of the Aryan ideal. In one of the film's most disturbing scenes, a Nazi eugenicist assesses the measurements and physical characteristics of a young boy in order to determine his Aryan eligibility, thereby clearly connecting it with themes of racial selection discussed in Act 2 of *Goya*, also set during Second World War Europe. Nyman includes a Wagner tuba at this point in the opera, echoing the brass and reed sonorities heard in *The Ogre*'s soundtrack.

### *Facing Goya*'s intertextual design

Certain conclusions may be drawn from the study of intertextual interactions found in *Facing Goya*. First, Act 1 employs mass inter-referential migration from *Vital Statistics* from number five onwards, creating in effect a kind of opera within an opera. The concept of the palimpsest is again suggested in the processes of layering and covering undertaken in relation to *Vital Statistics* and *The Kiss*. Nyman's repositioning of parts of *Vital Statistics* in Act 1 functions in broad terms as a statement of intertextual intent; an expository 'gesture', supplying the work with a kind of archaeological and genealogical depth and sense of stylistic chronology. In Act 2 this material undergoes a process of fragmentation. No longer are large slabs of pre-fabricated blocks inserted into existing structures, as was the case with Act 1, but themes are identified, scrutinized, then broken down and reformed – a kind of musical equivalent of genetic engineering. The development of these intertextual fragments only leads at the end of Act 2 to an atomization of such ideas, to a form of thematic meltdown.

Act 3 starts off where Act 2 ends by attempting to pick up and perhaps reshape these splintered intertexts, but it soon gives way to the introduction of new ideas. Act 3 is the least intertextual of the opera's four acts. It also coincidentally deals in greater detail with themes of inhumanity and cold-blooded rationality. Act 4 also initially sets out independently from any intertextual sources only to gradually readmit them during its closing sections. If the two central acts parallel each other in following independent paths, Acts 1 and 4 are also similarly constructed. Both use the 'Kiss' theme at almost identical moments and both refer to the 'parallel fourths' theme (though in the final act the latter precedes *The Kiss* reference). The final act's connections with Act 1 thus provide the opera with a sense of rapprochement, reconciliation and resolution at its end.

A discussion of the opera's intertextual narrative threads may easily lead one to believe that the work can only make sense in relation to its past connections with other works. While tracing the source of a musical idea through a family tree network sheds further light on its development and evolution in diachronic terms, its function and meaning synchronically – within a specific context – is also important in determining the overall relationship between text and intertext here.

Table 9.1's blank spaces, those moments where there are no intertextual correspondences, speak as much of presences as of absences. These absent spaces form their own intra-textual weave, providing a level of internal coherence through contrasts with the quoted material. Intertextual and inter-referential elements – outside influences and newly formed ones – coexist from the very beginning of the work. The *Gattaca* allusion heard during the opening measures is underpinned by a rhythmic figure that emphasizes the minor third interval, and consists of a long-short-long pattern (see Ex. 9.4).

**Example 9.4**    Facing Goya*: 'Goya' motive*

This pattern generates many of the musical ideas immediately following on from the Prelude. The first number, 'Dogs Drowning in Sand' converts the minor-third interval into an ostinato figure. Then at bar 10 it returns in its original rhythmic guise in the bass, with stacked minor thirds placed on top in an uncharacteristically dissonant seven-note configuration. This moment of harmonic conflict gives way at bar 16 to a series of rhythmic variations on this figure, but developed in relation to a pentatonic tetrachord consisting of $A^b$, $B^b$, $D^b$ and $E^b$.

At bar 24 yet another section is established, but again the rhythmic figure is prevalent, first quoted then extended using quartal harmonies. The minor third interval is retained for a melody heard at bar 33, its pentatonic shape suggesting bar 16. The opening material for 'Dogs Drowning in Sand' returns at bar 39, then at bar 48 the pentatonic shape encountered earlier is combined with the short rhythmic figure derived from the prelude. At 52 a three-note figure forms an incomplete pentatonic pattern while the bass punctuates a low B major seventh and $G^\#$ minor ninth chord. What appears as a new, chromatic melody in the voice at bar 61, accompanied by open fifths in the strings, may be traced to the minor third ostinato figure heard at the beginning of the first number. As if to confirm this connection, Nyman reintroduces the ostinato figure at bar 73 to end this section.

The minor third figure and its variations are unique to both *Goya* the opera and Goya the artist. It usually accompanies references to him or by him and is also included in Table 9.1 (simply as 'Goya') in order to show how other aspects outside the 'intertextual weave' of the opera function within it. Reappearing towards the end of Act 1, the Goya material finds its way in and amongst themes from *Vital Statistics*, cutting across an argument on craniometry by quoting from the artist's words. It also appears towards the end of Act 2 where the order of sequences has been reversed. The material appearing at bar 16 of Act 1 is now heard first before the ostinato pattern reappears, accompanying another Goya quote. The Goya motive returns briefly in the final number of Act 3 but its original identity has been transformed by rhythmic augmentation. Its positioning in the final act is similar to Act 1, accompanying Goya's entry during the first number and then signing off before the final sequence. Its final appearance thus signals the end of the work, at the point when Goya admonishes the art banker for her greed. The very last number (which is thematically less important in the work) thus functions as a kind of coda or epilogue.

If viewed as a musical trope within the work as whole, these passages of self-allusion and self-quotation create their own sense of growth through accumulation. Studying their order and function within each act draws attention to the opera's overarching shape beyond the plurality of localized references. An alteration to a DNA sequence according to gene theory typically occurs by means of deletion, insertion, inversion and substitution. Have these biological transgressions been transferred to Nyman's own musical sequences? Do they serve to delete the narrative 'progress' of the original music, subverting its attempt to create its own sense of logical unity and continuity? One reading might view the intertext as the opera's consciousness, redirecting the course of the opera by invoking a sense of the past.

The 'Goya' material heard at the beginning is more clearly 'evolutionary' and developmental in design, and may therefore be seen as the musical equivalent of genetic replication and mutation central to the opera's subject matter. On a more general level, the treatment of this material suggests the inexorable onward march of science and progress. Only after the 'Kiss' theme's appearance a third of the way through Act 1 do intertextual elements start to infiltrate the work and assimilate its contents. In this context, the intertext appears to function as a kind of rogue reference, disrupting the enclosed and self-sufficient logic of the work's hitherto internal narrative. An intertextual presence at the end of the opera might therefore suggest that its intrusion at various points in the work finally brings about the relentless logic of science to its senses.

In many respects *Facing Goya* represents a watershed in Nyman's intertextual development. Both hypo- and hypertextual forces battle it out for superiority during the course of the opera, but the outcome remains in the end inconclusive. The sprawling heteroglossic nature of the work provides an effective riposte to science's attempts to harness and control genetic theory. In addition, the idea of creating a perfect race through scientific means – powerfully presented both in *Facing Goya* and *Gattaca* – is countered by the textual diversity of the musical score and its avoidance of any rigorous musical 'logic'.

After the multi-layered approach adopted in *Facing Goya*, Nyman has since adopted a far more direct and transparent approach, as witnessed in his subsequent opera *Man and Boy: Dada*. While this may suggest that, having exhausted the function of quotation in *Drowning by Numbers*, the inter-referential aspect also seems to have run its course in Goya's final predicament, only time will tell.

# Conclusion

I have set out to demonstrate in this study that it is useful to understand Nyman's music as much through relationships established between his compositions as within them. This approach has proven particularly helpful in looking at works that specifically borrow from pre-existing melodic, thematic or harmonic ideas, because Nyman's own deep sense of historical awareness – already evident in his upbringing and music criticism – coupled with his two-way understanding of it (the present influences the past, and *vice versa*) enables him to set up highly effective stylistic, aesthetic and dramatic oppositions between text and intertext in his music. A study of Nyman's reworking of pre-existing material has also drawn notice to the diverse range of intertextual techniques employed by him, from the deconstructive methods of the early works of the late 1970s to the extension, elaboration and integration of these ideas a decade or so later. It thus became possible to draw parallels between Nyman's methods and the hypotextual, polytextual and metatextual practices of linguistic theory and analysis.

Furthermore, intertextual principles underlying these referential works were also applied on a wider scale to Nyman's non-referential compositions through a rich and varied application of self-quotation in his music. From these observations, one can conclude that Nyman's entire oeuvre in fact possesses a high degree of inter-referentiality and inter-connectedness, despite also being receptive to outside influences. The family tree network of associations proved useful in mapping out some of these connections, while also drawing attention to the fact that some compositions (and musical ideas contained therein) were more productive and proactive in this respect than others, generating further variations, recompositions and rearrangements. While a broadly intertextual approach such as the one adopted in this study may not prove directly relevant to the works of other composers (nor does it tell the 'whole story' about Nyman's music), my hope is that, in contextualizing his music by taking into account both aesthetic and compositional approaches, admirers and critics alike will have identified in Nyman's work a high degree of conceptual thought and level of technical application that marks him out as one of the late twentieth century's most significant composers.

# Bibliography

Abbate, Carolyn (1991), *Unsung Voices: Opera and Musical Narrative in the Nineteenth Century* (New Jersey, Princeton University Press).

Adlington, Robert (2004), *Louis Andriessen: De Staat* (Aldershot, Ashgate Publishing).

Agawu, V. Kofi (1991), *Playing With Signs: A Semiotic Interpretation of Classic Music* (New Jersey, Princeton University Press).

Allen, Graham (2000), *Intertextuality* (London, Routledge).

Allsen, J. Michael (1993), 'Intertextuality and compositional process in two cantilena motets by Hugo de Lantis', *Journal of Musicology*, 11/2, pp. 174–202.

Anderson, Virginia (1983), *British Experimental Music: Cornelius Cardew and His Contemporaries* (MA thesis, University of Redlands).

Antokoletz, Elliott (1984), *The Music of Bela Bartók: A Study of Tonality and Progression in Twentieth-Century Music* (Berkeley, University of California Press).

Ayrey, Craig (1994), 'Debussy's significant connections, metaphor and metonymy in analytical method', in Anthony Pople (ed.), *Theory, Analysis and Meaning in Music* (Cambridge, Cambridge University Press), pp. 127–51.

Bakhtin, M.M. (1981), *The Dialogic Imagination*, four essays trans. C. Emerson and M. Holquist, ed. M. Holquist (Austin, University of Texas).

Barthes, Roland (1974), *S/Z*, trans. Richard Miller (New York, Noonday).

—— (1977), *Image–Music–Text* (London, Fontana).

Baxandall, Michael (1974), *Painting and Experience in Fifteenth Century Italy* (Oxford, Clarendon Press).

Beard, David and Kenneth Gloag (2005), *Musicology: The Key Concepts* (London, Routledge).

Beirens, Maarten (2005), *The Identity of European Minimal Music* (PhD thesis, Katholieke Universiteit, Leuven).

Bergius, Hanne (1980), 'The ambiguous aesthetic of Dada: towards a definition of its categories', in Richard Sheppard (ed.), *Dada: Studies of a Movement* (Chalfont St Giles, Alpha Academic), pp. 26–38.

Bloom, Harold (1975), *A Map of Misreading* (Oxford, Oxford University Press).

Borges, Jorge Luis (1973), *A Universal History of Infamy*, trans. Norman Thomas di Giovanni (London, Allen Lane).

Boulez, Pierre (1971), *Boulez on Music Today* (London, Faber).

Bowen, Meirion (1995), 'Synthetic material', *The Guardian*, 10 April, p. 9.

Brown, Lesley (ed.) (1993), *The New Shorter Oxford English Dictionary* (Oxford, Clarendon Press).

Brown, Royal S. (1994), *Overtones and Undertones: Reading Film Music* (Berkeley and California, University of California Press).

Bush, Alan (1946), 'The crisis of modern music', *Keynote*, I/4, pp. 4–7.

—— (1980), *In My Eighth Decade and other Essays* (London, Kahn and Averill).

Cage, John (1961), *Silence* (London, Calder and Boyars).

—— (1973), *M: Writings 67–72* (Middletown, CT, Wesleyan University Press).

—— (1985), *A Year from Monday* (London, Calder and Boyars).

—— (1993), *Writer* (New York, Limelight Editions).

Calvino, Italo (1981), *If on a Winter's Night a Traveller* (London, Picador).

Campion, Jane (1993), *The Piano* (London, Bloomsbury).

Cardew, Cornelius (1961a), 'Report on Stockhausen's *Carré*', *The Musical Times*, September, pp. 619–22.

—— (1961b), 'Report on Stockhausen's *Carré* – Part 2', *The Musical Times*, November, pp. 698–700.

Cardinal, Roger (1994), 'Collecting and collage making: the case of Kurt Schwitters', in John Elsner and Roger Cardinal (eds), *The Cultures of Collecting* (London, Reaktion Books), pp. 68–96.

Cenciarelli, Carlo (2006), 'The Case against Nyman Revisited: "Affirmative" and "Critical" Evidence in Michael Nyman's Appropriation of Mozart', *Radical Musicology*, 1, <http://www.radical-musicology.org.uk>, accessed 17 May 2007.

Culler, Jonathon (1975), *Structuralist Poetics* (London, Routledge and Keegan Paul).

Cutler, Chris (1996), 'Plunderphonics', in Richard Kostelanetz and Joseph Darby (eds), *Classic Essays on Twentieth-Century Music* (New York, Schirmer), pp. 354–76.

Dahlhaus, Carl (1989), *Nineteenth-Century Music*, trans. J. Bradford Robinson (Berkeley, University of California Press).

Dart, Thurston [with A. Lewis, D. Arundell and A. Goldsbrough] (1957), [Purcell's] *Miscellaneous Odes and Cantatas*, Works, xxvii (London).

—— (1959a), 'Purcell's chamber music', *PRMA*, lxxxv (1958–9), 81.

—— (1959b), *Fantasias and other Instrumental Music*, Works, xxxi (London).

—— (1963), *J. Bull, Keyboard Music, II*, Musica Britannica, xix (1963).

De Gaetano, Domenico (1994), 'La musica di Greenaway', in Robert Santagostino (ed.), *Appuntamento Greenaway* (Piedmont, Circolo del Cinema), pp. 17–31.

Dean, Winton (1987), 'Review of *Vital Statistics*', *The Musical Times*, 128, p. 449.

Denham, Laura (1993), *The Films of Peter Greenaway* (London, Minerva Press).

Derrida, Jacques (1976), *Of Grammatology*, trans. Gayatri Chakravorty Spivak (Baltimore, Johns Hopkins University Press).

Eagleton, Terry (1983), *Literary Theory* (Oxford, Blackwell).

Ellis, William (1997), 'Interview with Michael Nyman', *American Record Guide*, March/April 1997, <http://www.december.org/nyman9703-04a.htm>, accessed 11 February 2003.

Eno, Brian (1975a), 'I want to be a magnet for tapes', *Time Out*, <www.enoweb.co.uk>, accessed 18 November 2005.

—— (1975b), 'Brian Eno talks about Obscure Records with Kenneth Ansell', *Impetus 4*, <www.enoweb.co.uk>, accessed 18 November 2005.

Epstein, David (1979), *Beyond Orpheus* (Oxford, Oxford University Press).

Erauw, Willem (1998), 'Canon formation: some more reflections on Lydia Goehr's *Imaginary Museum of Musical Works*', *Acta Musicologica*, 70/2, pp. 109–15.

Everett, Yayoi Uno (2004), 'Parody with an ironic edge: dramatic works by Kurt Weill, Peter Maxwell Davies, and Louis Andriessen', *Music Theory Online*, 10/4, <www.societymusictheory.org/mto/issues/mto.04.10.4/mto.04.10.4.yeverett.html>, accessed 18 November 2005.

Feuerbach, Ludwig (1957), *The Essence of Christianity*, trans George Eliot (New York, Harper and Brothers).

Ford, Andrew (1993), 'Jerry Lee Lewis plays Mozart', *Composer to Composer* (London, Quartet Books), pp. 192–5.

Foster, Hal, Rosalind Krauss, Yve-Alain Bois and Banjamin Buchloh (2004), *Art Since 1900: Modernism, Antimodernism and Postmodernism* (London, Thames and Hudson).

Frith, Simon and Howard Horne (1987), *Art into Pop* (London, Routledge).

Gelder, K. (1999) 'Jane Campion and the limits of literary cinema', in D. Cartmell and I. Whelehan (eds), *Adaptations from Text to Screen, Screen to Text* (London, Routledge) pp. 157–71.

Goehr, Lydia (1992), *The Imaginary Museum of Musical Works* (Oxford, Clarendon Press).

Gould, Stephen Jay (1981), *The Mismeasure of Man* (New York, Norton).

Graham, Robert (1998), 'Goya's last caprice', *Financial Times*, 28 March.

Griffiths, D. (1995), 'Report on the first UK Critical Musicology Conference, Salford, 1–2 April 1995', *Critical Musicology Newsletter*, 3, pp. 7–12.

Griffiths, Paul (1985), *New Sounds, New Personalities: British Composers of the 1980s* (London, Faber Music).

Haglund, Magnus (1994), 'Interview with Michael Nyman', *Filmmusik*, X/8, Filmkonst (Gothenbourg), trans. Johan Lif, <http,//www.december.org/pg/text/articles/nyman.htm> accessed 19 February 1998.

Hall, Michael (1984), *Harrison Birtwistle* (London, Robson).

Hallmark, Rufus E. (1979), *The Genesis of Schumann's Dichterliebe: A Source Study* (Michigan, UMI Research Press).

Hastings, Michael (2004), *Almeida Opera Programme*, 1–18 July, p. 8.

Heldt, Guido (1989), '"... Breaking the sequence down beat by beat", Michael Nyman's music for the films of Peter Greenaway', *Film und Fernsehwissenschaftliches Kolloquium, Berlin 1989* (Münster), pp. 177–88.

Hill, Dave (1991), 'Riddle of the sounds', *The Guardian*, 10 October, p. 26.

Hobbs, Christopher (1981), 'Cardew as teacher', *Perspectives of New Music*, 20/1, pp. 2–3.

Hudson, Richard (2006), 'Ground', *Grove Music Online*, ed. L. Macy, <http,//www.grovemusic.com>, accessed 17 February 2006.

le Huray, Peter and James Day (1988), *Music and Aesthetics in the Eighteenth and Early-Nineteenth Centuries* (Cambridge, Cambridge University Press).

Hutcheon, Linda (1985), *A Theory of Parody* (Routledge, London).

—— (1991), 'The politics of postmodern parody', in Heinrich F. Platt (ed.), *Intertextuality* (Berlin, Walter de Gruyter) pp. 225–36.

Jameson, Fredric (1972), *The Prison-House of Language* (New Jersey, Princeton University Press).

—— (1992), *Signatures of the Visible* (London, Routledge).

Jeffries, Stuart (1990), 'Romanian miracle', *Ham and High*, 16 February.

Jones, C.A. (1993), 'Cage and the abstract expressionist ego', *Critical Inquiry*, pp. 628–65.

Kant, Immanuel (1987) (1790), *Critique of Judgment*, trans. Werner S. Pluhar (Indianapolis, Hackett).

Karolyi, Otto (1994), *Modern British Music: The Second British Musical Renaissance* (London, Associated University Presses).

Kaup, M. (1993), *Mad Intertextuality: Madness in Twentieth-Century Women's Writing* (Trier, WVT).

Kenyon, Nicholas (1981), *The BBC Symphony Orchestra: The First Fifty Years, 1930–1980* (London, British Broadcasting Corporation).

Klein, Michael L. (2005), *Intertextuality in Western Art Music* (Bloomington and Indianapolis, Indiana University Press).

Komar, Arthur (ed.) (1971), *Dichterliebe* (London, Chappell and Company).

Korsyn, Kevin (1991), 'Towards a new poetics of musical influence', *Music Analysis*, 10/1–2, pp. 3–72.

Kozinn, Allan (1995), *The Beatles* (London, Phaidon).

Kramer, Jonathan D. (2002), 'The nature and origins of musical postmodernism', in J. Lochhead and J. Auner (eds), *Postmodern Music / Postmodern Thought* (New York, Routledge) pp. 13–26.

Kramer, Lawrence (2002), *Musical Meaning: Toward a Critical History* (Berkeley, University of California Press).

Kristeva, Julia (1980), *Desire in Language: A Semiotic Approach to Literature and Art*, trans. Thomas Gora, Alice Jardine and Leon S. Roudiez, ed. Leon S. Roudiez (New York, Columbia University Press).

Landy, Leigh (1991), *What's the Matter with Today's Experimental Music?* (Philadelphia, Harwood).

Lawrence, Amy (1997), *The Films of Peter Greenaway* (Cambridge, Cambridge University Press).

Lentricchia, Frank and Thomas McLaughlin (eds), 1990, *Critical Terms for Literary Study* (Chicago, University of Chicago Press).

Lerdahl, Fred and Ray Jackendoff (1983), *A Generative Theory of Tonal Music* (Cambridge, MA, MIT Press).

Leydon, Rebecca (2002), 'Towards a typology of minimalist tropes', *Music Theory Online*, 8/4, <http://mto.societymusictheory.org/issues/mto.02.8.4/mto.02.8.4.leydon_frames.html>, accessed 19 April 2006.

Lipsitz, George (1997), 'Cruising around the historical bloc', in Ken Gelder and Sarah Thornton (eds) *The Subcultures Reader* (London, Routledge), pp. 350–59.

Lyon, David (2004), personal correspondence, 27 January.

Lyotard, Jean-François (1984), *The Postmodern Condition* (Manchester, Manchester University Press).

McCartney, Andra (2000), *Sounding Places with Hildegard Westerkamp* (PhD thesis, University of York), <http://www.emf.org/artists/mccartney00/text.html>, accessed 19 April 2006.

McClary, Susan (2000), *Conventional Wisdom* (Los Angeles, University of California Press).

McCreless, Patrick (1988), 'Roland Barthes's *S/Z* from a musical point of view', *In Theory Only*, 10, pp. 1–30.

Macdonald, Ian (1995), *Revolution in the Head* (London, Pimlico).

Maconie, Robin (1976), *The Works of Karlheinz Stockhausen* (London, Marion Boyars).

—— (1998), 'Through the looking glass: Robin Maconie revisits Stockhausen's *Hymnen*', *The Musical Times*, September, pp. 4–11.

Margolis, M. (ed.) (2000), *Jane Campion's The Piano* (Cambridge, Cambridge University Press).

Marks, Anthony (1987), 'The Man who Mistook his Wife for a Hat', *The Musical Times*, January, pp. 34–5.

Mason, Colin and Hugo Cole (1980), 'Alan Bush', *New Grove Dictionary of Music and Musicians*, ed. Stanley Sadie, pp. 502–3.

Mellers, Wilfrid (1987), *Music in a New Found Land* (London, Faber).

Mertens, Wim (1988), *American Minimal Music* (London, Kahn & Averill).

Meyer, Leonard B. (1967), *Music, the Arts, and Ideas* (Chicago, University of Chicago Press).

Meyer, Thomas (1989), 'Von der Struktur zum Musik, von der Musik zum Film,' *Cinema*, 37, pp. 43–53.

Molino, Jean (1990), 'Music fact and the semiology of music', trans. J.A. Underwood, *Music Analysis*, 9/2, pp. 113–56.

Monelle, Raymond (1992), *Linguistics and Semiotics in Music* (Chur, Harwood Academic Publishers).

Moore, Allan (1992), 'Patterns of harmony', *Popular Music*, 11/1, January, pp. 73–106.

—— (1993), *Rock: The Primary Text* (Buckingham, Open University Press).

Nattiez, Jean-Jacques (1990), 'Can one speak of narrativity in music?', trans. K. Ellis, *Journal of the Royal Musical Association*, 115/ii, pp. 240–57.

Nielsen, Steen K. (1992), *Michael Nyman: En komponist & hans musik* (MA diss., Aarhus University).

Nimczik, Ortwin (2000), 'Im Spagat zwischen Bull und Schönberg', *Musik und Bildung*, 33/1, pp. 22–30.

Nyman, Michael (1964a), Programme note for the *Canzona* for solo flute (source unknown).

—— (1964b), Programme note for the *Divertimento* for wind trio (source unknown).

—— (1968a), 'We never close', *The Spectator*, 22 November, pp. 741–2.

—— (1968b), 'Britons at sea', *The Spectator*, 23 August, p. 269.

—— (1968c), 'About time too', *The Spectator*, 6 December, pp. 809–10.

—— (1968d), 'Minimal music', *The Spectator*, 11 October, pp. 518–19.

—— (1969), 'Purcell in his cups', *Music and Musicians*, 18, October, p. 30.

—— (1970a), 'Anachronisms', *The New Statesman*, 30 October, p. 574–5.

—— (1970b), 'John Cage in Paris', *The New Statesman*, 6 November, p. 617.

—— (1971a), 'Sign language', *The New Statesman*, 26 February, p. 282.

—— (1971b), 'Boulez's law', *The New Statesman*, 2 April, pp. 466–7.

—— (1971c), 'Heavy Duty', *The New Statesman*, 10 September, p. 343.

—— (1971d), 'Steve Reich, an interview with Michael Nyman', *Musical Times*, 112/1537, pp. 229–31.

—— (1971e), 'Uncommercial', *The New Statesman*, 20 August, p. 248.

—— (1971f), 'Believe it or not melody rides again', *Music and Musicians*, 20, October, pp. 26–8.

—— (1971g), 'Harrison Birtwistle', *London Magazine*, October–November, pp. 118–22.

—— (1971h), 'Dart's epitaph', *The New Statesman*, 17 December, p. 872.

—— (1971i), 'Disciplinarians', *The New Statesman*, 29 October, p. 599.

—— (1972a), 'SR – Mysteries of the Phase', *Music and Musicians*, 20, February, pp. 20–21.

—— (1972b), 'Cornelius Cardew's "The Great Learning"', *London Magazine*, December–January, pp. 130–35.

—— (1972c), 'Circle complete', *The New Statesman*, 31 March, p. 434.

—— (1975a), 'Peak district', *The Listener*, 9 October, p. 480.

—— (1975b), 'Experimental music and the American vernacular tradition', *First American Music Conference* (Keele University), pp. 149–52.

—— (1976a), 'Hearing/seeing', *Studio International*, November–December, pp. 233–43.

—— (1976b), 'Music', *Studio International*, March–April, pp. 186–8.

—— (1976c), 'Music', *Studio International*, May–June, pp. 282–4.

—— (1976d), 'Music', *Studio International*, July–August, pp. 71–2.

—— (1976e), 'Music', *Studio International*, January–February, pp. 64–5.

—— (1977), 'Music', *Studio International*, January–February, pp. 6–8.

—— (1988a), *The Kiss and Other Movements* (EEGCD40).

—— (1988b), *The Man Who Mistook His Wife*, CBS Masterworks (MK 44669).

—— (1989a), 'Taking stock', The Nyman / Greenaway Soundtracks (VEBN 55).

—— (1989b), *The Draughtsman's Contract*, CD 1989 (Virgin Records CASCD 1158), <http:// catalogus.volume12.net/item/206> accessed 5 February 2006.

—— (1991), 'The spice of ice', *What's On*, 30 January, p. 23.

—— (1993a), 'Against intellectual complexity in music', in *Postmodernism, a Reader*, ed. Thomas Docherty (London, Harvester Wheatsheaf), pp. 206–13.

—— (1993b), Composer's Note, *String Quartet No. 1* (Chester Music).

—— (1994), *The Piano Concerto* (Argo, 443 382-2).

—— (1998), *The Suit and the Photograph*, EMI Classics (7243 5 5674 8).

—— (1999), *Experimental Music, Cage and Beyond* (Cambridge, Cambridge University Press).

—— (2000), Interview with Sue Lawley on BBC Radio 4's *Desert Island Discs*, 7 January.

—— (2002), *Facing Goya*, Warner Classics (0927-45342-2).

—— (2004), 'Collector's items', *The Guardian*, 10 July, pp. 16–17.

—— with Peter Sainsbury and Peter Greenaway (1978), 'A Walk through H', *Catalogue of British Film Institute Productions 1977–8* (London, 1978), pp. 89–92.

Orr, Mary (2003), *Intertextuality: Debates and Contexts* (Cambridge, Polity Press).

Osborne, Nigel (1983), 'Recordings', *Tempo*, March, pp. 40–41.

Osmond-Smith, David (1985), *Playing on Words: A Guide to Luciano Berio's Sinfonia* (London, Royal Musical Association).

Pasler, Jann (1993), 'Postmodernism, narrativity, and the art of memory', *Contemporary Music Review*, 7/2, pp. 3–32.

Perloff, Marjorie (1994), '"A Duchamp unto my self": "Writing through" Marcel', in Marjorie Perloff and Charles Junkerman (eds), *John Cage: Composed in America* (Chicago, University of Chicago Press), pp. 100–124.

Perloff, Nancy (1993), *Art and the Everyday: Popular Entertainment and the Circle of Erik Satie* (Oxford, Oxford University Press).

Pierce, John R. (1983), *The Science of Musical Sound* (New York, Scientific American Library).

Poirer, R. (1971), *The Performing Self: Compositions and Decompositions in the Languages of Contemporary Life* (London, Chatto & Windus).

Potter, Keith (1990), 'New music', *Musical Times*, 131, pp. 212–13.

—— (2000), *Four Musical Minimalists* (Cambridge, Cambridge University Press).

Prendergast, Mark (2000), *The Ambient Century* (London, Bloomsbury).

Prévost, Eddie (2001), 'The arrival of a new music aesthetic: extracts from a half-buried diary', *Leonardo Music Journal*, 11, pp. 25–8.

Purkis, C. (1995), 'Postmodernity at the piano: nineteenth-century bodies and the limits of language', *Critical Musicology Newsletter*, 3, pp. 36–42.

Ratner, Leonard G. (1980), *Classic Music, Expression, Form, and Style* (New York, Schirmer).

Revill, David (1992), *The Roaring Silence: John Cage, a Life* (London, Bloomsbury).

Richter, Hans (1965), *Dada: Art and Anti-Art* (London, Thames and Hudson).

Rietveldt, Hillegonda (1995), 'Pure bliss: intertextuality in house music', <www.cia.com.au/peril/youth/purebliss.pdf>, accessed 8 January 2006.

Ritzel, Fred (1993), 'Planspiele, Zum Verhältnis von Bild und Musik bei Peter Greenaway und Michael Nyman', <http://www.staff.unioldenburg.de/ritzel/Material/PLANSPIELE0.htm>, accessed 1 February 2006.

Rivière, D. and D. Caux (1987), 'Entretien avec Michael Nyman', *Peter Greenaway* (Paris, Dis Voir), pp. 74–91.

Rosen, Charles (1976), *The Classical Style* (London, Faber and Faber).

Russell, Mark and James Young (eds) (2000), *Film Music Screencraft* (Woburn, MA, Focal Press).

Sacks, Oliver (1985), *The Man who Mistook his Wife for a Hat* (London, Picador).

Samuels, Robert (1995), *Mahler's Sixth Symphony: A Study in Musical Semiotics* (Cambridge, Cambridge University Press).

Schoenberg, Arnold (1984), *Style and Idea*, ed. Leonard Stein (London, Faber and Faber).

Schoonderwoerd, Pieter (2005), 'Beckham crosses, Nyman scores', paper given at the University of Nottingham, 24 May.

Schwarz, K. Robert (1996), *Minimalists* (London, Phaidon).

Simon, L. (1982), 'Music and film: an interview with Michael Nyman', *Millennium Film Journal*, 10/11, pp. 223–34.

Sisman, Elaine (ed.) (1997), *Haydn, Shakespeare, and the Rules of Originality* (New Jersey, Princeton University Press).

Sparks, E.H. (1975), *Cantus Firmus in Mass and Motet: 1420–1520* (New York, Da Capo Press).

Stangos, Nikos (ed.) (1981), *Concepts of Modern Art* (London, Thames and Hudson).

Straus, Joseph (1990), *Remaking the Past: Musical Modernism and the Influence of the Tonal Tradition* (Cambridge, MA, Harvard University Press).

—— (1991), 'The "anxiety of influence" in twentieth-century music', *The Journal of Musicology*, IX, pp. 430–47.

Street, Alan (1989), 'Superior myths, dogmatic allegories', *Music Analysis*, 8 1/2, pp. 77–123.

Strickland, Edward (1993), *Minimalism: Origins* (Bloomington, Indiana University Press).

Sutcliffe, Tom (1984), 'Confessions of a melody maker', *The Guardian*, 20 July, p. 9.

Sutcliffe, W. Dean (2003), *The Keyboard Sonatas of Domenico Scarlatti and Eighteenth-Century Music Style* (Cambridge, Cambridge University Press).

Viswanathan, T. and Matthew Harp Allen (2004), *Music in South India: The Karnatak Concert Tradition and Beyond* (Oxford, Oxford University Press).

Watkins, Glenn (1994), *Pyramids at the Louvre: Music, Culture, and Collage from Stravinsky to the Postmodernists* (Cambridge, MA, Belknap Press).

Watson, Ben (1994), *Frank Zappa: The Negative Dialectics of Poodle Play* (London, Quartet Books).

Webster, Jonathan (1995), 'The composer's contract', *Gramophone Magazine*, April, pp. 14–17.

White, Michael (1991), 'Commercial drive', *The Independent*, 8 November, p. 17.

Williams, Alastair (1989), 'Music as immanent critique: stasis and development in the music of Ligeti', in Christopher Norris (ed.), *Music and the Politics of Culture* (London, Lawrence & Wishart), pp. 187–225.

—— (1997), *New Music and the Claims of Modernity* (Aldershot, Ashgate Publishing).

Wills, David and Alec McHoul (1988), 'Zoo-logics, questions of analysis in a film by Peter Greenaway', *Textual Practice*, 5/1, pp. 8–24.

Woods, Alan (1996), *Being Naked Playing Dead: The Art of Peter Greenaway* (Manchester, Manchester University Press).

# Index